Contemporary Thoughts on Co.
Corporate Identity Management

Contemporary Thoughts on Corporate Branding and Corporate Identity Management

Edited by

T. C. Melewar
Brunel Business School, UK

Elif Karaosmanoğlu
ITU Faculty of Management, Turkey

First published 2008 by
PALGRAVE MACMILLAN

Palgrave Macmillan in the UK is an imprint of Macmillan
Publishers Limited, registered in England, company number
785998, of Houndmills, Basingstoke, Hampshire RG21 6XS.

Palgrave Macmillan in the US is a division of St Martin's Press LLC,
175 Fifth Avenue, New York, NY 10010.

Palgrave Macmillan is the global academic imprint of the above
companies and has companies and representatives throughout the
world.

Palgrave® and Macmillan® are registered trademarks in the
United States, the United Kingdom, Europe and other countries.

ISBN-13: 978–0–230–54314–0   hardback
ISBN-10: 0–230–54314–6   hardback

This book is printed on paper suitable for recycling and made from
fully managed and sustained forest sources. Logging, pulping and
manufacturing processes are expected to conform to the
environmental regulations of the country of origin.

A catalogue record for this book is available from the British
Library.

Library of Congress Cataloging-in-Publication Data

Contemporary thoughts on corporate branding and corporate
  identity management / [edited by] TC Melewar, Elif
  Karaosmanoğlu.
    p. cm.
  Includes bibliographical references and index.
  ISBN 0–230–54314–6 (alk. paper)
  1. Corporate identity.   2. Corporate image.   3. Branding
  (Marketing)
  I. Melewar, T. C.   II. Karaosmanoğlu, Elif, 1975–
  HD59.2.C66 2008
  659.2—dc22   2008015911

10   9   8   7   6   5   4   3   2   1
17   16   15   14   13   12   11   10   09   08

Printed and bound in Great Britain by
CPI Antony Rowe, Chippenham and Eastbourne

Contents

Figures, Tables and Appendices

List of Tables

List of Appendices

About the Contributors

Tatiana Anisimova completed her PhD at the Department of Marketing, Monash University, Australia. She received her Bachelor and Honours degrees at Moscow State University. Her research interests include corporate branding, corporate perception, stakeholder management, and consumer behaviour.

Patrick Cettier studied International Business at ESB Reutlingen (Germany) and Northeastern University (Boston, USA) before joining McKinsey & Company in their Munich office in 2001. His industry focus was mainly with financial institutions and his functional expertise centred around marketing and sales. He took a leave of absence in 2003 and completed his PhD in Finance from the University of Aachen in 2005. In 2006, Dr Cettier joined UBS Global Wealth Management and Business Banking in Zurich as an associate director.

Sue Vaux Halliday is a senior lecturer in the marketing group in the School of Management, University of Surrey. She recently published an extended case study in a textbook on organizational change and is currently working on a textbook on services marketing. She publishes on relationship marketing in a range of journals, including the *European Journal of Marketing* and the *Journal of Services Marketing*.

Salah S. Hassan is the Chairman and Professor of Marketing at the School of Business, George Washington University. He received his PhD from Ohio State University in 1984. Dr Hassan has published well over 40 articles and papers in leading academic journals and trade publications. He was granted the 'Highly Commended' best paper award by the *Journal of Consumer Marketing* in 2004. He was recognized as an 'Outstanding Marketing Teacher' award recipient in 2005 by the Academy of Marketing Science (AMS). His research interests include strategic brand management, international market segmentation and global marketing.

Elif Karaosmanoğlu is at Istanbul Technical University, Management Engineering Department (Turkey). She completed her PhD at Warwick Business School in 2007. She has contributed to leading marketing conferences' proceedings such as EMAC, WMC, CCIRC and co-authored articles with Professor T. C. Melewar, which have been published in the *European Journal of Marketing*, the *Journal of General Management* and the *Journal of Brand Management*. Her research interests cover consumer behaviour, image interface and corporate communications.

Sven Kuenzel is a senior lecturer in marketing at the University of Greenwich; he is a member of the Academy of Marketing and of the Institute of Direct Marketing. His main research interests are in relationship marketing, direct marketing, consumer behaviour and quantitative research techniques.

Roy Langer is Professor of Organizational and Marketing Communication at Roskilde University, Denmark. He received his PhD at Copenhagen Business School in 2000. His (co-)authored books, book chapters and articles, including contributions to journals such as *Harvard Deusto Business Review*, *Publizistik*, *Psychology & Marketing*, *Corporate Reputation Review* and *Corporate Communications – An International Journal*, address a wide range of topical interests. His research has received awards several times, most recently an Emerald Literati Award (2006). He has just finished a presentation of legitimacy-gap theory for the *The International Encyclopedia of Communication* (Blackwell, 2008, ed. by Wolfgang Donsbach).

Felix Mavondo is Professor of Marketing in the Department of Marketing at Monash University, Australia. He is also a certified management consultant. His research interests include marketing strategy, market orientation, relationship marketing, retailing and agribusiness.

Robert McMurrian is an associate professor at the University of Tampa and the director of the John H. Sykes College of Business Center for Ethics. He has previously published in such journals as the *Journal of Marketing*, the *Journal of Applied Psychology*, and *Psychology and Marketing*.

T. C. Melewar is Professor of Marketing and Strategy at Brunel Business School (UK). Formerly a lecturer in Warwick Business School, the MARA Institute of Technology, Malaysia and a senior lecturer at De Montfort University, Leicester. Dr Melewar has links with a number of companies including Corus, Sony and Safeway. He has published in leading journals in marketing including the *European Journal of Marketing*, the *Journal of International Business Studies* and the *Journal of Brand Management*. Current research interests include corporate identity, marketing communications and international marketing strategy.

Shaun Powell lectures in marketing within the School of Management and Languages at Heriot-Watt University, Edinburgh. He is also a director at the International Center for Corporate Marketing Studies (www.corporate-marketing.org). His research interests include corporate marketing, corporate branding, organizational creativity and organizational identity.

Bernd Schmitt is the Robert D. Calkins Professor of International Business and Executive Director of the Center on Global Brand Leadership at Columbia Business School in New York. The joint research in this volume was undertaken during Patrick Cettier's stay as an exchange scholar at the Center on Global Brand Leadership.

Hamed M. Shamma is an assistant professor of Marketing in the School of Business, Economics and Communication at the American University in Cairo. He formerly was an instructor of marketing and a PhD candidate at the School of Business, the George Washington University (GWU). He holds a BA with a specialization in marketing and an MBA in marketing and international business from the American University in Cairo. He has more than four years of experience in corporate performance valuation with Mobinil, a partially owned subsidiary of Orange Worldwide and Egypt's leading mobile telephone service operator. His research interests are in the areas of corporate marketing, strategic brand management, and customer relationship management (CRM).

David Stark is a former MBA student, supervised by Professor T. C. Melewar, studying at Warwick Business School.

Robyn Stokes lectures within the Faculty of Business at Queensland University of Technology (School of Advertising, Marketing and Public Relations) in Brisbane, Australia. She holds a PhD from Griffith University. Her current research interests are corporate branding, interorganizational relationships and networks and services marketing including tourism and events.

Richard Varey is Professor of Marketing at the Waikato Management School, New Zealand, and a specialist in investigating the impact of commercial marketing, social marketing, human interaction in market situations, and systems of managed communication. He is the editor of the *Australasian Marketing Journal*, and a member of the editorial boards of several academic journals including *Marketing Theory*, the *European Journal of Marketing* and the *Journal of Communication Management*. He is an ad hoc reviewer for the *Journal of Marketing* and the *Journal of Public Policy & Marketing*, and a guest reviewer for a wide range of management journals, conferences, and publishers. He is a member of the Advisory Committee of the Corporate Communication Institute at Baruch College, New York, and a contributing member of the TechCast virtual think-tank on technology futures (hosted at the George Washington University). Professor Varey is currently Principal Investigator on the Socially and Culturally Sustainable Biotechnology in New Zealand research programme.

Lee Chun Wah is an associate professor in the Wee Kim Wee School of Communication and Information at Singapore's Nanyang Technological University. His research areas are advertising management, brand communication and public communication. His teaching includes promotional communication and advertising campaigns. He is a member of the Education Council of the Association of Accredited Advertising Agents of Singapore as well as a member of the accreditation board of the Institute of Public Relations of Singapore. He received his doctorate in communication studies from Ohio University, USA.

Judith H. Washburn is an assistant professor at the University of Tampa. She has published articles on branding and business/nonprofit alliances in such journals as *Psychology and Marketing*, the *Journal of Marketing Theory and Practice*, and the *Journal of Services Marketing*.

Introduction

The concepts of corporate branding and corporate identity have gained considerable interest both in academic and practitioner circles. These concepts are particularly salient to strategic management and marketing disciplines, providing new lenses through which an organization's central attributes may be nurtured and altered.

In theory, a host of research contributing to corporate branding and management through academic journals (such as the *Journal of the Academy of Marketing Science*, the *European Journal of Marketing* and the *Journal of Brand Management*) and conferences (such as the International Conference on Corporate Communication, Identity and Reputation, the International Conference of the Corporate Identity/ Associations Research Group and the SIG on Corporate Branding under the Academy of Marketing) is rapidly increasing. Many higher universities and research centres, such as Brunel Business School, Birmingham Business School, Copenhagen Business School, the Corporate Communications Institute, Oklahoma State University and the Australian Graduate School of Management, have now become leading institutions generating research in the fields of corporate branding and corporate-identity management.

In practice, many national, multinational and even small and medium-sized enterprises (SMEs) have recognized that managing their corporate identities and corporate brands is a strategic tool that creates competitive advantage. Marketers have become increasingly concerned with the impact of increased environmental pressures such as the significance of reactions towards corporate scandals, the fast pace of product introductions and extensions, scarce investor-attracting opportunities, the demand for a highly qualified workforce, and the rise in mergers and acquisitions. Therefore, senior managers have started devoting a substantial amount of resources towards the management of corporate brands and corporate identities in order to benefit from the leveraging influences of corporate branding and management. For instance, in 2003 BT (British Telecom) spent about £5m to re-design and launch its new visual identity (the 'connected world') to express its internationalization, its coverage of a wide range of business activities and its capabilities in multimedia.

However, notwithstanding an increasing recognition of the importance of corporate branding and management both in theory and practice, there is still the need to further discuss these two concepts in order to provide a solid theoretical and practical infrastructure. This book takes this point into account and provides currency, coverage and practicality in the fields of corporate branding and management. Although readers may differ on whether other articles deserve inclusion within the collection, the editors were seeking a balance between three important points. First, contributions to this book had to address the conceptual debate in the areas of corporate branding and management. Second, they should foster new dialogues about further research opportunities. Third, they should offer ideas about the applications of corporate branding and management, and relevant managerial implications. In brief, this book attempts to broaden our understanding in these two areas by providing theoretical and practical insights from current academic research and practitioner approaches.

The book contains 11 articles which cover facets of corporate branding and management. The chapter by McMurrian and Washburn addresses the need for drawing theories from other disciplines to understand how brands and customers interact, and proposes that social-contract theory can be used as a framework to examine how ethical company actions may lead to a favourable image in the marketplace and hence increase customer-perceived value. Shamma and Hassan further the discussion on perceived value on the grounds of brand equity and examine the latter concept at corporate level. They provide a conceptual framework which illustrates that salient corporate values held by stakeholders to assess corporate brand equity may differ and that each stakeholder's valuation has an impact on corporate performance indicators.

Similarly, Anisimova and Mavondo's chapter takes into account the fact that corporate identity and its perception relate to multiple stakeholders. It draws attention to incongruence between the perceptions of internal and external stakeholders on corporate brand which may lead to undesirable outcomes for companies; it then proposes an integrative model which incorporates both managers' and customers' views on corporate brand.

The fourth chapter, by Stokes, attempts to challenge the general tendency of using corporate branding as an overarching concept, as it was presented in the preceding chapters. This article provides argument about the definition of corporate brand concept in comparison to vision, image, and the concepts of reputation and identity. The author discusses the conceptual distinctions and intersections between these concepts and corporate branding, supported by empirical data collected from an airport's staff.

Inspired by recent studies (for example, Bhattacharya and Sen, 2003), Halliday and Kuenzel bring the concept of identification into the area of corporate branding and develop a conceptual model of customer brand identification in business relationships, based on social identity theory. Their article offers a view on how customer brand identification can play a central role in linking corporate branding, identity and communications.

In the following paper Powell focuses on organizations' internal environment and integrates literatures from business-to-business and organizational identity research streams. It unfolds employees' views on issues related to the interconnections between creativity, identity and brand by adopting a case-study approach, in particular thematic network analysis. In this paper it is argued that small to medium-sized enterprises (SMEs) that encourage creativity among their workforces may enjoy a creative reputation and stronger organizational brand perception.

Another perspective is presented by Wah, who argues that earlier studies have failed to present strong relationships between the original constructs of strategy, structure and culture on the one hand and dimensions of management on the other. In addition to these determinants of management, he suggests a set of constructs related to management processes and environmental characteristics – corporate artifacts, symbolism, shared values, the nature of employee relationships, and mental schemata, among others.

Sowa directs the reader's attention towards integrated marketing communication, and in particular he questions how public relations should take place during this aligning of promotional activities and strategies in order to achieve a communicative transaction with corporate brand names.

The following two papers focus on the practice of corporate rebranding and the re-formation of a corporate identity during a merger. Cettier and Schmitt identify seven key factors for a successful corporate rebranding process by examining companies from the United States, UK and Germany for the period between 1995 and 2004. Furthermore, they compare two rebranding initiatives that were undertaken by UBS and the Swiss financial corporation. Melewar, Stark and Karaosmanoğlu provide another example of the re-creation and relaunch of a corporate identity by analysing the Renault-Nissan merger on the basis of another management model developed by Melewar and Jenkins (2000).

The last chapter, by Langer and Varey, provides another challenging view about the traditional role of corporate communication in corporate identity and image construction. By drawing on research on national images, media studies and corporate communication and providing company examples such as Hamburg-Mannheimer, Rambøll, Shell, Burger King and Scandinavian Airlines, they assert that corporate image or corporate identity cannot be built on the basis of product images or identities. They argue that corporate communication should be considered as an interactional tool and therefore its role in image and identity construction should be researched by integrating all stakeholders of an organisation, all the discursive history and former actions of a corporation, and the social memory of the respective public.

As editors we would like to mention that preparation of this book has been a very stimulating experience for us. We believe that we have managed to bring a special collection of thoughts from academics and practitioners who pursue their enthusiasm on resolving corporate branding and management issues all around the world. We hope that the papers compiled in this book expand the readers' knowledge and understanding in corporate branding and management and inspire them to conduct more challenging research.

References

Bhattacharya, C. B. and S. Sen (2003) 'Consumer-company Identification: A Framework for Understanding Consumers' Relationships with Companies', *Journal of Marketing*, 67, pp. 76–88.

Melewar, T. C. and E. Jenkins (2000) 'Defining Corporate Identity: the Search for a Holistic Model', *Advanced Issues in Marketing*, pp. 1–25.

1

Branding: A Social Contract between a Business and Its Customer

Robert McMurrian[1] and Judith H. Washburn

Abstract

This article proposes social-contract theory as a useful framework for understanding the relationship between businesses and customers. The authors suggest that customer-perceived value increases when businesses practice ethical behaviours that bridge the gap between business and customer communities. The authors make the case that customer value, created through brand-building efforts, leads to long-term profitability and competitive advantage. This article is the first to suggest that social-contract theory explains the mechanism by which customers perceive brands as promises.

Introduction

'Pretty is as pretty does' is an admonition that can be traced back as far as Chaucer, circa 1387. The proverb suggests that actions are much more important than appearances and pertains to both individuals and organizations. With respect to organizations, customers develop perceptions about a company and its image based on marketplace behaviours; these perceptions lead to the customer's value proposition. Customers respond to that which a company *actually does* as opposed to what it *says it will do*, forming perceptions based on prior experience, word of mouth, and marketplace activities.

This article explores the connections between a company's branding activities, customer perceptions of a company's ethical behaviour, and customer value. We review social-contract theory as it relates to a business and its customers and suggest that this theory offers a useful framework for examining the relationship between branding strategy and customers' perceptions of value. Our review of the literature suggests that ethical behaviour builds brand equity which in turn provides customer value. Conversely, unethical behaviour can damage brand equity and, consequently, customer value. Numerous recent examples (for example, Arthur Andersen, WorldCom and Tyco) illustrate the dissipation of brand equity for companies ensnared in ethical scandals.

We organize the article by first discussing the concepts of brand and brand equity and then exploring social-contract theory as it relates to branding. Next, we examine customer value, discussing both its antecedents and its outcomes, and explicitly pursue the link between customer value and ethics. The article concludes with a discussion of managerial implications and suggestions for future research that flow from the six propositions offered throughout the article.

Brands and brand equity

Brands play a vital role in the relationship between company and customer; they help customers navigate the decision process by reducing risk and providing a shortcut to product identification. In many cases, brands allow customers to make a personal statement about who they are. For companies, brands not only provide a legal means to identify and protect their products, but also provide the key to product differentiation, which ultimately leads to competitive advantage. In fact, the value of a company's brand can constitute as much as 70 per cent of its intangible assets. Putting this into perspective, the total value of many companies often comprises 90 per cent intangible assets (Keller, 2003). Thus, well over half a company's assets may be attributable to its brand(s).

In the eyes of many customers, the brand *is* the company. David Aaker has said that brand identity goes beyond brand as a product and includes brand as an organization, person and symbol (Aaker, 1996). In fact, at least 32 of the top 50 global brands boast names that are the same as or very similar to the organization's name (Clarke, 2004). Customers attach a high level of meaning to a brand, meaning that goes far beyond the brand's name and symbolism. To many customers a brand is a promise (Keller, 2000). This is the language that confirms the application of social-contract theory in branding. Customers form relationships with brands that are built on trust and often describe these relationships as being a type of bond, pact or contract. These bonds lead to brand loyalty and the '... implicit understanding that the brand will behave in certain ways and provide [the customer with] utility through consistent product performance and appropriate pricing, promotions, distribution programmes and actions' (Keller, 2003, p. 9). The success of longstanding, well-known brands such as Wedgwood, Estee Lauder, Starbucks and Dell has been attributed to the founders' abilities to forge deep relationships with customers (Koehn, 2001).

The goal of branding is to build brand equity, the definition of which continues to be debated in the marketing literature (e.g., Aaker, 1991; Farquhar, 1989; Srivastava and Shocker, 1991). Commonly, brand equity has been discussed as the value, over and above the tangible value of a product, passed on to customers (both individuals and companies) by the brand and its components. Aaker (1991) explained brand equity as consisting of brand assets and brand liabilities that contribute to or detract from a product's value to the firm and/or its customers. Aaker and Keller, among others, advocate managing, maintaining and measuring brand equity.

For the purposes of this paper, Keller's (1993) conceptualization of customer-based brand equity (CBBE) is most relevant. According to Keller, 'the power of a brand lies in what customers have learned, felt, seen, and heard about the brand as a result of their experiences over time.' To build CBBE, a company must take four sequential steps to form a brand pyramid. The first step answers the question, 'Who are you?' and requires creating brand salience or brand awareness. The next step addresses the question, 'What are you?' and involves delivering on brand performance and creating a brand image. The third question, 'What about you?' focuses on generating customer evaluations, opinions, and feelings about the brand. Finally, reaching the top of the pyramid, or achieving brand resonance answers the question, 'What about you and me?' and constitutes achieving customer loyalty, attitudinal attachment, a sense of community, and active engagement with the brand (Keller, 2003). As we will demonstrate, the steps involved in building customer-based brand equity are fully consistent with the tenets of social-contract theory.

This discussion on brands and brand equity provides the first of six propositions developed within this paper:

Proposition #1. In an economic community of business organizations and their customers, customers develop expectations that the promise a business communicates through its brand is the truth.

Social-contract theory and marketing ethics

Dunfee, Smith and Ross, Jr. (1999) suggest that social-contract theory is a normative approach to ethics that prescribes how managers should react when facing an issue with right and wrong implications. Of all business activities, marketing has developed a reputation of being among the worst offenders for unethical practice (LeClair, Ferrell and Ferrell, 1997). As academics and organizations have searched for explanations and prescriptions for business ethics, social-contract theory has emerged as a viable framework.

Donaldson (1982) was one of the first to propose social-contract theory as a basis for business ethics. In his book *Corporations and Morality* (1982), Donaldson made an application of social-contract theory to 'productive organizations' rather than the traditional application to political institutions. Donaldson identified two classes of business obligations – direct (explicit) obligations grounded in laws and contracts, and indirect (inexplicit) obligations that organizations have regarding stakeholders. Donaldson used social-contract theory to identify indirect obligations such as the scope of employees' rights, regulation goals, and consumers' unwritten rights. In his second book *The Ethics of International Business* (1989), Donaldson applied social-contract theory to international business and more clearly established inexplicit obligations as a basic contract. In business, social-contract theory sets a bar that represents a minimum responsibility.

Dunfee (1991) expanded social-contract theory to better reflect the applied nature of business ethics. He sees social contracts as including certain standards or norms. These norms are usually not fully defined in words and are related to notions of right and wrong behaviour that is shared by a group or community. Donaldson and Dunfee (1994) describe such a community as a 'self-defined, self-circumscribed group of people who interact in the context of shared tasks, values or goals, and who are capable of establishing norms of ethical behaviour for themselves' (p. 13). Donaldson and Dunfee (1994) merged their social-contract ideas into an integrative social-contract theory that envisions social contracts as existing between two communities. In the case of marketing ethics, one community is the business organization and the other is the business's customers. This economic integration is characterized by the business relationship that ties the community of customers to the business organization community in exchange practices. According to Dunfee (1991), the communities will specify group norms of behaviour. If these group norms are consistent with general moral standards, the norms become an ethical norm, and all members of the group have a basic duty to comply with ethical norms. In essence, this duty to comply is accepted by people who are members of a group, who benefit from the group, or who are beneficiaries of the norms of the group. Such is the case with branding of products, services, and even business organizations themselves. Branding conveys a promise by a member of one community (the business) to a member of the other community (the customer) and the promise eventually is accepted as an ethical norm.

Calton and Lad's (1995) treatment of social contracting as a network governance process offers another view of how social-contract theory relates to marketing practice. Calton and Lad (1995) define a network as the 'structure of ties among the actors of a social system' (p. 273). A market is characterized by economic exchanges between loyal, repeat customers and conscientious providers of goods and services; thus, a basic network exists. One of the most fundamental ethical norms found in a network is that network members will tell the truth in their communications with other network members. That is, members of a network share a belief that all network members will work for the common good of the network and thus have common objectives for the good of the network. As such, members feel they can rely on the truth in network communications from one member to another member. Calton and Lad (1995) contend 'that network sustainability depends on the creation and maintenance of a social context of mutual trust among participants in the collective learning, problem-solving process' (p. 281).

It is in this sense that we use social-contract theory as our basis for examining the role of ethics in branding. Businesses offer satisfying goods or services to defined groups of customers who make purchasing decisions on the basis of a product's (or an organization's) brand image. As such, a brand image carries with it implied promises. The automobile industry offers good examples. Through longstanding, consistent branding messages, customers believe that Volvo promises safety, Mercedes-Benz promises unsurpassed engineering, and BMW promises performance. Customers develop trust based on brand images and an inherent belief that organizations will uphold these implied promises.

Therefore, social-contract theory relates to both marketing ethics and branding strategy through the common theme of exchange. Donaldson's (1982, 1989) social contract suggests that an organization offers advantages to its stakeholders, including customers and employees, in exchange for the privilege to exist and be profitable. This exchange relationship between an organization and its customers is one of the most fundamental concepts in marketing (Hunt, 1983; Kotler, 1972). It seems logical to apply social-contract theory, an exchange-based model of ethics, to the ethical issues associated with the exchange-based discipline of marketing and particularly to the marketing function of branding. While social-contract theory has been referenced in the marketing literature with respect to social responsibility (Goolsby and Hunt, 1992), this article adds to the literature by applying social-contract theory to the act of branding.

Social-contract theory is the basis of our next two propositions:

Proposition #2. Ethical norms develop in business networks based on members' expectations of other members.

Proposition #3. Companies that uphold expected ethical norms form bonds of trust with their customers.

Customer value and branding

Branding is closely related to the process quality component of customer value because customers develop feelings and expectations based on their brand perceptions. Heskett, Sasser and Schlesinger (1997) suggest that the manner in which a product is provided can be as important to customers as the results a product actually delivers. Based on this belief, Heskett et al. (1997) developed the service profit chain model to explain the relationships between employees and customers in a service environment. The model suggests skilled employees who are highly satisfied with their jobs are much more loyal to the organization and far more productive in delivering high levels of quality service to customers. As a result of this high level of service, the organization's customers hold positive attitudes toward the company exhibited in high levels of customer satisfaction. In turn, customer satisfaction generates higher levels of loyalty, which is expressed in customers' behaviours such as repeat purchases and referrals of additional customers. This process results in long-term, stable revenue growth and profitability.

While the service profit chain was developed specifically for service organizations, we believe that the concept is both applicable to and useful for managing for growth and profitability in any organization where employees interact directly with customers. Thus, we have extended the service profit chain model to include organizations marketing physical goods. Our extended model is presented in Figure 1.1.

We extend this concept of customer value and argue that an organization's branding activities and resulting brand image or reputation are an important component of the process quality variable in the

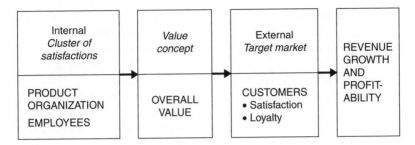

Figure 1.1 The value profit chain

value concept. The connection to a company's ethical behaviours is highlighted by Willmott (2003) in his discussion of citizen brands:

> Good citizenship encourages trust in the company, which leads to higher levels of satisfaction and retention and ultimately commercial success'... Citizenship is rapidly becoming an integral part of brand equity. (p. 367)

Willmott (2003) contends that branding, in addition to conveying information regarding a product or service, also is a source of information regarding an organization from which customers derive perceptions of value. When a brand is known for good corporate citizenship there is a direct positive impact on business operations (a more motivated workforce, better supplier relationships, and improved market intelligence, for example). Possibly of even more importance is the positive indirect impact of a well-perceived brand. Such a brand, conveying a perception of good corporate citizenship, builds reputation and trust in a market. Citizen brands increase customers' perceptions of quality and, in essence, create a 'goodwill bank' (p. 363). These results, in turn, create higher levels of perceived customer value leading to greater customer loyalty, which results in higher customer retention rates, repeat sales to existing customers, and referral from satisfied customers.

Central to our extended model is the concept of overall value that customers realize and perceive in relationships with organizations. In the services context, a customer's perceived value is dependent on contacts with service employees (Heskett et al., 1994). However, perceived value in a physical goods environment is the result of several relationships, or a cluster of satisfactions. When customers acquire a product, they anticipate and expect some level of utility value based on the implied contract with that company. That is, the customer expects the product to provide desired personal advantages and benefits, physical and/or psychological. To acquire these need-satisfying products, customers usually have some direct contact with an organization and its employees.

The cluster of satisfactions

While customers purchase products for the results or utility value they seek, current marketing thought indicates that customers today are better educated and more demanding, and expect more than utility value from a product. These customers are redefining products as combinations of the physical good, the organization from which the product was acquired, and the service received from the organization's employees. Customers seek a cluster of satisfactions that arise from the combination of product, organization and employees (see Manning and Reese, 2004). Customers expect this cluster of satisfactions to deliver high levels of perceived value from use of a product, interaction with an organization, and contact with an organization's representatives. Recall that the previous discussion of brand identity suggested similar underpinnings (that is, the organization, the person and the symbol).

The customer value equation

Heskett et al. (1997) developed a value *equation* to describe customer value as comprising two components – customer revenue and customer cost. The resulting customer profit (or loss) represents value to the customer in terms of: (1) benefits in utilizing the product, (2) the relationship with the company in purchasing the product, and (3) the relationship with the company's representatives. Value, as perceived by the customer, is represented as:

$$\frac{\text{Customer}}{\text{Value}} = \frac{\text{Results Produced for the Customer} + \text{Process Quality}}{\text{Price to the Customer} + \text{Costs of Acquiring the Product}}$$

The numerator in the customer value equation represents income or revenue, both real and psychological, to a customer. This customer revenue consists of results the customer realizes from actual use of a product or service and the overall quality of the process of initiating and maintaining a relationship with both the organization and the organization's representatives. Value, as perceived by customers, is the difference between the personal revenue (results + process quality) generated and the personal cost (price + acquisition cost). The greater the positive difference between customer cost and customer revenue, the greater the value of the product and relationships (organization and people) to the customer. The individual components of customer value are discussed below.

Results produced for the customer

In the end, customers buy results or utility value (e.g., a one-quarter inch hole), not features (e.g., a quarter-inch drill bit), when purchasing products and services.

Process quality

We define process quality as the perceived value of the business relationship between a customer and an organization and the personal relationship between a customer and representatives of the organization. Examples of process quality components include customers' perceived ease of negotiation in dealing with a business, the ease of obtaining product information, the ease of obtaining product service, the responsiveness of service personnel, and the ethical standards and behaviours that customers believe characterize business organizations.

Parasuraman, Zeithaml and Berry (1988) found that the quality and perceived value of such processes consists of the following five dimensions – dependability, responsiveness, authority, empathy and results. *Dependability*, or doing what you say you're going to do, is key to an organization's long-term growth and profitability because it is a determinant of customer trust that leads to higher levels of customer retention. In addition, customers must feel that companies *respond* to customer needs in a timely manner and that customer contact personnel have the *authority* to deliver on promises. Customers must also feel that the organization is *empathetic* or can see things from the customer's point of view. Finally, customers expect to achieve desired *results*, or tangible evidence, from the purchase and use of products.

Price to the customer

The price of a product can consist of more than just a financial price. Inherent in a product's price is a psychological component of risk. Customers expect that products with a higher inherent risk factor will also have higher prices.

Costs of acquiring the product

In addition to the economic price that customers pay to acquire products, customers must invest time and effort to physically acquire products.

Outcomes

When customers perceive the relationship with an organization to be of value, the organization benefits from several positive outcomes. These customers are highly satisfied. While most companies survey their customers and measure levels of customer satisfaction, satisfaction is only an attitude. To ultimately be profitable for an organization, these attitudes of satisfaction must result in specific customer behaviours that increase revenue and profitability. These behaviours represent levels of customer loyalty to the organization. For example, customers, based on high satisfaction levels, should continue to purchase products from the organization in the future. These customers usually buy more often and purchase larger quantities when they do buy. Additionally, these customers refer other potential customers to the organization. Referred customers usually develop higher levels of satisfaction and loyalty at faster rates than did the referring customers. These outcomes are directly related to the company's branding activities.

Customer value and ethics

A business's ethical behaviours strongly influence customers' perceptions of process quality that we defined previously. Customers' overall feelings regarding the quality of processes in maintaining a business relationship with an organization are based on customers' general perceptions of the five key items also described above, four of which are directly tied to organizational behaviours grounded in ethical business practices – dependability, responsiveness, empathy and results. First, an organization must be *dependable* in delivering on promises made to customers. Second, organizations must *quickly respond* to customers' issues (such as complaints). Third, organizations must understand the *customer's point of view* in any interactions. Fourth, organizations must consider the *results* of any actions or behaviours on customers. For example, Enron made bad internal management decisions that resulted in unethical practices. These unethical activities, while primarily internal to the company, had far-ranging impacts in the marketplace. It was not only customers that were negatively affected – the effects were felt by all stakeholders in the company.

Business ethics, the foundation of the processes by which customers develop feelings of trust in organizations, directly impact customers' perceptions of process quality. Customers might feel they are getting good results from using a company's products; that the market price of the products is reasonable compared to competitive products; and that the cost (time and effort) of obtaining the products is in line; however, their perceptions of value will be degraded if they do not trust the company. This discussion is the basis for the next proposition:

Proposition #4. Overall, customers would rather pay higher prices and maintain business relationships with ethical and trusted organizations than get good price deals from organizations that do not deliver outstanding process quality.

Brand ethics lead to customer value

Rust, Zeithaml and Lemon (2004) expanded on Keller's idea of customer-based brand equity. They advocate that, instead of focusing on brand equity, companies should be more interested in customer equity – the 'sum of lifetime values of all of the firm's customers, across all the firm's brands' (p. 113). Rust et al. (2004) depict customer equity as being the result of brand choice and customer lifetime value. According to their model, three forms of equity – value equity, brand equity and relationship equity – drive brand choice. Value equity is 'the objectively considered quality, price, and convenience of the offering,' while relationship equity 'factors in switching costs – the customer's reluctance to go elsewhere' (p. 116). In many cases, the key to developing brand choice, and ultimately customer equity, is brand equity. Rust et al. (2004) assert that while brand equity drivers vary from company to company, three common drivers are brand awareness, attitude toward the brand, and brand ethics or corporate citizenship.

We have reviewed several different models throughout this article, all of which suggest that ethical corporate behaviours contribute positively to brand equity, which in turn, leads to customer value. Alternatively, unethical behaviours denigrate a company's brand equity by creating brand liabilities. Social-contract theory is the framework that helps to explain the connections between brands, corporate ethics and customer value.

Proposition #5. A brand that is trusted by the marketplace leads to customer satisfaction and customer value.

Trust processes and ethical behaviour

Long-term relationships with customers depend on exchange processes that are characterized by high levels of trust between the parties involved in an exchange (Morgan and Hunt, 1994). There is some disagreement in the literature as to whether customers can develop trust in the organization itself (Morgan and Hunt, 1994) or whether customers actually develop trust in the representatives of an organization (such as sales representatives or customer service personnel) (Doney and Cannon, 1997). It is somewhat intuitive that customers would develop perceptions of trust (or distrust) in organizations through contact with organizational agents since these contacts actually represent the organizations to the customers.

Our definition of trust is a combination of two elements related to an exchange partner – perceived credibility and perceived benevolence (Kumar, Scheer and Steenkamp, 1995). Credibility relates to an expectancy that the exchange partner's word, written statement (contract), or actions can be relied on. Benevolence relates to the degree that one exchange partner (the organization) is genuinely interested in the wellbeing of the other partner (the customer) and is seeking to develop a win-win relationship.

Doney and Cannon (1997) suggest five distinct processes – calculative, prediction, capability, intentionality and transference – by which customers develop trust in business relationships and organizations. Of these five trust processes, perceived ethical behaviour is an important component of trust based on capability, intentionality and transference.

Capability focuses on the credibility element of trust and involves the organization's ability to meet its obligations and deliver on its promises. Customers infer a level of trust in an organization if the customer has reason to believe the organization can deliver products, services and support as promised. Ethical behaviour also signals an organization's *intentionality* when customers believe the organization will behave in ways that are in customers' best interests. Finally, a customer can develop trust in an organization through the process of *transference,* in which a customer trusts an exchange partner because of its relationship with a third-party (for example, a friend or relative) trusted by the customer. In sum, a business organization's ethical behaviours and actions are the foundation of these trust processes.

The impact of ethical behaviour on long-term profitability

Organizations that practice ethical behaviour and maintain high-quality relational processes with their customers have the potential to generate sustained growth and higher revenues over a longer period of time. Furthermore, these organizations incur lower marketing expenses resulting in increased profitability. The customer value profit chain model (Figure 1.1) posits that high levels of perceived customer value result in high levels of customer satisfaction, and customer satisfaction leads to higher levels of customer loyalty.

It is important to understand, however, that customer satisfaction and customer loyalty are two very different variables in the profit chain model. Customer satisfaction is an attitude that represents how a customer feels about the relationship with a business organization. Customer loyalty, on the other hand, is an action rather than an attitude; loyal customers consciously act to maintain business relationships with organizations. It is customer loyalty that leads to three very profitable behaviours by customers. First, loyal customers purchase more from organizations, generating higher levels of revenue compared to not-so-loyal customers. Second, loyal customers repeat purchases from organizations on a more frequent basis and for longer time periods than do other customers. Third, loyal customers refer other prospects (friends, relatives, neighbours) to the organizations they trust and are highly satisfied with. These referred customers then become more satisfied and more loyal in a shorter period of time than did the referring customers.

Highly satisfied, loyal customers are much more profitable than other less loyal customers because they generate more revenue and cost much less to maintain. Business organizations with high percentages of satisfied and loyal customers can invest fewer financial resources in costly marketing programmes aimed at these customers. For example, promotion directed at maintaining loyal customers is a less costly investment than promotion designed to attract customers away from competitors to build market share. Additionally, salespeople are not required to contact these loyal customers as often and the contacts that are made tend to maintain positive and profitable relationships rather than directly sell products. The final proposition captures these relationships:

Proposition #6. High levels of customer value lead to high levels of customer retention, repeat purchases and referrals.

Managerial implications

It is important that business organizations recognize the influence of branding activities on customer perceptions of value. It is the customer's value perception that leads to long-term profitability and competitive advantage for a business organization. Management decisions on branding activities are the building blocks that contribute to customer value.

As managers design programmes to build brands and brand equity, they must include activities that demonstrate the organization's commitment to ethical business practices in exchange transactions with their customers.

In current marketing literature, branding is associated with creating an image in customers' and potential customers' minds. Such an image is designed to identify a product or service with value associated with the product or service and to differentiate a product or service from those offered by competitors. In essence, positive brand equity becomes a competitive advantage. In another sense, branding is presented in marketing principles textbooks as a promise made by a company to customers regarding the overall product in terms of quality, utility value and psychological value. Through a company's branding activities, customers associate specific brands with the aforementioned qualities. Positively perceived branding activities result in brand recognition, brand loyalty and brand preference. As we have suggested in this article, as a result of branding activities, a company's brand is perceived by customers as constituting a promise to customers.

We believe, however, that branding and the resulting brand image is more than a promise to customers. With social-contract theory as our foundation, we suggest that a brand represents a contract between a company and its customers. That is, a brand and associated branding activities are perceived by customers to be a promise of quality, utility and psychological value made by a company. As social-contract theory posits, this promise by one community member to another community member is seen as a social contract in which terms of the agreement (promises) are expected to be upheld and delivered. Each action taken by management either contributes to or takes away from the customer's level of trust in the company to live up to its promise and support the contract. Such is the case with branding activities.

Social-contract theory is even more relevant today with our focus on relationship marketing (Dunfee et al., 1999). Relationship marketing focuses on closely linked relationships between buyers and sellers. Implicit in relationships is the role of shared values. Managers charged with the task of 'branding' products and services must recognize customers' expectations regarding an organization's marketplace behaviours. These expectations will have an influence on future interactions and even become part of norms that frame relationships with customers. Managers must understand that, as suggested by social-contract theory, these close-knit marketing relationships may even become communities with their own norms.

In our marketing classes, we teach that one of the most basic foundations of relationship marketing is trust. Norms that are a part of informal social contracts are important for trust to exist in exchange relationships. Social norms, as explained by social-contract theory, provide a more flexible and more permanent basis for relationships than do alternative bases, such as litigation or government regulations. Social-contract theory provides managers with a framework for understanding and heading off branding actions that customers (partners in the community) perceive as violating conditions of the social contract with its existing norms of acceptable behaviours. This can lead to long-term relationships that result in customer satisfaction, customer loyalty, customer retention, and growth and profitability.

Future research

Current research and theory development related to marketing ethics has not typically been supported with multidimensional models. Additionally, while there exists marketing literature addressing the relationship between ethics, brand equity and customer perceptions of products and companies, this literature has omitted social-contract theory as a possible theoretical base with which to examine these relationships. Such research has focused on moral philosophies and provided descriptive statistics about ethical beliefs. Our research will contribute to existing theory by using social-contract theory to develop multidimensional decision-making models.

This paper lays the conceptual underpinnings of future efforts to develop a decision-making model for managers charged with making branding decisions that lead to increased customer value. While marketing literature has addressed the correlation between a brand, branding activities, and customer perceptions and actions, current research has not examined social-contract theory as a possible explanation for the connection between a brand and customer perceptions. We believe social-contract theory provides a useful foundation for such research. We have offered six propositions throughout the paper that can be further refined and developed into hypotheses for empirical testing. Future research should focus on answering the following questions:

What is the connection between customer expectations and ethical norms? Businesses and customers exist in integrated communities that develop ethical norms over time based on their expectations. Future research should unravel the process by which expectations evolve into ethical norms.

What branding activities are the most critical in building trust among customers? Customers learn to trust businesses when they perceive the business as upholding ethical norms. In other words, customers trust businesses when they see that the promises the business makes via their branding activities are true.

What is the nature and direction of the relationships among trust, customer satisfaction, customer value, and customer commitment? Can a model be developed that clearly illustrates these relationships? This trust bond leads to customer satisfaction and increased customer value, which leads to committed customers and referrals.

Can it be empirically demonstrated that customers are willing to make sacrifices (i.e., pay higher prices) to form relationships with ethical companies that they can trust? Anecdotal evidence suggests that, in many cases, customers are less concerned about price than about performance in a brand they trust.

Can a model be developed that is useful to managers in making ethical branding decisions? Absent from the available set of managerial tools is a decision tree designed to lead managers to making branding decisions that convey trust and contribute to customer value. Future research should contribute to the development of such a decision process that managers can call on when developing branding strategies. Such a decision process and tree should provide managers with a branding tool to ensure that branding strategies project an ethical image that leads to a value proposition that customers view as exceeding their expectations and contributing to higher retention, repeat business and referral.

Note

1. Both authors contributed equally to this chapter.

References

Aaker, D. (1991) *Managing Brand Equity* (New York, NY: The Free Press).
Aaker, D. (1996) *Building Strong Brands* (New York, NY: The Free Press).

Calton, J. M. and L. J. Lad (1995) 'Social Contracting as a Trust-Building Process of Network Governance', *Business Ethics Quarterly*, 5(2), pp. 271–95.

Clarke, B. (2004) 'Behaviour = Trust', *Brand Strategy*, March, pp. 34–5.

Donaldson, T. (1982) *Corporations and Morality* (Englewood Cliffs, NJ: Prentice Hall).

Donaldson, T. (1989) *The Ethics of International Business* (New York: Oxford University Press).

Donaldson, T. (2003) 'Adding Corporate Ethics to the Bottom Line', *Business Ethics 03/04*, 15th edn, John E. Richardson, ed. (Guildford: McGraw-Hill).

Donaldson, T. and T. Dunfee (1994) 'Towards a Unified Conception of Business Ethics: Integrative Social Contracts Theory', *Academy of Management Review*, 19(2), pp. 252–84.

Donaldson, T. and T. Dunfee (1999) *Ties that Bind: A Social Contract Approach to Business Ethics* (Boston, MA: Boston Business School Press).

Doney, P. M. and J. P. Cannon (1997) 'An Examination of the Nature of Trust In Buyer-Seller Relationships', *Journal of Marketing*, 61 (April), pp. 35–51.

Dunfee, T. W., N. C. Smith and W. T. Ross Jr (1999) 'Social Contracts and Marketing Ethics', *Journal of Marketing*, 63 (July), pp. 14–33.

Dunfee, T. W. (1991) 'Business Ethics and Extant Social Contracts', *Business Ethics Quarterly*, 23 (1), pp. 23–51.

Farquhar, P. H. (1989) 'Managing Brand Equity', *Marketing Research*, pp. 24–33.

Goolsby, J. R. and S. D. Hunt (1992) 'Cognitive Moral Development and Marketing', *Journal of Marketing*, 56 (January), pp. 55–68.

Heskett, J. L., W. E. Sasser Jr. and L. A. Schlesinger (1997) *The Service Profit Chain* (New York: The Free Press).

Heskett, J. L., T. O. Jones, G. W. Loveman, W. E. Sasser Jr and L. A. Schlesinger (1994) 'Putting the Service-Profit Chain to Work', *Harvard Business Review*, March/April, pp. 164–74.

Hunt, S. D. (1983) *Marketing Theory: The Philosophy of Marketing Science* (Homewood, IL: Richard D. Irwin).

Keller, K. (1993) 'Conceptualizing, Measuring, and Managing Customer-Based Brand Equity', *Journal of Marketing*, 57(1), pp. 1–22.

Keller, K. (2000) 'The Brand Report Card', *Harvard Business Review*, Jan–Feb, pp. 147–57.

Keller, K. (2003) *Strategic Brand Management: Building, Measuring, and Managing Brand Equity* (Upper Saddle River, NJ: Prentice Hall).

Koehn, N. (2001) *Brand New: How Entrepreneurs Earned Consumers' Trust from Wedgwood to Dell* (Harvard Business School Publishing Corporation).

Kotler, P. (1972) 'A Generic Concept of Marketing', *Journal of Marketing*, 36 (April), pp. 46–54.

Kumar, N., L. K. Scheer and J. Steenkamp (1995) 'The Effect of Perceived Interdependence on Dealer Attitudes', *Journal of Marketing Research*, 3 (August), pp. 348–56.

LeClair, D. T., O. C. Ferrell and L. Ferrell (1997) 'Federal Sentencing Guidelines for Organizations: Legal, Ethical and Public Policy Issues for International Marketing', *Journal of Public Policy and Marketing*, 16 (Spring), pp. 26–37.

Manning, G. L. and B. L. Reece (2004) *Selling Today*, 9th edn (New Jersey: Prentice Hall), p. 126.

Morgan, R. M. and S. D. Hunt (1994) 'The Commitment-Trust Theory of Relationship Marketing', *Journal of Marketing*, 58 (July), pp. 20–38.

Parasuraman, A., V. A. Zeithaml and L. Berry (1988) 'SERVQUAL: A Multiple-Item Scale for Measuring Consumer Perceptions of Service Quality', *Journal of Retailing*, Spring, pp. 12–40.

Rust, R., V. Zeithaml and K. Lemon (2004) 'Customer-Centered Brand Management', *Harvard Business Review*, September, pp. 110–18.

Srivastava, R. and A.D. Shocker (1991) 'Brand Equity: a Perspective on its Meaning and Measurement', *Marketing Science Institute Working Paper Series*, Report Number 91-124 (Cambridge, MA: Marketing Science Institute).

Willmott, M. (2003) 'Citizen Brands: Corporate Citizenship, Trust and Branding', *Brand Management*, 10 (4–5), pp. 362–69.

2

A Multiple Stakeholder Perspective for Measuring Corporate Brand Equity: Linking Corporate Brand Equity with Corporate Performance

Hamed M. Shamma and Salah S. Hassan

Abstract

Research on corporate brand equity has not gained much attention from marketing scholars. This chapter aims to fill this gap in the literature by: 1) highlighting the importance of corporate brand equity; 2) proposing a measure for corporate brand equity; and 3) linking corporate brand equity with corporate performance. A conceptual model is presented which integrates the multiple stakeholders' salient values in corporate brand equity valuation. By linking corporate brand equity components with elements of corporate performance, a framework is developed that sets the pace for a series of testable propositions. The chapter concludes with managerial implications, the challenges presented by the study and an agenda for future research.

Introduction

Kevin Keller (1998) defined corporate brand equity (CBE) as the 'differential response by consumers, customers, employees, other firms, or any relevant constituency to the words, actions, communications, products or services provided by an identified corporate brand entity' (p. 539). A company is said to have strong CBE when stakeholders hold 'strong, favourable and unique associations' about the corporate brand in their memories (p. 540). CBE therefore includes all those intangible aspects of a corporate brand that are presented in the form of corporate reputation, corporate image, corporate associations and relationships that add value to an organization's corporate identity (Motion, Leitch and Brodie, 2003). CBE depends highly on perceptions about a corporate brand and thus any valuation of CBE should be based on the different stakeholders' perceptions about a corporate brand.

A corporate brand is 'more than just the outward manifestation of an organization, its name, logo and visual representation, it is the core of values that define it' (Ind, 1997, p. 13). It is the overall perception about an organization, reflected by its overall corporate identity (Balmer, 2001). Marketers have become increasingly concerned about assessing perceptions about corporate brands. The increased environmental pressure faced by marketers has highlighted the importance of managing and evaluating corporate brands.

Several environmental trends taking place in the marketplace have increased the significance of corporate branding. The fast pace of product introductions and extensions, the broadening and diversity of sales channel members, the multiplicity of communication channels, the movement towards globalization, and mergers and acquisitions all have increased the reliance on corporate branding strategies as means of communicating information to external and internal parties about an organization (Hatch and Schultz, 2003). Also, the growing importance of capital markets, the need for attracting talented employees and executives and the increased demand for transparency puts more emphasis on the image of corporate brands (Einwiller and Will, 2002).

Increased corporate scandals and anti-corporatism have shifted the significance of corporate branding from a purely marketing communication perspective to a strategic and corporate-wide initiative. Consequently, the marketing and management of corporate brands has become a strategic necessity in today's highly regulative and turbulent business environment. Thus, a need was identified to assess the value of corporate brands as a means to help in strategically assessing their impact on corporations. Without an effective means for measuring corporate brands, corporations will not be able to evaluate how corporate brands strengthen or weaken company performance and also how they add or subtract value from corporations' overall reputation and credibility.

A review of corporate-based measures

Several consulting firms have proposed various methods for assessing perceptions about corporations. Corebrand, a consulting company that specializes in building and leveraging corporate brands, developed the Corporate Branding Index©(www.corebrand.com). This index measures the impact of corporate advertising on corporate reputation and financial performance over a certain period of time. It provides an indication to management on assessing the return on investment (ROI) from corporate advertising.

Fortune magazine has also developed a survey instrument for determining corporate reputation. They ask financial analysts, executives and outside directors to rate companies within their own industry based on the following characteristics: 1) financial soundness; 2) value as a long-term investment; 3) wise use of corporate assets; 4) innovativeness 5) the ability to attract, develop and keep talented people; 6) quality of products or services; 7) quality of management; and 8) community and environment responsibility (Sobol, Farelly and Taper, 1992). The results of this survey become the basis upon which Fortune magazine determines the ranking of America's Most Admired Corporations.

The Reputation Institute and Harris-Interactive jointly conduct an annual study that assesses the reputation of well-known companies. The Reputation Quotient®(RQ) is utilized for measuring corporate reputation which assesses companies on six key areas: 1) emotional appeal; 2) product/service quality; 3) financial performance; 4) social responsibility; 5) vision and leadership; and 6) workplace environment (www.reputationinstitute.com). The survey asks the general public about their opinions on corporations based on 20 attributes related to these six dimensions. While the measures utilized in measuring the RQ provide a quantitative measure for corporate reputation, standard item measures are applied in assessing the perceptions of one stakeholder group, the general public.

From the academic perspective, several measures have been developed in the marketing literature that assess perceptions at the corporate level. These include corporate associations, corporate image, corporate identity and corporate reputation. A summary of the major studies related to measuring corporate-level perceptions are presented in Table 2.1 below in chronological order.

Measuring CBE requires the assessment of different stakeholders' perceptions about a corporate brand. Using the same evaluation instrument for all stakeholders contradicts the central principle that each stakeholder group's perceptions should be based on their respective salient values. As Bromley (2002) mentioned, a common survey that is distributed to the general public or one particular group 'may not sample the stakeholder groups best informed about the survey items' (p. 36).

Table 2.1 Corporate level perceptions: concepts and measures

Authors (s)	Concept	Measures
Javalgi et al. 1994	Corporate image	Goods service Management Profit motive Community involvement Response to consumer needs Work environment

Brown and Dacin (1997)	Corporate associations	Corporate ability associations
		  • Leadership in industry
		  • Research and development capability
		  • Progressiveness of company
		Corporate social responsibility associations
		  • Concern for the environment
		  • Involvement in local communities
		  • Corporate giving to worthy causes

Keller (1998)	Corporate-image associations	Common product attributes, benefits or attitudes People and relationships Values and programs Corporate credibility
Fombrun, Gardberg and Server (2000)	Reputation quotient	Emotional appeal Products and services Vision and leadership Workplace environment Social and environmental responsibility Financial performance
Davies et al. (2001)	Personification metaphor	Sincerity Excitement Competence Sophistication Ruggedness
Melewar and Jenkins (2002)	Corporate identity	Communication and visual identity Behaviour Corporate culture Market conditions Firm, product and services
Brady (2003)	Corporate reputation	Knowledge and skills Emotional connection Leadership, vision and desire Quality Financial credibility Social credibility Environmental credibility

(Continued)

Table 2.1 (Continued)

Authors (s)	Concept	Measures
Cravens, Oliver and Ramamoorti (2003)	Reputation index	Products Employees External relationships Innovation and value creation Financial strengths and viability Strategy Culture Intangible liabilities
Davies et al. (2004)	Corporate character	Agreeableness Enterprise Competence Chic Ruthlessness Informality Machismo
Helm (2005)	Corporate reputation	Quality of products Commitment to protection of the environment Corporate success Treatment of employees Customer orientation Commitment to charitable and social issues Value for money of products Financial performance Qualification of management Credibility of advertising claims

This is because each stakeholder group is likely to hold different perceptions about an organization.

Any valuation of CBE should be derived by the stakeholders' valuable elements that are specifically important to each stakeholder group. Different stakeholders have different interests and concerns that need to be addressed independently. In this study, values of employees, customers, owners, regulators, the general community and partners will be examined in determining CBE. The purpose of this chapter is to: 1) propose a model for measuring CBE that integrates the stakeholders' value propositions into CBE valuation; and 2) assess the relationship between CBE and corporate performance (CP). This relationship can be presented as shown in Figure 2.1 below.

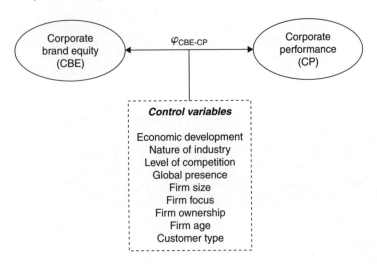

Figure 2.1 Relationship between corporate brand equity and corporate performance

The stakeholder perspective

It is important to highlight that any valuation for CBE requires assessing stakeholders' perspectives about a corporate brand. Stakeholders are 'persons or groups that have, or claim, ownership, rights, or interests in a corporation and its activities, past, present or future' (Clarkson, 1995, p. 106). Stakeholders include: employees, customers, stockholders, creditors, suppliers, vendors, regulators, governments, media, interest groups and the community at large. The stakeholder theory, a theory that is often cited in the strategic management literature, highlights the importance of establishing and maintaining effective relationships with all corporate stakeholders to achieve corporate goals and objectives (Freeman, 1984). The marketing literature, however, has primarily focused on managing relationships with the customer as the key stakeholder group to address. This is emphasized in the market-orientation approach, where the primary interest is in addressing and serving customer groups (Day, 1994; Jaworksi and Kohli, 1993; Slater and Narver, 1994). Yet in a highly regulated and interdependent business environment it is unreasonable to ignore the demands of other non-customer groups. This has triggered the attention of marketing scholars to reconsider the role of marketing within an organization.

In August 2004, the Board of Directors of the American Marketing Association developed a new definition of marketing as 'an organizational function and a set of processes for creating, communicating and delivering value to customers and for managing customer relationships in ways that benefit the organization and its stakeholders' (www.marketingpower.com). Further, in December 2007, the Board of Directors of the American Marketing association updated the definition of marketing as 'the activity set of institutions, and processes for creating, communicating, delivering and exchanging offerings that have value for customers, clients, partners and society at large.' (www.marketingpower.com). This new definition addresses the interests of stakeholders and includes the stakeholders' demands as part of the marketing function. The new definition assumes that shared responsibilities and mutual trust between a company and its stakeholders helps in achieving their common objectives in the long term (Dwyer, Schurr and Oh, 1987).

The pressure exerted by a company's stakeholders drives corporations to satisfy and meet stakeholders' demands. The more responsive organizations are towards stakeholders' needs, the better the overall image and credibility of an organization in the eyes of its stakeholders (Skyes, 2002). This will be reflected internally, on the overall corporate performance (CP) of an organization and externally on the corporate reputation perceived by an organization's publics. This paper will address the impact of stakeholder perceptions about the value of a corporate brand (reflected in CBE) on the internal CP of an organization.

Corporate performance

Assessing performance on financial indicators is not sufficient to evaluate a company's overall corporate performance (CP). Financial performance addresses the financial capability of an organization and is based on accounting systems and standards that aim to satisfy the requirements of capital markets (Atkinson, Waterhouse and Wells, 1997). Also, financial indicators do not provide sufficient guidance for internal management decision making and control (Atkinson et al., 1997). CP measurement includes elements of evaluation that assess performance from a corporate perspective which includes financial and non-financial measures. A corporate-based measure offers a more comprehensive method for evaluating performance which can be traced to stakeholder-specific values.

There are several CP measurement frameworks that have been developed which are based on a 'balanced-performance' perspective. These include: 1) the Business Excellence Model; 2) Performance Dashboards; 3) Baldrige Quality Award Criteria; and 4) the balanced scorecard. The balanced scorecard (BSC) evolved as a strategic tool to align strategy with operations and communicate with stakeholders. More than 50 per cent of the *Fortune* 500 companies use the BSC as a performance measurement tool (Gumbus, 2005). It is also commonly used for determining the degree to which organizations adopt the stakeholder approach (Gumbus, 2005).

The BSC approach developed by Robert Kaplan and David Norton has gained popularity as a method for measuring CP. Their tool, developed in 1992, realized the weakness of relying on financial indicators as a means of measuring performance, and thus developed a 'balanced' approach that includes non-financial measures. The BSC suggests developing a measure for CP that consists of: 1) the learning and growth perspective; 2) the customer perspective; 3) the business process perspective; and 4) the financial perspective (Kaplan and Norton, 1996).

While each company is expected to design its own scorecard that is in line with its corporate goals and objectives, the four quadrants of the BSC can be generally associated with certain stakeholder groups. The quadrants of the BSC demonstrate that the employees' impact is reflected in the growth and learning quadrant, the customers' in the customer quadrant, shareholders' in the financial quadrant and suppliers' in the business process quadrant (Cooper, 2004; Figge et al., 2003; Kaplan and Norton, 1996). It should be noted that these quadrants do not relate to these stakeholder groups only. Other stakeholders' perspectives, such as regulators and the community, also impact the quadrants of the BSC. Furthermore, relationships with different stakeholders may have an impact on one or more of the quadrants due to their mutual effects on the quadrants of the BSC (Kaplan and Norton, 1996). Thus, the BSC is able to capture all the different dimensions that are of value to different corporate stakeholders and assess performance accordingly (Sirgy, 2002). The BSC will be consulted in the proposed model as a 'stakeholder-based performance measurement system' (Cooper, 2004, p. 22).

A proposed model

It is important to highlight that any CBE valuation is one that is based on the respective stakeholders' perceptions about the degree to which their interests are being satisfied. In this study, the equity components of CBE denote the perceived value by the relevant stakeholder groups. Aggregately, CBE represents the degree to which an organization fulfils different stakeholder values. CP represents the implications of stakeholders' perceptions on internal performance indicators.

The model presented is based on the *instrumental* aspect of the stakeholder theory, which links stakeholders' relationship to corporate performance (Donaldson and Preston, 1995). The instrumental aspect of the stakeholder theory suggests that by responding to stakeholders' demands and interests, a company will realize significantly better corporate performance results than others that do not adhere to the stakeholder management approach.

Previous models of stakeholder orientation have tested its overall impact on business performance, mainly financial results (e.g. Greenley and Foxall, 1998). These studies considered the impact of stakeholder orientation on a subset of corporate performance measures, mainly financial and marketing measures, such as market share and return on investment (ROI). This paper addresses how an organization's relationship with each stakeholder group impacts specific components of CP. The multiple stakeholder relationships are in line with Greenley et al.'s (2004) multiple stakeholder orientation profile (MSOP) theory, which emphasizes the importance of addressing the interests of different stakeholder groups.

The proposed model presents the relationship between CBE and CP. The CBE construct is manifested in the following six sub-constructs: 1) employee equity; 2) customer-based brand equity; 3) owner equity; 4) regulator equity; 5) community equity; and 6) partner equity. These sub-components of CBE were developed to identify the 'value-added' aspects that respective stakeholders recognize as salient. Together, the CBE components form the value of corporate brands that appeal to an organization's stakeholders, namely employees, customers, owners, regulators, the community and partners. The six stakeholder groups included in the model include both primary and secondary stakeholder groups. The primary stakeholders include employees, customers, owners and partners, and the secondary stakeholders include the regulatory and the community groups. By incorporating both primary and secondary stakeholder groups the model offers a comprehensive overview about stakeholders' perceptions toward corporate brands.

On the other hand, the CP construct is manifested in the following four sub-constructs: 1) people results; 2) customer results; 3) financial results; and 4) operational results. People results are related to employee performance, customer results relate to customer-related performance indicators, financial results reflect financial performance, and operational results reflect business process operations. These measures are based on the BSC quadrants for measuring overall CP (Kaplan and Norton, 1996). Following are the specific CBE components that relate to each stakeholder group and the research propositions that are to be tested in future empirical research (see Figure 2.2).

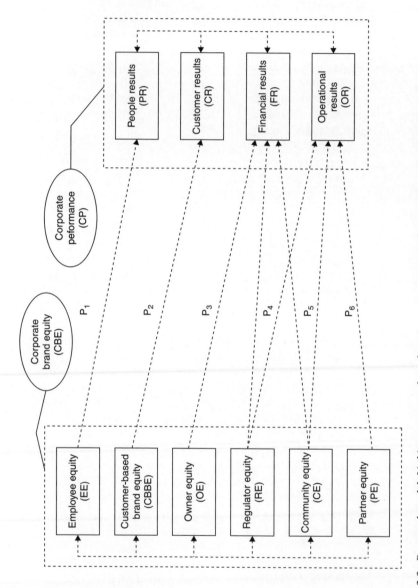

Figure 2.2 Proposed model: Linking corporate brand equity components with corporate performance elements

Employee stakeholders

The employee stakeholder group includes individuals that form the working body of an organization. Employees evaluate their equity according to the perceptions they have about the corporate brand. Employee equity reflects the employees' perceptions of how well an organization delivers values that are most significant to them. Job satisfaction is a major component of employee equity (Sirgy, 2002). This includes a healthy and safe working environment, fair and competitive compensation, advancement of knowledge and skills, and opportunities for career advancement (Maignan and Ferrell, 2004).

Research in Human Resource Management (HRM) provides evidence of a high positive relationship between employees' perceptions of job satisfaction and organizational effectiveness. Gelade and Ivery (2003) found a significant positive relationship between a healthy work environment and professional development and performance, as reflected in employee productivity and efficiency. A major study conducted by Huselid (1995) provided statistically significant results to support the positive relationship between effective HRM practices (that include providing attractive incentives, training and decision-making responsibility) and increased employee productivity and lower employee turnover.

Santos and Stuart (2003) also highlight the importance of employees' perceptions of the work environment, reward systems, training and promotion. These perceptions have an impact on employee performance-related issues such as organizational commitment and loyalty. Koys (2001) found similar results on the relation between human resource (HR) outcomes (employee satisfaction, employee attitude) and organizational effectiveness (turnover rate). Value-based organizations realize that employee satisfaction is directly associated with HR performance (van Marrewijk, 2004). Mathieu and Zajac's (1990) meta-analysis provided strong evidence of the positive relationship between job commitment and attendance. Also, several studies suggest that employees with strong commitment perform better (in terms of productivity) than those less committed (e.g. Bycio, Hackett and Allen, 1995; Leong, Randall and Cote, 1994).

The degree to which a firm is perceived to have employee equity has specific implications on employees' turnover, absenteeism and productivity (Melewar, Karaosmanoğlu and Paterson, 2005). Rodwell, Kienzle and Shadur (1998) provided evidence to support the relationship between perceptions of work-related factors such as teamwork, communication, participation in decision-making and employee performance.

Therefore, there is an expected positive relationship between employee equity and people results. Accordingly, the following proposition is presented:

P₁: There is a positive relationship between the degree of perceived employee equity and the level of people results.

Customer stakeholders

Customers are primarily concerned with the degree to which a corporate brand delivers a quality product that meets their desires and needs. Aaker (1996a) identified four main dimensions for product brand equity: brand awareness, perceived quality, brand associations and brand loyalty. Keller (1998) developed the concept of customer-based brand equity (CBBE), which he defined as 'the differential effect that brand knowledge has on consumer response to the marketing of that brand' (p. 60). Keller (1998) emphasized the importance of: the brand knowledge component, which expresses the degree of brand awareness and brand image; and the consumer response component, which refers to the degree of customer preference and customer behaviour towards the branded product in determining CBBE. Furthermore, Keller (1998) identified the benefits of CBBE in terms of breeding value for growth (attracting new customers, resisting competitive action, extending product lines and entering foreign markets) and brand profitability (brand loyalty, premium pricing and lower price elasticity).

Previous research provided evidence that high CBBE results in high market performance (Lassar et al., 1995). Therefore, customers' perceptions about the corporate offering of the product brands will have an impact on customer results. Several studies provided evidence to support the positive relationship between product brand equity and brand performance. Aaker (1996b) supported the positive relationship between brand equity and brand market performance. Brand market performance is composed of market share, price premium and distribution coverage. Also, Keller (2001) provided evidence to support the positive relationship between brand equity and its impact on market leadership and market share. Further, Baldauf, Cravens and Binder (2003) justified the positive relationship between brand equity and brand market performance, specifically on brand profitability, market performance, customer values and purchase intentions.

Also, the market orientation concept has been proven to result in higher customer-related performance measures (Kirca, Jayachandran and

Bearden, 2005). This is reflected in terms cost-based measures such as profitability, and revenue-based measures, such as sales and market share. This leads to the following proposition:

P$_2$:   There is a positive relationship between the degree of perceived customer-based brand equity and the level of customer results.

Owner stakeholders

Owners include individual shareholders and institutional investors that own a share of a company, and thus become company owners. The owners are particularly interested in a firm's financial value. They are primarily concerned with increasing their shareholder value by gaining an acceptable rate of return on their investments. Their desires are realized through corporate profits, corporate growth, dividend distribution, increases in stock value, and market opportunities (Waddock, Bodwell and Graves, 2002). The higher the perceptions of owner's equity about the value of their stock, the higher the expected share price. MacMillan and Downing (1999) also suggest that efficient exchange relationships with shareholders bring in more potential cash for investment, and also increase shareholder value. MacMillan and Downing provide evidence to prove that monetary exchanges with shareholders result in increased potential flow of cash into a company from shareholders, due to the increased trust and credibility of the future stock value. This increases trust and commitment in investment, leading to higher share prices, which reflect higher corporate equity value.

There is strong evidence of the relation between previous gains (earnings/share, increase in stock value) and future stock price (O'Hara et al., 2000). Fombrun and Shanley's (1990) research provided support for the positive relationship between stockholders' perceptions of company profitability and dividend distribution. Accordingly, the following proposition is posited:

P$_3$:   There is a positive relationship between the degree of perceived owner equity and the level of financial results.

Regulatory stakeholders

A regulator is responsible for governing business operations under a defined set of laws and regulations (Carroll and Buchholtz, 2003). The government has a dominant role as a regulative entity, especially for issues related to the collection of taxes, the disclosure of financial statements and making sure that companies abide by business laws and regulations. Regulators could be considered part of the government authority – for example, the FAA (Federal Aviation Administration) in the United States – but in other cases they could be independent entities, such as the FCC (Federal Communications Commission) or the SEC (Securities Exchange Commission) (Carroll and Buchholtz, 2003).

Verschoor (1999) provides evidence to support the strong positive connection between CP (financial and non-financial) and the conduct of business in an ethical way. Also, previous research supports the relationship that non-market actions, such as ensuring a healthy relationship with the government, results in high performance as reflected in operational efficiency and financial performance. Cochran and Nigh (1990) suggest that illegal corporate actions are negatively correlated with a firm's profitability. Moreover, an ethical culture has a direct impact on business operations, in that it helps eliminate any fines or legal fees a corporation may face otherwise, thus reducing a company's operating costs (Fombrun and Foss, 2004). Hence, the following proposition is posited:

P_4:   There is a positive relationship between the degree of perceived regulator equity and the level of financial and operational results.

Community stakeholders

Community stakeholders are concerned about organizations' involvement in non-business activities that help support the community. A term that is commonly used to denote this role is 'corporate social responsibility' (CSR). Davis (1973) defined CSR as the 'firm's consideration of, and response to, issues beyond the narrow economic, technical, and legal requirements of the firm to accomplish social benefits along with the traditional economic gains which the firm seeks' (p. 312). This definition includes issues related to providing employment opportunities, caring for the environment, corporate donations, and providing support for the improvement of communities. Community equity refers to the degree of public satisfaction with community-related activities, such as corporate giving, community support and support for the environment.

Studies that examine the relationship between CSR and financial performance have provided evidence of a strong positive relationship between them (e.g. Preston and O'Bannon, 1997; Waddock and Graves, 1997; Griffin and Mahon, 1997). This is because a company with high

CSR attracts stakeholders to engage in a relationship with the company. Moreover, a high CSR will result in higher corporate credibility of company stakeholders, which enhances perceptions about the corporation from the community's perspective and helps guard against negative public reactions (Shrivastava, 1995). This favourable perception adds credibility to the market value of a company's stocks.

The more environmentally concerned a business is, the less costly it becomes for a firm to comply with environmental regulations (Shrivastava, 1995; Hart, 1995). Environmental concerns bring about operational efficiencies which lead to a reduction in operating costs. A company's proactive approach toward environmental concerns safeguards an organization from the present and future costs of complying with environmental regulations. This results in improvement in the long-term operational efficiency of an organization (Dechant and Altman, 1994). Accordingly, the following proposition can be posited:

P_5:   There is a positive relationship between the degree of perceived community equity and the level of financial and operational results.

Partner stakeholders

Partners are those entities that deal directly with corporations in the provision of goods and services. Partners value the degree of business commitment and sustained business relationships with organizations (Waddock et al., 2002). Partners expect a smooth and long-term healthy relationship with their clients (the corporation). This usually means fewer supply-chain disruptions, quick inventory turnover and minimal lead time. Research has demonstrated the benefits of close and lasting relationships with organizational partners on the operational efficiency of an organization (Dwyer et al., 1987).

Brown's (1995) research provided support to show that positive supplier perceptions about a corporation resulted in improved attitudes of suppliers. A strong 'inter-firm relationship' (Johnson, 1999, p. 4) is thought to result in efficient business operations. The more strategically integrated the partners are with a firm, the higher the operational performance. Operational performance is reflected in operational efficiency, which impacts an organization's internal processes and procedures.

Research conducted by Kaynak (2002) specifically tested the effect of the supplier-buyer cooperation and the timely delivery of materials on firms' operational performance. The results showed that effective and long-term relationships with suppliers result in a reduction in delivery lead time, high inventory turnover and better lead-time performance. Also, studies by Petersen, Ragatz and Monczka (2005) and Tan, Kannan and Handfield (1998) also confirmed that effective collaboration with suppliers results in lower operating costs, lower inventory stock and fewer defects. Accordingly, the following proposition is posited:

P$_6$: There is a positive relationship between the degree of perceived partner equity and the level of operational results.

Overall

CBE can be assessed by adding together employee equity, customer-based brand equity, owner equity, regulator equity, community equity and partner equity, while accounting for the interaction that takes place between the stakeholders' equity components. Due to the high degree of interaction expected between the components of CBE, a multicollinearity model would be the proper method for valuating CBE. This can be graphically presented as shown in Figure 2.3.

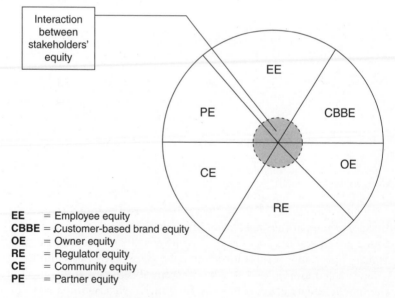

EE   = Employee equity
CBBE   = Customer-based brand equity
OE   = Owner equity
RE   = Regulator equity
CE   = Community equity
PE   = Partner equity

Figure 2.3 Corporate brand equity

CP is composed of people, customer, financial and operational results. These four quadrants are also highly interdependent due to the cause-and-effect nature of the quadrants of the BSC (Kaplan and Norton, 1996). Overall, there is a positive relationship between CBE and CP. The higher the aggregate perceived value by stakeholders as reflected in CBE, the higher the expected CP. This can be represented in terms of a high correlation coefficient ($\varphi_{CBE\text{-}CP}$) expected between CBE and CP (refer to Figure 2.1).

Control variables

While it is hypothesized that there is a positive relationship between CBE and CP, any future empirical study should take into account the following measures as control variables (refer to Figure 2.1). The level of economic development may moderate the relationship between CBE and CP. If this study is to be conducted across markets, it is expected that developed market economies would be more prone to the stakeholder orientation than less-developed markets. The nature of the industry, whether it is goods or services, will impact the relative importance of CBE. The level of competition will also determine the importance of the reputation and credibility of the corporate brand as a source of competitive advantage. The more involved a company is with global operations, the more significant corporate branding strategies are. The size and focus of the firm may determine the significance and value of CBE. Also, the form of ownership (public versus private) may impact the degree to which an organization serves the interests of multiple stakeholder groups. Also, it is anticipated that the older the firm, the more importance a firm places on corporate branding to ensure sustainability and long-term competitiveness. Customer type, whether consumer or business, will also determine the importance of CBE.

Conclusion

A strong corporate brand is a source of competitive advantage for firms in the highly competitive, regulative and turbulent environment that faces businesses today (Balmer, 1995). Measuring CBE requires a broader set of dimensions that goes beyond the customer's perspective and more towards the stakeholders' perspective. In this study, corporate brand equity is conceptualized in terms of employee equity, customer-based brand equity, owner equity, regulator equity, community equity and partner equity. By assessing the stakeholders' perspective of CBE, the proposed framework is able to integrate the value propositions of different stakeholder groups into the valuation of CBE.

Corporate performance is manifested in terms of people results, customer results, financial results and operational results. A company that has strong CBE is thought to generate a high CP. This is because a strong corporate brand is a source of competitive advantage that pertains not only to one group, but offers valuable unique propositions to different stakeholder groups. In summary, the study has made two major contributions: 1) proposed a model for measuring CBE; and 2) assessed the link between CBE and CP.

Managerial implications

Corporate branding strategies entail that marketers look beyond the marketing of a company's products/services and more towards the marketing of the entire business. This is the new function of marketers. They should develop and manage relationships not only with customers, but with all company stakeholders to ensure efficiency of the entire business's operations. Thus, the role of brand managers is broadened to encompass relations with customers, employees, owners, regulators, the community and partners (Jones, 2005).

Once the proposed model is applied, managers will be able to use it as a tool for identifying areas of strengths and weaknesses in the stakeholders' relationships. They can detect areas of strength that need to be sustained and identify areas of weakness that need to be better managed and nurtured. Such detection conveys signals about current stakeholder-company relations, which foretells the company's competitive position and sustainability in the marketplace. Thus, the model acts as a corporate monitor for business development and continuity.

Study challenges and future research

Studies pertaining to corporate branding have a higher degree of complexity than those relating to product branding, primarily due to the multiplicity of stakeholders involved; this makes the research more demanding. While the unit of analysis in the framework set forth here is the individual stakeholder, a study involving an adequate number of stakeholders within an organization would provide the statistically significant/insignificant results required for generalization. Previous research studies in this area have focused on an adequate sample of stakeholders in a few companies. This was the case in Davies et al.'s (2001) study where two stakeholder groups, customers and employees, were studied across three companies. Chun and Davies' (2006) study also examined these two stakeholder groups across two companies. Although they did not conduct their study across many companies, they set a good example by using an adequate sample size of individuals as the sampling frame within an organization.

Individuals can have an interest in a company by holding more than one stakeholder title. For example, an individual can be both a customer and employee. This raises the issue of 'unit of analysis' validity and inter-stakeholder bias. Future research should cover this issue.

This study relies heavily on the availability of a variety of indicators such as people, customer, financial and operational indicators within a firm. While retrieving information about employee, customer, financial and operational-level data could pose a challenge, more companies nowadays are investing in information and data warehouse systems to assess performance. These systems allow companies to better identify gaps and attempt to solve them in order to meet the demands of the increasingly highly regulated business environment, which also requires firms to release information about overall business performance. Therefore, it is strongly recommended that companies use information systems and data-warehouse applications as sources for assessing corporate performance.

More research needs to be undertaken in marketing to address the stakeholders' perspective and its implications for corporate outcomes, specifically, CP. This will greatly enhance the value of marketing within an organization from a function that purely serves customers only, to one that is concerned about relationships with all an organization's stakeholders. Moreover, it will highlight the important role marketers play in enhancing the value of a corporation and their role in creating stakeholder value and improving operational efficiency. This will change the perception of marketing by non-marketers, who do not see the return on investment that marketers provide. This model will help marketers convince non-marketers of the value of marketing.

References

Aaker, D. (1996a) *Building Strong Brands* (New York: Free Press).

Aaker, D. (1996b) 'Measuring Brand Equity Across Products and Markets', *California Management Review,* 38 (3), pp. 102–20.

American Marketing Association (2008), 'What are the Definitions of Marketing and Marketing Research', accessed at http://www.marketingpower/com/4620.php, 29 May.

Argenti, P. and B. Druckenmiller (2004) 'Reputation and the Corporate Brand', *Corporate Reputation Review*, 6 (4), pp. 368–74.

Atkinson, A. A., J. J. Waterhouse and R. B. Wells (1997) 'A Stakeholder Approach to Strategic Performance Measurement', *Sloan Management Review*, 38 (3), pp. 25–37.

Baldauf, A., K. S. Cravens and G. Binder (2003) 'Performance Consequences of Brand Equity Management: Evidence from Organizations in the Value Chain', *Journal of Product and Brand Management*, 12 (4) pp. 220–36.

Balmer, J. M. T. (1995) 'Corporate Branding and Connoisseurship', *Journal of General Management*, 21 (1), pp. 24–26.

Balmer, J. M. T. (2001) 'Corporate Identity, Corporate Branding and Corporate Marketing: Seeing Through the Fog', *European Journal of Marketing*, 35 (3/4), pp. 248–91.

Brady, A. K. (2003) 'How to Generate Sustainable Brand Value from Responsibility', *Journal of Brand Management*, 10 (4/5), pp. 279–89.

Bromley, D. (2002) 'Comparing Corporate Reputations: League Tables, Quotients, Benchmarks or Case Studies?', *Corporate Reputation Review*, 5 (1), pp. 35–51.

Brown, S. (1995) 'The Moderating Effects of Insupplier/Outsupplier Status on Organizational Buyer Attitudes', *Journal of the Academy of Marketing Science*, 23 (3), pp. 170–81.

Bycio, P., R. D. Hackett and J. S. Allen (1995) 'Further Assessment of Bass's (1985) Conceptualization of Transactional and Transformational Leadership', *Journal of Applied Psychology*, 80 (4), pp. 468–78.

Carroll, A. B. and A. Buchholtz (2003) *Business and Society: Ethics and Stakeholder Management* (Mason: South-Western).

Chun, R. and G. Davies (2006) 'The Influence of Corporate Character on Customers and Employees: Exploring Similarities and Differences,' *Journal of the Academy of Marketing Science*, 34 (2), pp. 138–46.

Clarkson, M. B. E. (1995) 'A Stakeholder Framework for Analyzing and Evaluating Corporate Social Performance', *The Academy of Management Review*, 20 (1), pp. 92–117.

Cochran, P. L. and D. Nigh (1990) 'Illegal Corporate Behaviour and the Question of Moral Agency: An Empirical Investigation', in W. C. Frederick and L. E. Preston (eds), *Business Ethics: Research Issues and Empirical Studies* (Greenwich: Jai Press).

Conti, T. (2002) 'Stakeholder Based Strategies to Enhance Corporate Performance', *Annual Quality Congress Proceedings*, p. 373.

Cooper, S. (2004) *Corporate Social Performance: A Stakeholder Approach* (Burlington: Ashgate).

Corebrand (2006) 'Our Services', accessed at http://www.corebrand.com/services/services.html, 10 November.

Cravens, K., E. G. Oliver and S. Ramamoorti (2003) 'The Reputation Index: Measuring and Managing Corporate Reputation', *European Management Journal*, 21(2), pp. 201–12.

Davies, G., R. Chun, D. S. Rui and R. Stuart (2001) 'The Personification Metaphor as a Measurement Approach for Corporate Reputation', *Corporate Reputation Review*, 4 (2), pp. 113–27.

Davies, G., R. Chun, D. S. Rui and R. Stuart (2004) 'A Corporate Character Scale to Assess Employee and Customer Views of Organization Reputation', *Corporate Reputation Review*, 7 (2), pp. 125–46.

Davis, K. (1973) 'The Case For and Against Business Assumption of Social Responsibilities', *Academy of Management Journal*, 16 (2), pp. 312–22.

Daub, C. H. and R. Ergenzinger (2005) 'Enabling Sustainable Management Through a New Multi-disciplinary Concept of Customer Satisfaction', *European Journal of Marketing*, 39 (9/10), pp. 998–1012.

Day, G. (1994) 'The Capabilities of Market-driven Organizations', *Journal of Marketing*, 58 (4), pp. 37–52.

Dechant, K. and B. Altman (1994) 'Environmental Leadership: From Compliance to Competitive Advantage: Executive Commentary', *The Academy of Management Executive*, 8 (3), pp. 7–20.

Donaldson, T. and L. E. Preston (1995) 'The Stakeholder Theory of the Corporation; Concepts, Evidence and Implications', *Academy of Management Review*, 20 (1), pp. 65–91.

Dwyer, R. P., H. Schurr and S. Oh (1987) 'Developing Buyer-Seller Relationships', *Journal of Marketing*, 51 (2), p. 11–27.

Einwiller, S. A., A. Fedorikhin, A. R. Johnson and M. A. Kamins (2006) 'Enough is Enough! When Identification No Longer Prevents Negative Corporate Associations', *Journal of the Academy of Marketing Science*, 34 (2), pp. 50–5.

Einwiller, S. A. and M. Will, 'Towards an Integrated Approach to Corporate Branding: An Empirical Study', *Corporate Communications*, 7 (2), pp. 100–09.

Figge, F., T. Hahn, S. Schaltegger and W. Marcus (2002) 'The Sustainability Balanced Scorecard-Linking Sustainability Management to Business Strategy', *Business Strategy and the Environment*, 11 (5), pp. 269–84.

Fombrun, C. and C. Foss (2004) 'Business Ethics: Corporate Responses to Scandal', *Corporate Reputation Review*, 7 (3), p. 284–88.

Fombrun, C., N. Gardberg and J. M. Server (2000) 'The Reputation Quotient: A Multi-Stakeholder Measure of Corporate Reputation', *Journal of Brand Management*, 7 (4), p. 241–55.

Fombrun, C. and M. Shanley (1990) 'What's in a Name? Reputation Building and Corporate Strategy', *Academy of Management Journal*, 33 (2), pp. 233–58.

Freeman, R. E. (1984) *Strategic Management: A Stakeholder Approach* (Boston: Pitman).

Gelade, G.A. and M. Ivery (2003) 'The Impact of Human Resource Management and Work Climate on Organizational Performance,' *Personnel Psychology*, 56 (2), pp. 383–404.

Griffin, J. J. and J. F. Mahon (1997) 'The Corporate Social Performance and Corporate Financial Performance Debate: Twenty Five Years of Incomparable Research', *Business and Society*, 36 (1), pp. 5–31.

Greenley, G. E. and G. Foxall (1998) 'External Moderation of Associations among Stakeholder Orientations and Company Performance', *International Journal of Research in Marketing*, 15 (1), pp. 51–69.

Greenley, G. E., G. J. Hooley, A. J. Broderick and J. M. Rudd (2004) 'Strategic Planning Differences among Different Multiple Stakeholder Orientation Profiles', *Journal of Strategic Marketing*, 12 (3), pp. 163–82.

Gumbus, A. (2005) 'Introducing the Balanced Scorecard: Creating Metrics to Measure Performance', *Journal of Management Education*, 29 (4), pp. 617–30.

Harris Interactive (2006) accessed at www.harrisinteractive.com, 6 March 2008.

Hatch, M. J. and M. Schultz (2003) 'Bringing the Corporation into Corporate Branding', *European Journal of Marketing*, 37 (7/8), pp. 1041–64.

Helm, S. (2005) 'Designing a Formative Measure for Corporate Reputation', *Corporate Reputation Review*, 8 (2), pp. 95–109.

Huselid, M. A. (1995) 'The Impact of Human Resource Management Practices on Turnover, Productivity and Corporate Financial Performance', *Academy of Management Journal*, 38 (3), pp. 635–72.

Ind, N. (1997) *The Corporate Brand* (New York: New York University Press).

Javalgi, R. G., M. B. Taylor, A. C. Gross and E. Lampan (1994) 'Awareness of Sponsorship and Corporate Image: An Empirical Investigation', *Journal of Advertising*, 23 (4), pp. 47–58.

Jaworski, B. and A. K. Kohli (1993) 'Market Orientation: Antecedents and Consequences', *Journal of Marketing*, 57 (3), pp. 53–70.

Johnson, J. (1999) 'Strategic Integration in Industrial Distribution Channels: Managing the Interfirm Relationship as a Strategic Asset', *Journal of the Academy of Marketing Science*, 27 (1), pp. 4–18.

Jones, R. (2005) 'Finding Sources of Brand Value: Developing a Stakeholder Model of Brand Equity', *Journal of Brand Management*, 13 (1), pp. 10–32.

Kaplan, R. and D. Norton (1996) *The Balanced Scorecard: Translating Strategy into Action* (Boston: Harvard Business School Press).

Kaynak, H. (2002) 'The Relationship between Just-in-Time Purchasing Techniques and Firm Performance', *IEEE Transaction on Engineering Management*, 49 (3), pp. 205–17.

Keller, K. (1998) *Strategic Brand Management: Building, Measuring and Managing Brand Equity* (Upper Saddle River: Prentice Hall).

Keller, K. (2000) 'Building and Managing Corporate Brand Equity', in M. Schultz, M. J. Hatch and M. Larsen (eds) *Expressive Organization: Linking Identity, Reputation and the Corporate Brand* (New York: Oxford University Press).

Keller, K. (2001) 'Branding and Brand Equity', in R. Wensley and B. Weitz (eds) *Handbook of Marketing* (London: Sage Publications).

Kirca, A., S. Jayachandran and W. O. Bearden (2005) 'Market Orientation: A Meta-Analytic Review and Assessment of its Antecedents and Impact on Performance', *Journal of Marketing*, 69 (2), pp. 24–41.

Koys, D. J. (2001) 'The Effects of Employee Satisfaction, Organizational Citizenship Behaviour, and Turnover on Organizational Effectiveness: A Unit-Level Longitudinal Study', *Personnel Psychology*, 54(1), pp. 101–14.

Lassar, W., B. Mittal and A. Sharma (1995) 'Measuring Customer-Based Brand Equity', *Journal of Consumer Marketing*, 12 (4), pp. 11–19.

Leong, S. M., D. M. Randall and J. A. Cote (1994) 'Exploring the Organizational Commitment-Performance Linkage in Marketing: A Study of Life Insurance Salespeople', *Journal of Business Research*, 29 (1), pp. 57–63.

MacMillan, K. and S. Downing (1999) 'Governance and Performance: Goodwill Hunting', *Journal of General Management*, 24 (3), pp. 11–21.

Maignan, I. and O. C. Ferrell (2004) 'Corporate Social Responsibility and Marketing: An Integrative Framework', *Journal of the Academy of Marketing Science*, 32 (1), pp. 3–19.

Mathieu, J. E. and D. Zajac (1990) 'A Review and Meta Analysis of the Antecedents, Correlates and Consequences of Organizational Commitment', *Psychological Bulletin*, 108 (2), pp. 147–58.

Melewar, T. C., E. Karaosmanoğlu and D. Paterson (2005) 'Corporate Identity: Concept, Components and Contribution', *Journal of General Management*, 31 (1), pp. 59–81.

Melewar, T. C. and E. Jenkins (2002) 'Defining the Corporate Identity Construct', *Corporate Reputation Review*, 5 (1), pp. 76–90.

Motion, J., S. Leitch and R. Brodie (2003) 'Equity in Corporate Co-branding: The Case of Adidas and All Black', *European Journal of Marketing*, 37 (7/8), pp. 1080–94.

O'Hara, H. T., C. Lazdowski, C. Moldovean and S. T. Samuelson (2000) 'Financial Indicators of Stock Price Performance', *American Business Review*, 18 (1), pp. 90–100.

Petersen, K. J., G. L. Ragatz and R. M. Monczka (2005) 'An Examination of Collaborative Planning Effectiveness and Supply Chain Performance', *Journal of Supply Chain Management*, 41 (2), pp. 14–25.

Preston, L. E. and D. P. O'Bannon (1997) 'The Corporate Social-Financial Performance Relationship: A Typology and Analysis', *Business and Society*, 36 (4), pp. 419–29.

Rao, V., M. Agarwal and D. Dahloff (2004) 'How is Manifest Branding Strategy Related to the Intangible Value of a Corporation?', *Journal of Marketing*, 68 (4), pp. 126–41.

Reputation Institute, 'Reputation Quotient' accessed at www.reputationinstitute. com/main/index.php?pg=res&box= reputation_quotient

Rodwell, J. J., R. Kienzle and M. A. Shadur (1998) 'The Relationship Among Work-Related Perceptions, Employee Attitudes, and Employee Performance: The Integral Role of Communications', *Human Resource Management*, 37 (3/4), pp. 277–93.

Santos, A. and M. Stuart (2003) 'Employee Perceptions and Their Influence on Training Effectiveness', *Human Resources Management Journal*, 13 (1), pp. 27–45.

Schultz, D. and P. Kitchen (2004) 'Managing the Changes In Corporate Branding and Communication: Closing and Re-opening the Corporate Umbrella', *Corporate Reputation Review*, 6 (4), pp. 347–66.

Shrivastava, P. (1995) 'The Role of Corporations in Achieving Ecological Sustainability', *Academy of Management Review*, 20 (4), pp. 936–60.

Sirgy, M. J. (2002) 'Measuring Corporate Performance by Building on the Stakeholder Model of Business Ethics', *Journal of Business Ethics*, 35(3), pp. 143–62.

Skyes, S. (2002) 'Talent, Diversity and Growing Expectations', *Journal of Communication Management*, 7 (1), pp. 79–86.

Slater, S. F. and J. C. Narver (1994) 'Does Competitive Environment Moderate the Market Orientation-Performance Relationship?', *Journal of Marketing*, 58 (1), pp. 46–55.

Sobol, M., G. Farrelly and J. Taper (1992) *Shaping the Corporate Image: An Analytical Guide for Executive Decision Makers* (New York: Quorum Books).

Tan, K. C., V. R. Kannan and R. B. Handfield (1998) 'Supply Chain Management: Supplier Performance and Firm Performance', *International Journal of Purchasing and Materials Management*, 34 (3), pp. 2–9.

van Marrewijk, M. (2004) 'A Value-Based Approach to Organization Types: Towards A Coherent Set of Stakeholder-Oriented Management Tools', *Journal of Business Ethics*, 55 (2), pp. 147–58.

Vershoor, C. C. (1999) 'Corporate Performance is Closely Linked to a Strong Ethical Commitment', *Business and Society Review*, 104 (4), pp. 407–15.

Waddock, S., C. Bodwell and S. Graves (2002) 'Responsibility: The New Business Imperative', *Academy of Management Executive*, 16 (2), pp. 132–48.

Waddock, S. and S. Graves (1997) 'The Corporate Social Performance-Financial Performance Link', *Strategic Management Journal*, 18 (4), pp. 303–19.

3
Aligning Corporate Brand Perceptions: Does it Matter?

Tatiana Anisimova and Felix Mavondo

Abstract

Corporate branding theorists view incongruency between the company and its consumers as undesirable and that it can have detrimental consequences for performance outcomes. However, the proposition of negative performance implications of corporate brand misalignment is yet to be empirically supported. This paper seeks to overcome this limitation through: 1) conceptualization and operationalization of misalignment in terms of the profile deviation; and 2) an empirical test of the performance impact of misalignment. The results of this study generally support the proposition that deviation from the manager-construed profile (referred to as a corporate perspective) has significant and negative implications for customer satisfaction and loyalty, thus raising the strategic importance of the alignment of corporate and consumer perspectives within corporate branding. An organization engaged in corporate branding in the Australian automotive industry was chosen as a unit of analysis.

Introduction

To survive in today's hyper-competitive markets, where product performance is perceived by consumers as a given, particularly in complex durable products such as automobiles, companies need to discover new ways of generating customer satisfaction and loyalty. As consumers are becoming increasingly demanding and knowledgeable, to stand out in the marketplace, organizations need to capitalize on unique characteristics of corporate culture and corporate values. Corporate branding represents an opportunity for organizations to enhance their distinctiveness through linking unique and credible corporate characteristics to products and services, thus enabling important synergies to be developed.

Corporate brands provide various benefits to organizations, such as economies of scale in marketing (Rao, Agarval and Dahlhoff, 2004) and credible means of differentiation in the marketplace (Hatch and Schultz, 2003). Often, corporate brands serve as substitutes for product information and identity construction to customers (Brucks, Zeithaml and Naylor, 2002). While corporate-branding literature (Balmer, 1998; Ind, 1997; Urde, 2003) advocates the multidimensional nature of the corporate brand, there has been little reflection of this in the empirical research. One common thesis that exists in corporate branding literature is that corporate-brand performance is contingent upon the ability of managers to align internal and external perspectives within corporate branding. However, there has been a lack of empirical support for such an argument. This paper argues that a stricter conceptualization and operationalization of misalignment is needed to allow this concept to be less equivocal and more useful both academically and managerially. The objectives of this paper are as follows:

1. Conceptualize and operationalize the concept of misalignment;
2. Operationalize the corporate brand;
3. Empirically test customer performance outcomes and the implications of misalignment.

The paper opens by providing of an overview of the gaps in the literature and continues with an overview of the congruency and misalignment of corporate branding. The concept of profile deviation and its performance implications are then examined. Finally, multiple dimensions of the corporate brand are demonstrated and the associated hypotheses are formulated.

Gaps in corporate-branding literature

The first gap that appears in corporate branding literature is that the studies are predominantly conceptually focused (Balmer, 1998; Balmer and Gray, 2003; de Chernatony, 2000) and the research is largely exploratory (Burghausen and Fan, 2002; Einwiller and Will, 2002). While there has been recognition regarding the value that corporate branding represents for organizations, there is a lack of consistency regarding corporate brand-management practices. This empirical paper provides practical insights for companies engaged in corporate branding.

Although corporate branding implies a stakeholder orientation, there is a lack of research that is based on the perceptions of internal and external stakeholders. Balmer (1998) categorizes the contributions to corporate-brand literature in two main streams (corporate identity and corporate image). This is reflected in the existing empirical studies on corporate branding that largely take either a consumer perspective (Saunders and Guoqun, 1997; Schoenfelder and Harris, 2004) or a managerial perspective (Daffey and Abratt, 2002; Einwiller and Will, 2002) This paper overcomes the one-perspective deficiency by incorporating managers and customers within the research framework.

A third gap relates to the discrepancy between the conceptualization and operationalization of the corporate brand. While corporate brand is claimed to be a multidimensional construct, its measurement has primarily been one-dimensional (Davies and Chun, 2002). Davies and Chun (2002) have made a valuable contribution in terms of the measurement of the discrepancies between customers (referred to as image) and companies (referred to as identity) using the Corporate Personality scale. However, while corporate personality is a crucial dimension it should be recognized that the corporate brand encompasses dimensions beyond personality alone (Azoulay and Kapferer, 2003). As Aaker (1991) maintains, 'using personality as a general indicator of brand strength will be a distortion for some brands, particularly those that are positioned with respect to functional advantages and value' (p. 113); this category includes automobiles. Therefore, to comprehensively measure the corporate brand, this paper builds on the frameworks suggested by Keller (2003) and Urde (2003) who maintain the multidimensionality of the corporate brand image.

Finally, although it is common for theorists to postulate the relationships between stakeholders and the corporate brand using expressions such as congruence and alignment, translation of these notions to analytical schemes have not been provided. A proposition that exists in the theoretical corporate branding literature is that a lack of alignment in stakeholder perceptions can be detrimental for corporate-brand performance (Harris and de Chernatony, 2001; Hatch and Schultz, 2003). However, the empirical support for such a proposition has been neither sufficient nor unequivocal. This paper overcomes this deficiency by undertaking an empirical test of performance implications of misalignment.

The notion of congruency in corporate branding

It has been implied throughout the previous discussion that the corporate branding phenomenon has its roots in both marketing and organizational perspectives (Knox and Bickerton, 2003). It has also been acknowledged that corporate branding has a multi-stakeholder orientation (Balmer and Gray, 2003; Schultz and de Chernatony, 2002). Diverse interests of stakeholders imply having misalignments between the company-desired, -construed and -projected corporate brand and perceptions by relevant stakeholders (Balmer and Greyser, 2002; Hatch and Schultz, 2001).

Corporate identity and corporate branding literature argues that development of perceptual *coherency* through aligning internal and external perspectives is an important factor in achieving better corporate brand performance (Harris and de Chernatony, 2001; Hatch and Schultz, 2001). In particular, Mohr and Bitner (1991) propose that cognitive similarity between internal and external stakeholders leads to more effective communication and higher customer satisfaction. Hatch and Schultz (2001) take the latter point further by arguing that organizations will achieve a competitive advantage provided that the corporate brand is established, based on the integration and continuous adjustment of their vision and image. For Olins (1989) coherency is one of the key factors in organizational success as it enables an organization to send unified brand messages to multiple audiences. A similar point is made by Fombrun (1996) in relation to the importance of the development of coherent messages to a company becoming well regarded by the public and its customers.

Because the notion of alignment lacks theoretical support in the corporate-branding literature, it was deemed appropriate for the present study to examine studies on fit or congruency in a related discipline, strategic management, where this concept has been extensively discussed (Venkatraman, 1989, 1990; Venkatraman and Prescott, 1990).

Linking the studies in strategic management to the unit of analysis in this study also appears relevant due to the pan-company perspective that corporate branding implies, which transforms 'corporate branding from marketing-communication activity to strategic framework' (Schultz and de Chernatony, 2002, p. 105). Although theorists recognize the inevitability of the different interests of internal and external stakeholders (Balmer and Greyser, 2003; Dowling, 2001; Schultz and de Chernatony, 2002), overall, there has been a tendency to view multiplicity in perceptions as undesirable in building strong corporate brands.

The impact of a lack of stakeholder perceptual alignment (also termed misalignment) on performance is a central point raised in this paper. To better understand the concept of misalignment, it is important to review the underlying premise and existing methodological perspectives of misalignment.

The concept of profile deviation and its performance implications

According to Venkatraman (1990), fit or co-alignment represents a 'desirable property that has significant performance implications' (p. 20). He suggests three perspectives of fit: interactionist; profile-deviation; and co-variation. In essence, the interactionist approach is specified in terms of joint effects, while the co-variation perspective regards fit as a pattern of internal consistency between dimensions.

Since the present study is concerned with examining *multiple* corporate-brand variables' effects on customer performance outcomes, the interaction perspective was not followed because it depends on only two variables at a given time. Although co-variation views fit in terms of internal consistency among a set of related variables, this approach was not considered appropriate since this study was fundamentally designed to examine the degree of adherence of customers' perceptions to the manager-specified internal-ideal profile. Thus, the profile-deviation perspective most appropriately fits with the objective of this study as this perspective is associated with the development of the 'ideal' profile, which can be derived either theoretically or empirically (Ferry, 1979). Profile deviation specifies fit in terms of adherence to a particularly specified profile (Venkatraman and Prescott, 1990), which is akin to Drazin and van de Ven's (1985) and van de Ven and Drazin's (1985) pattern-analytic approach. Thus, if fit can be specified in terms of adherence to the ideal profile, the underlying thesis posits that deviation or divergence from a developed ideal profile implies a weakness in, and negative effect on, performance (Venkatraman and Prescott, 1990). As was noted by Venkatraman and Prescott (1990), 'the attractiveness of the profile-deviation method lies in its capacity to recognize the multivariate deviation' (p. 5) in the particular pattern from an ideal profile.

This paper defines profile deviation as follows: managers responsible for corporate-branding strategy and practices specify the attributes of the corporate brand that are identifiable to all stakeholders as well as the attributes that are experienced by customers. Then a deviation from the manager-specified pattern represents a misalignment between managerial and customer perceptions, which is hypothesized to be significantly and negatively related to customer satisfaction and loyalty. The proposition concerning the impact of customer perceptual misalignment on customer satisfaction and loyalty is formulated as follows:

Deviation from manager-construed corporate brand will have significant and negative impact on customer satisfaction and loyalty

Corporate brand

According to Knox and Bickerton (2003), during the past 30 years the definition of the brand has been refined, resulting in the extension of the applications and scope of branding to the level of corporate agenda. However, a consensus definition of corporate brand image is yet to be established (Stern, Zinkhan and Morris, 2002). As Hsieh, Pan and Sentiono (2004) maintain, despite some commonalities, the definitions and operationalization of corporate brand image have been fairly irregular. This may be attributable to the relative newness of the concept and thus there is some ambiguity about what corporate brand entails, in both business and academia. Instead, literature generally provides characteristics-based descriptions of corporate brands (Balmer, 1998; Ind, 1997).

Ind (1997) has been one of the first author-practitioners who pointed to the issues of intangibility, complexity and responsibility within the corporate brand. While these characteristics provide a broad picture of corporate brands, further specifying of corporate brand dimensions is important in order to enable the measurement and management of the corporate brand. In an attempt to reflect what dimensions comprise a corporate brand, Urde (2003) and Keller (2003) have developed brand measurement frameworks. Using a case study of Volvo, Urde (2003) identifies three major categories of dimensions that underlie the corporate brand, namely, *organizational*, *brand* and *customer-experienced* values. This paper builds on Urde's (2003) and Keller's (2003) frameworks but expands the domain of the corporate brand to include corporate activities and corporate associations, important theoretical components lying at the heart of corporate branding (Dacin and Brown, 2002). The following sections will explicate the concepts of corporate associations and activities, corporate values and customer-experienced values.

Corporate brand associations

As Keller (1998) notes, corporate image is contingent on corporate actions and the manner in which an organization treats its customers.

Understanding the content and the structure of consumer perceptions of the corporation is critical for determining what consumers think about the brand in general and about the company's marketing activities (Keller, 1993). One important reason why corporate image and reputation concept are important to organizational success is that, in contrast to products and services, intangibles such as image and reputation are not easily imitable by competitors. This puts corporate associations at the level of a sustainable competitive advantage (Brown, 1998).

In a similar vein, Fombrun (1986) argues that favourable reputation can imbue an organization with a competitive advantage similar to brand equity. Furthermore, research in corporate associations suggests that corporate image (Andreassen and Lindestad, 1998) and reputation (Yoon, Guffey and Kijewski, 1993) have a favourable effect on customer loyalty. Thus, it appears important to maintain congruency between the company-projected and consumer-perceived corporate brand. Thus the first two hypotheses are as follows:

H_1: Perceptual mis-fit (misalignment) between managers and customers about corporate activities will result in reduced customer satisfaction and loyalty.

H_2: Perceptual mis-fit (misalignment) between managers and customers about corporate associations will result in reduced customer loyalty.

Organizational values

Urde (2003) describes organizational values as authentic differentiators that allow a company to distinguish itself from competitors. Knox, Maklan and Thompson (1999) write in terms of a unique organizational value proposition that they describe as a visible set of credentials throughout the supply chain in relation to the core processes in an organization. Campbell and Tawaday (1990) define corporate value in terms of senior management beliefs. Aaker (2004) takes a wider perspective, characterizing organizational values as the essence of a whole company and of what it considers important. He suggests innovation, quality and customer concern among the primary drivers of the corporate brand. The rise of organizational associations driven by values in corporate branding implies that strategic managerial vision, organizational values and corporate image need to be strongly aligned, and there is a need in perceived long-term mutual correspondence between these (Hatch and Schultz, 2003). Therefore, discrepancies between the corporate-brand constituents regarding values may have negative implications for corporate-brand performance. This leads to the third hypothesis:

H$_3$:   Perceptual mis-fit (misalignment) between managers and customers about corporate values will result in reduced customer satisfaction.

Corporate brand benefits

This study examines the effects of misalignment on the customer stakeholder group in the Australian automotive industry. Ultimately, customers are the most powerful group (Doyle, 1992) that generates sales and favourable word-of-mouth, thus maintaining the corporate brand's existence (Samli, Kelly and Hunt, 1998). Until recently there has been a significant amount of attention paid to the notion of consumer value in marketing literature. Whether one is discussing intangibles such as brand image or quality and product dimensions, understanding and delivery of consumer value is often at the crux of these issues.

Keller (2003) views consumer benefits as a multidimensional construct, defining it as 'personal value and meaning that consumers attach to the brand's product attributes (e.g. functional, symbolic, or experimental consequences from the brand purchase or consumption)' (p. 596). By creating differential consumer responses and affecting brand campaigns, brand benefits are the source of the consumer-based brand equity (Vázquez, Río and Iglesias, 2002). Similarly, Park, Jaworski and MacInnis (1986) distinguished between three categories of consumer benefits, namely, functional, symbolic and experimental. Vázquez et al. (2002) also maintain the importance of functional and symbolic brand utilities for consumer-based brand equity. They classify symbolic utility into two categories; the utility associated with the product (i.e. vehicle style, colours, design); and symbolic utility, associated with the corporate brand and reflected in consumer ability to communicate to important others desirable image and thereby enhance one's self-concept. Since purchase of complex durable consumer goods such as automobiles requires high-involvement decision-making (Brucks et al., 2000), assessment of consumer benefits as a multidimensional construct was deemed appropriate. In this paper, it is expected that perceptual discrepancies between managers and customers on the attributes of customer-experienced values have unfavourable consequences for customers' performance outcomes. This leads to the last three hypotheses of this study:

H$_4$:   Perceptual mis-fit (misalignment) between managers and customers about functional values will result in reduced customer loyalty.

H$_5$:   Perceptual mis-fit (misalignment) between managers and customers about emotional values will result in reduced customer loyalty.

H$_6$:   Perceptual mis-fit (misalignment) between managers and customers about symbolic values will result in reduced customer loyalty.

Methodology

Due to the relative newness of the corporate branding concept and a lack of measurement instruments, theory-building case-study research design appears to be appropriate for this study (Gill and Johnson, 1981). A case method was employed in this study as this allows the obtaining of a better understanding of the corporate brand domain within its real-life context (Yin, 2002). Another advantage of the case study method is that it allows the unit of analysis to be investigated with thorough attention to detail specific to an individual case, and enables a researcher to search for necessary information in the process of the investigation (Zikmund, 1997). To enable a more complete, holistic picture of the phenomenon under investigation, a case survey method (Larsson, 1993) was adopted in this study, which consisted of exploratory (qualitative) and cross-sectional stages. In order to gain the knowledge necessary for the development of corporate-brand constructs, exploratory research in the form of qualitative interviews with managers was undertaken. The interviews were particularly important in identifying the corporate brand themes and aiding the development of the corporate brand constructs in the quantitative manager and customer survey questionnaires.

Sample

The survey questionnaire was distributed to both managers and customers of the participating company. The management respondents of the survey were middle- to senior-level managers and represented all functional areas of the company. The aim was to gather a representative sample of managers' perceptions that could represent the collective psyche of the organization in such issues as corporate brand, values and associations. Altogether 50 usable manager questionnaires were received, representing a 33 per cent response rate. Due to confidentiality issues the actual managerial specializations cannot be revealed.

Two mailouts yielded 235 useable responses for the customer sample, representing a 38 per cent response rate. Respondents to the mailouts were compared across most of the measures and there were no significant differences observed across the early and late respondents. This suggests non-response was not a major issue. The demographic characteristics of managers and customers are presented in Table 3.1.

The validation process was undertaken using AMOS 5, and, as can be seen from the fits indices provided in Table 3.2, the modes fit the data well.

The testing approach

The ideal profile in this study was developed in two phases: via benchmarking the results of the exploratory stage of the in-depth interviews and then incorporating the findings into the managerial survey. The next aspect was to determine the degree of deviation from this profile and its effects on customer-based performance. This required calibrating the set of *manager-construed* corporate-brand dimensions as the benchmark and comparing it with *customer-perceived* corporate-brand dimension taken from the data set gathered from the surveys. This study employed conceptualization and operationalization suggested by Venkatraman and Prescott (1990). Consistent with these researchers, misalignment was operationalized in terms of weighted *Euclidian distance* for the 'ideal' profile along customer-based performance variables. This measure can be more appropriately conceptualized as *misalignment*, since statistically significant and negative correlations point to the incidence of *misalignment* (rather than co-alignment or fit), which is termed in this study 'misalign', and is calculated using the following formula that builds upon van de Ven and Drazin (1985), Venkatraman and Prescott (1990) and Vorhies and Morgan (2005),

$$\text{MISALIGN} = \sqrt{\sum_{J}^{N} (X_{sj} - \overline{X}_{mgmt})^2} \qquad (1)$$

Table 3.1 Samples' characteristics

Stakeholder	Characteristic	Category	Percentage
Managers	Department/Section	Sales and marketing	46
		Fleet	18
		Dealership management	12
		Product development	6
		Finance	4
		Retail	4
		Communications	4
		Customer first division	2
		Franchise development	2
		Strategic planning	2
Customers	**Characteristic**	**Category**	**Percentage**
	Gender	Males	56
		Females	44
	Education level	No formal qualifications	8.1
		Year 10/Year 11*	16.6
		HSC or VCE**	19.6
		TAFE/Trade qualifications	20.9
		University degree	19.3
		Postgraduate qualification	12.3
	Age group	18–24 years	6.8
		25–29	7.7
		30–34	9.4
		35–44	16.6
		45–54	20.4
		55–64	22.1
		65–70	16.6
		71–75	4

Note: *in the UK, GCSE.
**in the UK, A Levels.

where X_{sj} corresponds to the score for the stakeholder in the study sample along the jth dimension; $\overline{X}_{mgmt}$ is a mean for the ideal profile on the jth dimension and j equates the number of profile dimensions. This allowed the calculation of profile deviation scores between the corporate-brand benchmark and stakeholder perceptions of this. The performance impact of misalignment was measured using Pearson Correlations (see Venkatraman and Prescott, 1990). The results of the assessment of the corporate-brand misalignment on customer satisfaction and loyalty performance are presented in Table 3.3.

Table 3.2 Convergent validity results for the corporate brand constructs

Construct	SH	χ^2	DF	Prob. Level	CMIN/DF	GFI	AGFI	RMSEA	TLI	NFI	CFI
Corporate activities	M	34.201	31	.317	1.103	.890	.804	.046	.968	.819	.978
Corporate associations	C	88.026	32	.000	2.751	.930	.880	0.86	.950	.946	.965
	M	21.580	18	.251	1.199	.915	.829	.064	.972	.905	.982
	C	30.070	16	.018	1.879	.970	.933	.061	.979	.975	.988
Core values	M	22.382	19	.266	1.178	.908	.825	.060	.960	.852	.973
	C	40.666	16	.001	2.542	.961	.911	.081	.964	.967	.980
Functional brand values	M	.585	1	.444	.585	.994	.941	.000	1.000	.989	1.000
	C	.144	1	.704	.144	1.000	.997	.000	1.000	1.000	1.000
Emotional brand values	M	15.900	16	.460	.994	.929	.840	.000	1.000	.930	1.000
	C	21.834	10	.016	2.183	.978	.919	.071	.982	.989	.994
Symbolic, brand values	M	16.195	15	.369	1.080	.927	.825	.040	.994	.961	.997
	C	32.527	14	.002	2.502	.967	.908	.080	.982	.986	.991

Note: SH corresponds to stakeholders; M to managers, C to customers.

Table 3.3 Correlation matrix for the relationship between the misalignment measure and customer performance outcomes

Corporate brand variables	Overall satisfaction with the corporate brand	Customer satisfaction	Customer loyalty
Corporate activities – H_1	−.179**	−338**	−.367**
Corporate associations – H_2	−.330**	−.568**	−.587**
Core values – H_3	−.489**	−.481**	−.457*
Functional values – H_4	−.296**	−.193**	−.167*
Emotional values – H_5	−.163*	−.035	−.013
Symbolic values – H_6	.041	−.117	.068

Note: $^*p < 0.5$, $^{**}p < 0.01$.
n = 235.

Results and discussion

This paper set out to examine the performance implications of misalignment of the corporate brand. Generally, the proposition of the negative performance implication of misalignment was supported. Strong support was found in the areas of corporate activities, corporate associations and corporate values. This reflects a positive support of the expectations that these are salient aspects of consumer relationship building. Four of the six hypotheses (H_{1-4}) were supported. Those in the area of organization-specific factors that reflected corporate reputation and image (H_{1-3}) were strongly supported, whereas of those factors that reflect product values (H_{4-6}) only one (H_4) was strongly supported.

Corporate activities (H_1)

According to Keller (1998) consumers may be interested in issues beyond product attributes that include the actions of an organization. These actions may include strong environmental considerations and partnering with local communities. The results in Table 3.3 illustrate that if customers' perceptions significantly differ from managers' views about corporate activities this misalignment is strongly and negatively associated with customer satisfaction ($p < 0.01$) and loyalty ($p < 0.01$). This suggests that automobile manufacturers need more effective communication in regard to the programmes and activities designed to address issues apart from common product attributes and benefits. Therefore the misalignment between managers and customers about corporate activities will likely result in reduced customer satisfaction and loyalty.

Corporate associations (H₂)

Automobile manufacturers undertake a number of activities such as sports sponsorship, car racing, activities closely associated with the Australian outback, and advertising to appear family-oriented. Such associations are intended to support the corporate brand positioning. Strong support was found for H_2. The results indicate that if there is a misalignment of corporate associations between managers and customers, this will result in reduced satisfaction ($p < 0.01$) and loyalty ($p < 0.01$) with the corporate brand. This suggests that companies need to choose the associations that are consistent with customer expectations and effectively support corporate brand positioning. This result supports Brown's (1998) and Berens and van Riel's (2004) views that the way in which customers perceive an organization is critical to its success, while also suggesting the benefits of aligning customer perceptions to managerial perceptions about the organization.

Core values (H₃)

Results from Table 3.3 also provide support for H_3. Significant and negative association was found between misalignment and customer satisfaction ($p < 0.01$) and loyalty ($p < 0.01$). This result suggests that customers do react to the misalignment of core values with reduced satisfaction and loyalty. The results point to the strategic importance of organizational values. In Urde's (2003) view, organizational values can often be attributed not only to the nature of the product or service but also serve as a basis for the emotional dimension of the corporate brand. This view is supported by Aaker (2004), who states that corporate values are the essence of the company that underlie branding strategy and drive the corporate brand.

Functional benefits (H₄)

The results provide support for H_4. This suggests that if customer perceptions on functional, more intrinsic benefits differ from those of managers, this is strongly and negatively associated with satisfaction and loyalty towards the corporate brand. This finding suggests that the company enhance and strengthen the communication related to the unique tangible attributes of the offer as well as to the utility associated with the actual brand name. As Vázquez et al. (2002) maintain, functional brand utility is a central component of consumer-based corporate brand equity. However, in the hyper-competitive automotive industry, where car manufacturers are vying for customer attention, innovation not just in product development but in communication of functional benefits is crucial.

Emotional (H$_5$) and symbolic benefits (H$_6$)

The results of H$_6$ revealed a lack of significant and negative association. Therefore, H$_6$ has been disconfirmed. In regards to H$_5$, support was only found in relation to overall satisfaction with the corporate brand ($p < 0.05$). This finding could imply that the participating organization is yet to develop symbolic or social meanings for their corporate brand. As one of the senior managers commented during an in-depth interview:

> 'We have not established a strong emotional connection with people. We need to be connected to people's lifestyles, we need to be fun'

In the opinion of several respondents, hedonistic benefits such as 'fun and exciting to drive' and those related to end-user feelings of 'joy' and 'popularity' are important to the postmodern consumer. The implication for car manufacturers might be to engage in more emotionally focused relationships with customers through social-symbolic corporate brand positioning strategies, which would allow car companies to make a purchase a more enjoyable experience for customers.

Contributions of the study

This paper makes a theoretical contribution through the conceptualization and operationalization of the concept of misalignment within corporate branding. There have been a handful of empirical and conceptual studies relating to the notion of misalignment. Typically, this concept or its manifestations have been employed in metaphorical terms. Performance implications of misalignment between internal and external stakeholder perceptions are gaining interest among academics, although not directly within the field of corporate branding (see Venkatraman and Prescott, 1990; Vhories and Morgan, 2005). These studies employed 'profile deviation' as a methodological perspective and a testing approach, and found a significant and negative relationship between the degree of deviation (from the profile of high performers) and performance outcomes. However, rather than choosing an external benchmark, this study makes a methodological contribution by starting with an internally determined benchmark of the corporate brand. Thus, the collective corporate-brand perception of management defines how the company wishes to be seen by customers. Using this as a benchmark, customers' perceptions were then compared to the internal managerial perceptions. From the perspective of customers, management is an external benchmark. This has a major advantage over approaches that take the highest performers as the benchmark, since it reduces the potential for subjectivity in choosing the percentage of top performers (Venkatraman, 1990; Venkatraman and Prescott, 1990) and tackles the problem of what to do with the lowest performers in order to minimize bias.

The findings of this study also have managerial implications. Deviation of customers from management in such areas as emotional and symbolic values may not have major implications for customer loyalty and customer satisfaction. This suggests that the automobile manufacturers would benefit most by aligning customer perceptions to managerial perceptions in critical areas such as corporate activities, corporate associations, functional values and core values. This suggests effective communication is critical and that different forms of communication are required to achieve performance outcomes. Communication approaches could range from sports sponsorship to engagement with the community through supporting worthy causes. Finally, core values are the real essence of the corporation and need to be communicated effectively to the public, as well as being shared and held strongly within the organization. Communicating core values is difficult, but once achieved, builds a long-term bond with the community and its customers.

Conclusion, limitations and suggestions for future research

This paper conceptualized and operationalized misalignment in terms of profile deviation and tested its performance impact. Overall, the results of the empirical test supported the proposition that the deviation from the manager-construed corporate brand has negative and significant implications for customer-performance outcomes. However, further research into corporate branding is essential. This paper has closed some important gaps; however, many more remain.

This study has a limitation associated with a case study research design's restricted ability to generalize across industries other than the automotive industry. The cross-sectional nature of the data collection method also limits the data to one-point-in-time information about the phenomenon under investigation. A longitudinal design would provide deeper insight into the relationship between misalignment and customer-performance outcomes. The scope of the current paper was the Australian automobile industry; as such, applications of the profile-deviation approach within contexts other than the automotive industry that are engaged in corporate branding strategy (e.g. banking, retail, services) would be beneficial. In order to obtain a comprehensive insight into the performance implications of misalignment, it would also be desirable to incorporate business-based measures within the research framework.

Acknowledgment

Special gratitude to S. Bruce Thomson for his valuable suggestions.

References

Aaker, D. A. (1991) *Managing Brand Equity. Capitalizing on the Value of a Brand Name* (New York: Free Press).

Aaker, D. A. (2004) 'Leveraging the Corporate Brand', *California Management Review*, 46, pp. 6–18.

Andreassen, T. W. and B. Lindestad (1998) 'The Effects of Corporate Image on the Formation of Customer Loyalty', *Journal of Services Research*, 1, pp. 82–92.

Azoulay, A. and J. N. Kapferer (2003) 'Do Brand Personality Scales Really Measure Brand Personality', *Brand Management*, 11, pp. 143–55.

Balmer, J. M. T. (1998) 'Corporate Identity and the Advent of Corporate Marketing', *Journal of Marketing Management*, 14, pp. 963–96.

Balmer, J. M. T. and S. A. Greyser, (2002) 'Managing the Multiple Identities of the Corporation', *California Management Review*, 44, pp. 72–86.

Balmer, J. M. T. and E. R. Gray (2003) 'Corporate Brands: What Are They? What of Them?', *European Journal of Marketing*, 37, pp. 972–97.

Berens, G. and C. B. M. van Riel (2004) 'Corporate Associations in the Academic Literature: Three Main Streams of Thought in the Reputation Measurement Literature', *Corporate Reputation Review*, 7, pp. 161–78.

Brown, T. J. (1998) 'Corporate Associations in Marketing: Antecedents and Consequences', *Corporate Reputation Review*, 1, pp. 215–33.

Brucks, M., V. A. Zeithaml and G. Naylor (2000) 'Price and Brand Name as Indicators of Quality Dimensions for Consumer Durables', *Journal of Academy of Marketing Science*, 28, pp. 359–74.

Burghausen, M. and Y. Fan (2002) 'Corporate Branding in the Retail Sector: A Pilot Study', *Corporate Communications: An International Journal*, 7, pp. 92–9.

Campbell, A. and K. Tawaday (1990) *Mission and Business Philosophy* (Oxford: Heinemann).

Dacin, P. and J. J. Brown (2002) 'Corporate Identity and Corporate Associations: A Framework for Future Research', *Corporate Reputation Review*, 5, pp. 254–63.

Daffey, A. and R. Abratt (2002) 'Corporate Branding in a Banking Environment' *Corporate Communications: An International Journal*, 7, pp. 87–91.

Davies, G. and R. Chun (2002) 'Gaps between the Internal and External Perceptions of the Corporate Brand', *Corporate Reputation Review*, 5, pp. 144–58.

de Chernatony, L. (2000) 'Developing Corporate Brand through Considering Internal and External Stakeholders', *Corporate Reputation Review*, 3, pp. 268–74.

Doyle, P. (1992) 'What Are Excellent Companies?', *Journal of Marketing Management*, 8, pp. 101–16.

Dowling, G. (2001) *Creating Corporate Reputations* (Oxford University Press).

Drazin, R. and A. van de Ven (1985) 'Alternative Forms of Fit in Contingency Theory', *Administrative Science Quarterly*, 30, pp. 514–39.

Einwiller, S. and M. Will (2002) 'Towards an Integrated Approach to Corporate Branding – An Empirical Study', *Corporate Communication: An International Journal*, 7, pp. 100–09.

Ferry, D. L. (1979) 'A Test of a Task Contingent Model of Unit Structure and Efficiency', Unpublished Doctoral Dissertation, University of Pennsylvania.

Fombrun, C. J. (1996) *Reputation: Realizing Values from the Corporate Image*, (Boston: Harvard Business School Press).

Gill, J. and P. Johnson (1991) *Research Methods for Managers* (London: Paul Chapman Publishing).

Harris, F. and L. de Chernatony (2001) 'Corporate Branding and Corporate Brand Performance', *European Journal of Marketing*, 35, pp. 441–56.

Hatch, M. J. and M. Schultz (2001) 'Are the Strategic Stars Aligned for Your Corporate Brand?', *Harvard Business Review*, 79, pp. 128–34.

Hatch, M. J. and M. Schultz (2003) 'Bringing the Corporation into Corporate Branding', *European Journal of Marketing*, 37, pp. 1041–64.

Hsieh, M. H., S. L. Pan and R. Sentiono (2004) 'Product-, Corporate-, and Country-image Dimensions and Purchase Behavior: A Multicountry Analysis'. *Journal of the Academy of Marketing Science*, 32, pp. 251–70.

Ind, N. (1997) *The Corporate Brand* (Oxford: Macmillan).

Keller, K. L. (1993) 'Conceptualizing, Measuring and Managing Customer-based Equity', *Journal of Marketing*, 57, pp. 1–22.

Keller, K. L. (1998) *Strategic Brand Management: Building, Measuring and Managing Customer-based Brand Equity* (New Jersey: Prentice-Hall International).

Keller, K. L. (2003) 'Brand Synthesis: The Multidimensionality of Brand Knowledge', *Journal of Consumer Research*, 29, pp. 595–60.

Knox, S., S. Maklan and K. Thompson (1999) 'Pan-company Marketing and Process Management', *Irish Marketing Review*, 12, pp. 36–45.

Knox, S. and D. Bickerton (2003) 'The Six Conventions of Corporate Branding', *European Journal of Marketing*, 37, pp. 998–1116.

Larsson, R. (1993) 'Case Study Survey Methodology: Quantitative Analysis of Patterns across Case Studies', *Academy of Management Journal*, 36, pp. 1515–46.

Mohr, L. A. and M. Bitner (1991) 'Mutual Understanding between Customers and Employees in Service Encounters', *Advances in Consumer Research*, 18, pp. 611–71.

Olins, W. (1989) *Corporate Identity: Making Business Strategy Visible through Design* (London: Thames and Hudson).

Park, C. W., B. J. Jaworski and D. J. MacInnis (1986) 'Strategic Brand Concept – Image Management', *Journal of Marketing*, 50, pp. 135–45.

Rao, V. R., M. K. Agarwal and D. Dahlhoff (2004) 'How is Manifest Branding Strategy Related to the Intangible Value of a Corporation?', *Journal of Marketing*, 68, pp. 126–41.

Samli, C. A., P. J. Kelly and K. H. Hunt (1998) 'Improving the Retail Performance by Contrasting Management and Customer-perceived Store Images:

A Diagnostic Tool for Corrective Action', *Journal of Business Research,* 43, pp. 27–38.

Saunders, J. and F. Guoqun (1997) 'Dual Branding: How Corporate Brands Add Value', *Journal of Product and Brand Management,* 6, pp. 40–48.

Schoenfelder, J. and P. Harris (2004) 'High-tech Corporate Branding', *Qualitative Marketing Research: An International Journal,* 7, pp. 91–9.

Schultz, M. and L. de Chernatony (2002) 'The Challenges of Corporate Branding'. *Corporate Reputation Review,* 5, pp. 105–12.

Stern, B. B., G. M. Zinkhan and B. H. Morris, 'The Netvertising Image: Netvertising Image Communication Model (NICM) and Constant Definition', *Journal of Advertising,* 31, pp. 15–28.

Urde, M. (2003) 'Core Value-based Corporate Brand Building', *European Journal of Marketing,* 37, pp. 1017–40.

van de Ven, A. H. and R. Drazin (1985) 'The Concept of Fit in Contingency Theory', in L. L. Cummings and B. M. Staw (eds) *Research in Organizational Behavior* (New York: JAI Press) pp. 333–65.

Vázquez, R., A. B. D. Río and V. Iglesias (2002) 'Consumer-based Brand Equity: Development and Validation of a Measurement Instrument', *Journal of Marketing Management,* 18, pp. 27–48.

Venkatraman, N. (1989) 'The Concept of Fit in Strategy Research: Toward Verbal and Statistical Correspondence', *The Academy of Management Review,* 14, pp. 423–44.

Venkatraman, N. (1990) 'Performance Implications of Strategic Co-alignment: A Methodological Perspective', *Journal of Management Studies,* 27, pp. 19–41.

Venkatraman, N. and J. E. Prescott (1990) 'Environment-strategy Co-alignment: An Empirical Test of Its Performance Implications', *Strategic Management Journal,* 11, pp. 1–23.

Vorhies, D. W. and N. A. Morgan (2005) 'Benchmarking Marketing Capabilities for Sustainable Competitive Advantage', *Journal of Marketing,* 69, pp. 80–94.

Yoon, E., H. J. Guffey and V. Kijewski (1993) 'The Effects of Information and Company Reputation on Intentions to Buy a Business Service', *Journal of Business Research,* 27, pp. 215–28.

Yin, R. K. (2002) *Case Study Research. Design and Methods,* Applied Social Research Method Series, Third Edition (Thousand Oaks: Sage Publications).

Zikmund, W. G. (1997) *Business Research Methods,* Fifth Edition (Fort Worth: Dryden).

4

Vision, Image, Reputation and Relationships: Critical Drivers in Developing an Airport City

Robyn Stokes

Abstract

This paper focuses on the vision, image, reputation and relationships of an Australian airport corporation developing an airport city. The four constructs (vision, image, reputation and relationships) and links between them underpinned a conceptual model for this pre-structured case research (Yin, 1994). Depth interviews with 60 government and business stakeholders were supplemented with interviews and focus groups among middle managers. A reputation scale based on the Harris-Fombrun Reputation Quotient (Fombrun, Gardberg and Sever, 2000), Australia's Reputex research (Reputation Measurement, 2004) and other studies featured in this research. Results showed mixed understandings of the vision, and strong viewpoints about the negotiating style of airport executives impacted upon image, reputation and relationships. However, high reputation scores were attached to leadership, management and economic stability, with lower scores attributed to social responsibility and inclusiveness. Reputation scores were marginally lower in government where more negative images and debates about the vision featured.

Introduction

Privatization of airports globally has brought with it the need to create new corporate visions, chart new territory with organizational relationships and shift the image of airports from one of government-owned, air-transport facilities to that of privately owned, 'multi-point, multi-service' transport centres (Jarach, 2001). With deregulation, many airports are complementing traditional business with a greater emphasis on non-aviation-related business. Such is the case with Australia's major city airports. In particular, the airport corporation in this research, influenced by Amsterdam's Schiphol Airport, has developed a vision and master plan for an 'airport city' (Rooijmans, 2003). This vision will take the airport experience beyond air travel to a myriad of leisure, retail, business and industrial services within its precincts. Approved by the Australian government, whose ownership of airport land gives it regulatory control, this 'airport city vision' affects and is affected by the views of multiple stakeholders, including local and state governments (who have limited regulatory control), existing and potential tenants on airport land, industry associations, interest groups, residents and businesses.

The need to explain and illustrate what is meant by this airport city vision is omnipotent, given that this development, described by Kasarda (2000/2001) as an 'aerotropolis', is a totally new concept in Australia. The emergence of an aerotropolis signals a fast-developing marriage between aviation, digitization, globalization and time-based competition in which airports have become powerful economic engines (Canaday, 2000). In a deregulated environment, private corporations owning and operating airports are a major beneficiary of the aerotropolis, but significant benefits also accrue to the region and adjacent cities. In this Australian case, stakeholder understandings of the airport city remain developmental despite a steady flow of new developments around the airport. While stakeholder input to strategies was a requirement for government approval of the master plan, a degree of residual uncertainty about the corporation's external relationships, image and reputation among business and government stakeholders prompted this research in late 2004. Notably, views of city residents and ratepayers with an interest in airport developments have been tracked with research outside the scope of this work.

Research questions addressed by this study were: 'How and why do stakeholders' interpretations of the airport corporation's vision, image and reputation interrelate?' and, 'How and why do the corporation's stakeholder relationships impact on these interpretations?' To begin, the paper explores the theoretical linkage of vision to image; debates about overlaps and differences between the constructs of image and reputation; links between identity and brand; and the impact of stakeholder relationships on those constructs. This discussion is aided by a conceptual model of proposed linkages between the constructs based on literature and observations within the airport corporation. This model is followed by a micro-level research and consultancy framework, within which this study is seated. Methods of exploring and analysing interview and focus group data, results of the study and their theoretical and practical implications for the airport are subsequently outlined.

Modelling the links between vision, identity, image, relationships, reputation and brand

A review of the theoretical debates that surround the definitions of core constructs in this study was a necessary precursor to its design. Here, the growing body of literature about vision, corporate image, identity and branding, stakeholder analysis, relationships and reputation was explored. It is apparent that interest in the disciplinary foundations of work in this domain, in particular overlaps and distinctions between the constructs, grew markedly throughout the 1990s. However, there is still little consensus about terminology (Wartick, 2002). Campbell's (1963) observation that 'varying definitions begin to reflect a proliferation of authors rather than a case of numerous phenomena' is worth pondering (cited in Ferrand and Pages, 1999, p. 387). For any research in this complex field, a 'sense-making' process relative to the constructs is needed to lay a theoretical foundation for research.

At the core of this research is a corporate vision created with the privatization of the airport and championed by the chief executive and senior management. But what is meant by 'vision'? Often, a vision of an organization is articulated in a statement that links to its mission and incorporates where it wants to be and how it wants to strategically position itself in the future. For this study, the following definition can be used to sum up the central meaning:

> Vision is a mental perception of the kind of environment an individual or an organization aspires to create within a broad time horizon and the underlying conditions for the actualization of the perception (El-Namaki, 1992, p. 25).

Although the majority of firms claim to have a vision (O'Brien and Meadows, 2003), in this case the entire focus of the organization's activities is the enactment of a widely publicized 'airport city' vision. The chief executive officer maintains an ongoing 'roadshow' of presentations (both within and outside the corporation) that orally and visually depict the vision to diverse audiences. However, such communication inevitably reaches some but not all stakeholders and differences of opinion about the value and credibility of the vision can breed misrepresentations of its intent. Where a major development such as an airport city impacts on a regional population, it is easy to conclude that the clarity of the vision among stakeholders must be monitored. Such was the backdrop to this study.

In El-Namarki's (1992) definition of vision, the 'underlying conditions' for actualizing it will include an organization's values, culture and image (Hatch and Schultz, 2003). That the claimed values must equate with those used on an everyday basis is an important priority and one that has been in focus within the airport corporation. Most theorists agree that there are close links between vision and image (Matt Zaid, 1994; O'Brien and Meadows, 2003). Indeed, definitions of vision sometimes include the word 'image'; a good example being that vision is an 'ideal and unique image of the future' (Testa, 1999, p. 154). In this research, one of the goals of airport management was to detect and understand any internal and external tensions or discrepancies between the strategic vision and images held by key stakeholders.

Despite widespread definitional debates, some tentative consensus exists about the meanings of 'image' and 'reputation'. For example, image has been referred to as a mental model or description that consists of cognitive, affective and sensorial information (Schuler, 2004). There appears to be little argument that image connotes the mental impressions that audiences may have about an organization's people, its products or the organization as a whole. However, the question of whose mental impressions are of interest appears to separate theorists to some degree, with marketers mostly referring to externally held impressions (Bromley, 1993) and organizational theorists focusing on internal image interpretations (Hatch and Schultz, 1997, 2003). A commonly cited definition of corporate image (for example, Fillis, 2003) refers to 'a holistic and vivid impression held by an individual or group towards an organization that is the result of sense-making by the group and communication by the organization of a fabricated and projected picture of itself' (Hatch and Schultz, 1997, p. 359). Notably, some authors do not differentiate between corporate image and reputation (Schwalger, 2004), but a total overlap between these constructs is not commonly argued.

Reputation has been studied from diverse disciplinary perspectives ranging from finance and accounting to strategy, marketing, economics, organizational behaviour and sociology (Balmer, 1998). However, assertions that reputation 'emerges over a period of time' (compared with image, which may be a snapshot of current impressions), that it is an aggregation of perceptions, and that it facilitates comparisons with other organizations feature in many definitions. Some definitions appear to imply quantitative measurement, while others imply multiple measures. For example, an early definition by Weigelt and Camerer (1988) tends to fit with later quantitative measures of reputation, such as the Harris-Fombrun Reputation Quotient (Fombrun et al., 2000) which dominates the literature. Weigelt and Camerer (1988) defined reputation as 'a set of attributes ascribed to a firm inferred from a firm's past actions' (p. 443). Thus, reputation is more often seen as an attitudinal construct; image frequently includes much more of an affective component (Schwalger, 2004). However, both reputation and image draw upon the beliefs and impressions of audiences and for both constructs, 'good' and 'bad' perceptions and those that are too complex to be labelled can emerge (Berens and van Riel, 2004). To illustrate, a reputation that is non-problematic may exist within an organization's external audiences based on an assumption of ethical practice, although no image, either 'good or bad', has been formed. While a single negative image of an organization may or may not harm its corporate reputation, a poor reputation derived from non-ethical behaviour may well eliminate the positive image of an organization. Accordingly, there are overlaps, but good reasons to believe that these are distinctive, albeit related constructs. Both reputation and image can be measured within internal and external audiences, with a combination of 'outside-in' and 'inside-out' approaches advocated by various authors (Hatch and Schultz, 2003; Mahon, 2002).

That there is an impact of stakeholder relationships (a further construct in this study) on both image and reputation is the very foundation of the public-relations discipline, and steps towards a co-orientation of stakeholder and organizational views have long been advocated (for example, Grunig, 1993). In related literature, stakeholder theories (Donaldson and Preston, 1995; Friedman and Miles, 2002; Pesqueux and Damak-Ayadi, 2005) initially championed by Freeman (1984) continue to pervade strategic-management research. Analyses of relationships that go beyond markets to stakeholders and beyond stakeholders to networks are also a 'hot topic' in the management and marketing disciplines (for example, Awuah, 2001; Batonda and Perry, 2002; Beeby and Booth, 2000; Healy and Hastings, 2001). However, it is interesting to note that papers dedicated to the role of reputation and image make only limited reference to the relationships that shape them. Authors that do acknowledge the importance of relationships in reputation formation are Cravens, Goad-Oliver and Ramamoorti in their Reputation Index (Cravens et al., 2003) and Mahon (2002), who says that reputation is formed 'not only over time, but as a function of complex interrelationships and exchanges' (Mahon, 2002, p. 423). Many investigations of stakeholder theories relative to corporate identity (for example, Scott and Lane, 2000) only tacitly highlight this impact of stakeholder relationships on organizational performance (Balmer, 2001). In this paper's research, relationships with multiple stakeholders are heavily featured, not only to qualitatively assess links with image and reputation, but to gauge overall relationship satisfaction.

Turning to other constructs relevant to this enquiry, a close look at corporate 'identity' (often seen to embrace many constructs) shows that consensus about its meaning is not at all apparent. Balmer (2003) observes that the three theoretical perspectives of 'visual identity', 'internal organizational identity' (including culture and values) and 'corporate identity' all colour the debate. His creation of the term 'business identity' to embrace all three perspectives is valuable in at least summarizing this construct in a global sense. However, it is the expressed meanings of 'corporate identity' alongside 'corporate brand' that appear to display the most overlap of all constructs. For example, Melewar (2003) embraces corporate marketing strategies and brand architecture among his sub-components of corporate identity. Others, such as Knox and Bickerton (2003), point to a convergence of thinking about corporate branding where the marketing perspective focused on brand image, positioning, identity and corporate association has gradually converged with other multidisciplinary work on image, personality, identity and reputation. This convergence, it is argued, brings all perspectives into what is broadly termed 'corporate branding'. Balmer (2001) has also acknowledged this evolution and concluded that, in time, 'a new cognitive area of management called corporate marketing' (p. 249) is likely to gain greater strength. According to Balmer (2001) it is a lack of dialogue between different disciplines among other factors that impedes theoretical progress.

In reflecting upon meanings of the study's core constructs, the airport's private-sector environment prompted the author to reflect on the place of corporate marketing and branding alongside the other constructs. It has already been suggested that all constructs may contribute to a corporate marketing discipline. Yet there are many different models of how constructs could relate to each other set out in Balmer's paper (2001) on 'seeing through the fog'. One of these models simply depicts overlaps between corporate brand, image, identity and reputation rather than a bundling of all concepts under the heading of 'corporate brand'. After considering the internal and external environment of the airport corporation, the author concluded that these theoretical models may only be as robust as their practical application. For example, ways in which the relationships between the constructs are 'lived out' may be organization-specific, at once driven by the internal and external environments of an organization.

To illustrate, during the airport corporation's previous life as a government-operated entity, anecdotal evidence suggests that the organizational identity (dominated by a bureaucratic culture) was the all-encompassing construct that drove the organization's direction. In turn, the organizational culture and operating environment as widely accepted elements of identity (Hatch and Schultz, 1997) were thought to impact on the organization's image and reputation as a transport provider. Potentially more stable relationships may have existed at that time within government quarters that have been somewhat challenged by airport privatization. Following privatization and the advent of the airport city vision, the working relationship between vision, organizational identity and image within the corporation was thought to have shifted, although not immediately.

The communication of the airport city vision from a powerful chief executive downwards has been accompanied by staff participation in corporate value creation and shifts in human-resource management. Although some differences between espoused values and values in use (Schein, 1999) must be expected, the author's participant observation in meetings and interviews prior to the study suggested small rather than large discrepancies. The fact that very few staff members remain from the days when the airport was government-operated and most have been employed to enact the current vision is likely to be influential in current linkages between vision and organizational identity, including culture. Focus-group data arising from this study's research among staff (discussed later) offers some additional support for this position. Indeed, general observations in the lead-up to this research pointed to a model where an overall convergence or 'feeding in' of knowledge about the corporate vision, image, reputation and relationships builds the platform for corporate branding. Interestingly enough, the branding of the airport or airport city is recognized as a separate strategic exercise, albeit related to the corporate-branding process.

In the absence of any deliberate branding exercise to date, the latent 'corporate brand' of the airport corporation is likely to embody stakeholder understandings and opinions about what the organization represents, including its vision, identity (internal culture being one component), image and reputation. Theoretically, Hatch and Schultz (2003) make a strong argument that the interplay between a well-articulated vision and informed insights into image and culture underpins successful corporate branding. An expectation that the airport corporation's brand

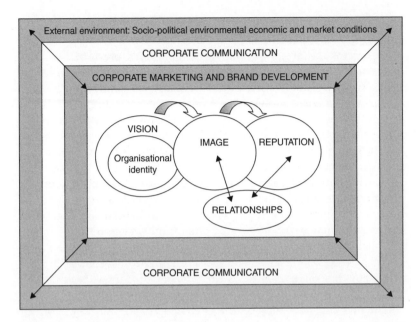

Figure 4.1 Vision, image, reputation and relationships as sub-components of corporate marketing

will be driven forward through its articulation of the vision and other constructs studied here also closely aligns with Knox and Bickerton's (2003) view of the corporate brand-development process. Figure 4.1 depicts the conceptual framework developed for the research with theoretical links demonstrating the author's interpretation of how constructs might be observed in this organizational setting. To some scholars, the positioning of organizational identity within the vision may appear to be a questionable decision. However, as noted earlier, prior interaction with airport staff overwhelmingly supported the notion that the organizational identity, that is, strategies, culture, values and traditions, have been deliberately and successfully seated within the vision. Overlaps between vision, image and reputation are noted in the figure along with the stakeholder relationships that contribute to both constructs.

Methods

The research framework, presented as Figure 4.2, shows practical linkages between this exploratory investigation of vision, image, relationships

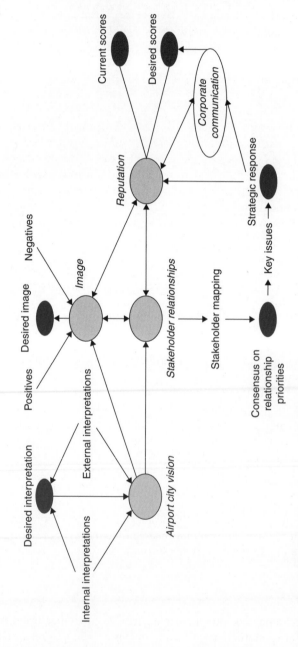

Figure 4.2 Framework for the airport corporation research and consultancy

and reputation and the strategic steps and decisions that hinge on the knowledge acquired. This paper's research embraces all aspects of the framework except the post-research actions of consensus-building about the desired interpretation of vision, the desired image, stakeholder mapping (now the subject of action research), issue positioning and corporate communication strategies. Not specified in this operating framework is the expected linkage of the research to the corporate brand development process.

To design this study, the author reviewed academic literature and documentation on the airport city master plan and visited Amsterdam's Schiphol Airport to become familiar with issues faced in developing an airport city. Here, semi-structured interviews with five senior airport executives and a guided tour of infrastructure and services rounded out the author's orientation to the airport city concept. Themes that framed these interviews were interpretations of an airport city, challenges confronted in developing the airport city, and stakeholder research and communication that prefaced and followed Amsterdam's airport city development.

Subsequently, the first phase of research in Australia included in-depth interviews with the chief executive officer and nine corporate executives of the airport corporation. These internal interviews with executives (although small in number) were essentially used to stimulate 'self-analysis' about how the airport city vision was interpreted and to gain internal perspectives on the corporate image and reputation. Examples of unstructured questions in this preliminary research were: 'the vision of the corporation is to "turn a city airport into an airport city". What does that statement mean to you?'; 'How would you define the current image of the airport corporation?'; and, 'Tell me your thoughts about the reputation of the corporation with regard to X or Y, for example, sharing information or involving stakeholders in shaping strategies.' Data arising from interviews with executives (albeit small in number) helped to frame the interviewer's guide for the external study.

The 60 interviews conducted with external stakeholders included: 23 senior government officials (state and local); 15 airport tenants, eight corporate leaders (CEOs of large organizations); five federal agencies (customs, quarantine services and others); and nine membership-based industry bodies (tourism, transport, retail, property, commerce development). Later, a series of focus groups with staff in marketing, operations, human resources and administration within the airport corporation provided further data from inside the corporation to facilitate a comparison of internal and external viewpoints.

The first section of the external interview guide explored the corporate image as well as stakeholders' images of the airport city vision itself. Reflecting questions in the preliminary research, the primary question about image was: 'When I refer to the airport corporation, what immediate images or impressions come into your mind? In relation to the airport city, the question presented was: 'The corporation's stated goal is to turn a city airport into an airport city – what images does the phrase "airport city" bring to your mind?' The next section of the questionnaire looked at corporate relationships and here free-flowing descriptions of the firm's relationship and its strengths and weaknesses were sought along with a rating of relationship satisfaction. This rating of satisfaction (1 = Strongly Disagree and 7 = Strongly Agree) was obtained from the statement: 'Overall, I would say that our organization is very satisfied with its current relationship with the airport corporation.'

The third and final section of the questionnaire measured the corporation's overall reputation among its stakeholders on 17 attributes using the same seven-point agreement scale. Clearly, the ratings were intended to serve as indicators only within this qualitative study. Nevertheless, a close examination of published reputation scales underpinned the instrument design. Here, the author reviewed Harris-Fombrun Reputation Quotient constructs (Fombrun et al., 2000), items from Australia's Reputex annual reputation surveys (Reputation Measurement, 2004), and constructs from Germany's Manager/Magazin reputation scale (Schwalger, 2004) to develop the instrument.

The 17 items employed were those that remained after an academic peer review and a pre-test of the questionnaire among a select group of five airport stakeholders (business and government). The goal was to ensure that the items were meaningful and useable in their wording, that they were relevant to the business of managing an airport and that they were representative of economic and non-economic criteria. Statements within the instrument embraced: corporate leadership and management; employees, economic stability and growth; reliability as a corporate partner; trustworthiness; ability to offer viable business opportunities; creativity, innovation and entrepreneurship; price/quality of services; stakeholder participation in vision and strategies; equitability in addressing stakeholder views; transparency; complaint resolution; social responsibility; environmental responsibility; overall management of non-economic business impacts; overall reputation among businesses; and finally, overall reputation within government. After implementing the external questionnaire, staff focus groups were used to further explore the meaning of the airport city vision, the corporate image and reputation, and any perceived linkages. Other relationship-management research with staff is ongoing.

Data analysis for this research was performed using N-Vivo software to code electronic transcripts based on audio recordings of one-hour internal and external interviews. Within the software, the ability to create 'nodes' and 'attributes' enabled both open-ended data and rating scores to be contained within the one database. Finally, the staff focus groups were video-recorded (with the permission of participants) and subsequently transcribed for analysis. The coding structure was both predetermined and fluid, in the sense that new codes were added as any unexpected themes or important sub-themes were identified. This online coding was supplemented with a manual review of the themes within the data where illustrative quotations were also selected for use in final reporting.

Results

Research findings are presented in the sequence of vision and image, reputation and relationships. Results from the internal interviews with executives, the external stakeholder interviews and the focus groups are integrated in the following discussion of the study's outcomes.

Findings about the airport city vision and corporate image

From the outset, it was clear that the external stakeholder interviewees did differentiate between their 'image' of what the airport city vision involved and their image of the corporation. However, it was somewhat surprising to find that airport executives had quite different ways of articulating the airport city vision. Some used a broad, city analogy such as 'a physical city, where the corporation is like a council, with environmental, social and community dimensions that are part of that city alongside the airport', while others had a more focused interpretation, such as 'a business city with activities attracted to that area because of aviation'. Of interest in future airport brand development were the specific images chosen to describe the airport city, such as 'a place where you can go without catching a plane – there are lots of reasons to come to the airport'. The fact that vision was expressed through verbalized images of what the airport would become did show an overlap between 'vision' and 'image' as concepts. However, images in this case depicted the future of the airport, rather than the image of the corporation. In comments about corporate image, words such as 'dynamic', 'aggressive' and 'win-win' were used by executives to characterize the organization, but other images such as a 'a major transport provider' and 'a growing land developer' simply reflected roles played by the corporation. Most executives referred to a future image of the organization as a quasi-local government entity or 'mini-Council' managing a city, albeit with a multiplicity of tenants rather than residents.

Interestingly, keywords such as 'win-win' used by executives in response to questions about the organization's image are cited values of the organization. It often appeared that there was little differentiation in the minds of the executives between 'who we are' (identity), 'how we appear' (image) 'what we value' (values) and 'how we operate' (culture). Their immediate tendency was to talk about their image of the organization and aspects of organizational identity in the one breath. The researcher needed to probe further to discover differences between 'what our self-image is right now' and 'what our external image might be'. With regard to external images, phrases that summed up the results were 'committed partners', 'highly collaborative' and 'sometimes distant and aloof' (with government being top-of-mind here). A clear conclusion among executives was that images held by businesses and governments as distinct audiences would contrast based on current issues and relationships, a finding that underlines the 'immediacy' of corporate image noted in the literature.

Most airport executives thought there would be limited external awareness of the airport city. However, mixed understandings of the airport city were found among external stakeholders in line with their degree of involvement in airport activities. More often, interviewees understood a single development within the vision with which they were closely associated for example, the runway project, but had a nebulous grasp of the overall vision. At higher levels within government and within select businesses where airport interaction was more frequent, a generic but accurate understanding of the airport city was evident: 'they are moving from just aircraft arrivals and departures to broader sets of activities and markets.' Four interpretations of the airport city's relationship to the existing metropolitan city emerged. These images were of: 1) an airport city that is a central hub leading the existing city's developments; 2) the airport as a separate city not necessarily integrated with central business district planning; 3) the airport as a city with diverse activities where air transport remains central; and 4) a city with diverse activities where aviation combines with other land developments to satisfy multiple stakeholders.

Dramatic changes in power relationships between the airport corporation and the city council as well as major land developers were implied in these vision interpretations. Thus, these findings pointed to an urgent need to clarify which of the four perspectives best represented the corporation's view in order to optimize its government relationships. Interpretations of the phrase 'airport city' also varied widely, illustrated by comments such as: 'It's simple and conveys the idea of an airport with urban activities' to 'I can see 80s-designed reception lounges and air hostesses walking around in something akin to a James Bond set ... it doesn't tell me anything specific about what is planned.' In general, it appeared that the airport city terminology was not particularly well understood. The limited appeal of the phrase within government circles was clearly influenced by some reticence about the use of the word 'city' where a capital city already existed and was managed by a large local-government authority. Overall, these data suggested that insights into the airport city vision and the phrase 'airport city' itself were superficial, with obvious implications for corporate communication.

Images of the airport corporation itself obtained from unaided and open-ended questions among government and business stakeholders produced attitudinal attributes already contained in the reputation scales, as well as affective images. Data analysis revealed 12 image descriptors of a positive nature, two descriptors that could be viewed as either positive or negative and six negative descriptors (See Appendix 4.1). Among the most commonly cited positive images were those that referred to the corporation as 'progressive, cutting-edge risk-takers' (35 mentions from the 60 participants) and 'dynamic and proactive marketers' (20 mentions). Other positive corporate images attracting a smaller number of mentions included: 'a growing force in the property domain beyond aviation'; 'leadership/top management abilities'; 'a corporate economic driver'; 'well-organized and efficient'; 'informative and consultative' and 'professional'. Images that could be classified as positive or negative were 'aggressive, determined tough negotiators' and 'very commercially oriented, but with some residual bureaucracy'. Negative images were fewer in number, but expressed in much stronger terms. Some of these images referred to corporate arrogance and inflexibility as well as weaknesses with stakeholder engagement and relationship management. In effect, many responses to the image question quickly suggested that overlaps between corporate image and reputation ratings could be expected and that relationships were likely to reflect the tone of those results.

In staff focus groups involving middle management, there was some consensus across departments that the vision was quite well understood internally, although its verbal statement needed more clarity. Participants thought that the general meaning of the vision from a site-development perspective was clear, but it was agreed that character-istics of the airport city concept could be spelled out further. At a generic level, use of the phrase, 'more than a place to catch a plane' mirrored the images offered by both executives and those external stakeholders interacting more frequently with the corporation.

The degree to which the airport city vision impacted on the working environment was evidenced by the ability of most staff to talk freely about it, even though some were unaware of where the vision was actually published. There was a consciousness that every action went towards achieving the airport city outcome. However, managers con-ceded that the understanding and relevance of the vision was likely to be much greater at executive level, with its meaning and related interest diminishing at lower levels. It was felt that 'technical and maintenance staff, car-parking attendants and others would have little knowledge and enthusiasm for the airport city vision'. An observation that there was a solid understanding of the vision among a nucleus of the 'well-informed' that fast dissipated beyond this core group was not dissimilar to findings among external stakeholders.

By comparison, middle managers believed that communication of the vision to convey images to external stakeholders was more successful. 'I think it's successful because it shows a certain development push … that we are not just talking about an airport, but a much more com-plex business environment with urban elements'. Most participants felt that the airport city vision was a good marketing tool. Some suggested that the vision was primarily needed to project 'how we want to be seen by others' (the corporate image). More cautious participants noted that there were image-related risks in publicizing a vision with very specific aspirations: 'we need to be able to follow through on everything stated'. The belief that the vision was mostly needed for external audiences was further emphasized by those who thought that ongoing reference to the vision in the working environment may not be important now when 'people know what jobs they need to do to carry it out and are doing those jobs anyway'. A related comment was 'although there is a broader vision statement, the vision always narrows off to what each person is concerned with in their everyday work'. The vision and values linkage was seen to be important, along with uniform adoption of the values, in efforts to achieve the vision: 'we need to decide whether we are going to seek to achieve it at any price or act in a considered way.' There was some debate about whether the vision-values linkage was 'lived out' to its fullest extent; a doubt that emerged again in external stake-holder research about the corporate image. For example, there was some agreement that the corporation could be inflexible in its negotiations: 'We tend to try to push it through our way, even though we have this 'win-win' value. I don't know that we live up to that value, despite our good intentions.'

Findings about the corporate reputation

As indicated earlier, stakeholders were invited to rate 17 attributes of corporate reputation and comment on their responses. Findings for all items are presented as Appendix 4.2. In considering the leadership item, top management was described as 'visible', 'passionate', 'visionary' and somewhat 'brash'. This perception of toughness and/or 'arrogance' in business negotiations was raised here, as in the image questions, by a number of vocal interviewees: 'No one is questioning their ethical standards . . . they are just a bit too aggressive at times.' However, the professionalism of executives and other employees was also acknowledged. With respect to creativity and innovation, the corporation's attempts to do something commercially attractive outside the traditional role of airports was seen to be innovative.

Scores for trustworthiness and reliability were sound, but perceptions of the corporation's reliability in partnerships were impacted by the views of stakeholders who had experienced difficulties in dealing with the corporation. Most of these negative views were held within government where debates about responsibilities for essential services to support the airport city have been ongoing. Some suggested that the organization was 'a bit unsympathetic to an alternative point of view'. The perceived responsiveness of the organization to complaints was linked to delays in getting things done and occasional difficulty in getting middle management to respond to concerns. In considering stakeholder participation in strategies, contrasts were drawn between information-sharing and an invitation to participate in strategy-making. Select stakeholders were thought to have had input into strategy and it was suggested that some people 'would be more in the loop than others'. Transparency and information-sharing with key stakeholders was thought to have been recently lost due to the preoccupation of the corporation with development challenges, but findings showed healthy support for a new platform of engagement.

The corporation's economic stability rated quite highly along with its ability to be a substantial generator of economic growth in the region. Some interviewees agreed that there were viable opportunities at the airport, but posited that many businesses would not yet understand how they could do business in airport city: 'You don't traditionally think about relocating near an airport and if you're not there, you sometimes don't know who else is there.' The rating of the price/quality relationship of services on-airport was completed by only 36 interviewees (those who felt sufficiently knowledgeable to comment). Pricing was seen to be set at a premium level for property (a predictable response from tenants), although the marketing offer to airlines was perceived in a more positive light.

Overall, the ratings on the corporation's management of non-economic impacts of its business, including social responsibility, were on the lower side. Concern for profits was thought to be a very strong factor driving the corporate reputation and, therefore, the rating on the corporation's relative interest in other business impacts was somewhat lower. A number of issues were mentioned here including a perception of limited community engagement about some of the airport's major developments. With regard to environmental responsibility, most inter-viewees noted that the corporation had a sound reputation, but few could name actual initiatives. Stakeholders appeared to show a higher regard for the corporation's environmental responsibility than for its social responsibility in this study.

Finally, the corporation's overall reputation within the business sector was compared with its reputation among local and state government stakeholders. Here, management expectations of a somewhat higher score within the business sector were supported, although there was a marginal rather than a major difference. Government departments and agencies had more challenging issues to negotiate with the airport and most stakeholders were aware of highly publicized tensions between the airport and government about infrastructure development. Hence, it was likely that some business leaders' views would also be impacted by these conflicts.

Findings about stakeholder relationships

In the data analysis, the airport corporation's relationships with senior representatives in local and state government, business leaders and membership-based industry bodies were compared. The climate of con-flict with local government and some arenas of state government at the time of the research did colour the relationship scores given by these stakeholders. In contrast, chief executive officers of private corpora-tions were more lenient in their relationship scores. Not surprisingly, relationship satisfaction ratings varied in line with the atmosphere of cooperation/conflict at the time of the research. Accordingly, the lowest score was produced among local government stakeholders (mean of 4.7, sd = 1.1), with ratings accompanied by the expression of strong negative opinions about ways in which the corporation had managed past conflicts. However, some positive ratings that reflected the recent resolution of the conflict tended to push the score a little higher than might have been achieved several months earlier. Here, a comment was: 'I think there's been a positive change. I think that we can see a cultural change. There is a recognition that if the corporation wants to succeed with its vision, they need to work with us and listen.'

At the state government level, a score of 5.0 (sd = 1.6) showed somewhat stronger relationships, but stakeholders were not homogenous in the nature of their interaction with the airport, often dealing with quite dissimilar issues. Here, there was no level playing field within the group in terms of the element of vision of concern to them. Consequently, the mean score was not particularly reflective of the strength of either negative or positive comments. Comments ranged from 'there is no reticence by the airport corporation to come to the bargaining table' to 'we've really got some issues and the corporation needs to give a bit'. Overall, it was clear that these relationship scores also reflected stakeholder agreement/disagreement with the airport's mode of negotiating to advance the vision. As indicated earlier, relationships with business leaders reflected greater satisfaction levels (mean of 5.3, sd = .97), but many of these stakeholders were not directly affected by airport-development challenges and looked forward to the economic spin-offs from the vision. A stakeholder group with more interaction with the corporation that also produced the highest satisfaction score (mean of 5.4, sd = 1.1) was membership-based industry bodies. These stakeholders (for example, the Taxi Council, the Property Council, National Retailers Association) had regular dialogue with senior managers and noted that issues of common interest and points of departure were well known to both parties. Nevertheless, this group still sought a more meaningful engagement with the airport and sought an invitation to negotiate further on issues of direct interest to them.

Conclusion

When considering the study's research questions, a tight linkage between vision, image and reputation was apparent. Internally, the vision was seen to be central to all corporate activities and understood by most staff, although some additional clarity in its statement was needed. Executives and middle managers did expect to only observe a sound, external under-standing of vision among a nucleus of stakeholders heavily involved in the airport city development. Their view was not misguided in that a co-orientation of understanding about the corporation's purpose and images of an airport city 'as more than a place to catch a plane' was mainly evident within a select group. Varying levels of awareness of the airport vision and contrasting views about ways in which executives sought to enact it were more common in the wider body of stakeholders.

A mix of positive and negative image descriptors was also expected by executives, and here the strength of emotion attached to negative images of the corporation showed direct links to their adopted approaches to vision implementation. There was no question that images of the corpo-ration were impacted by the atmosphere of negotiation about who was responsible for essential service infrastructure both before and during the research process. Negative images of the corporation did reflect external perceptions of how the corporate culture and operating style (aspects of organizational identity in Figure 4.1) shaped these negotiations to advance the vision. Findings also pointed to a misalignment between the corporation's 'win-win' value and the management style of execu-tives. As a result, doubts at middle management level about whether the promised value was being 'lived out' were also mirrored in the findings among external stakeholders.

Based on these findings, the umbrella position of the vision with orga-nizational identity (culture, mode of operation, values, traditions) firmly seated within it, as shown in Figure 4.1, cannot be discounted. Execu-tives' views that the corporation could be described on the one hand as 'highly collaborative' and on the other as 'distant and aloof' were not totally supported. More of a 'distant' image tended to prevail among all but those stakeholders with positive working partnerships or business relationships with executives. In this context, it was interesting to see that the lowest reputation scores were attached to the corporation's equi-tability in dealing with different stakeholders and its encouragement of stakeholders to contribute to its vision and corporate strategies. Percep-tions about the corporation's concern for profits over other impacts and its social responsibility suggested a need for it to explore how it could build a more 'people-friendly', 'open' and 'flexible' reputation among government and business stakeholders.

Internal expectations of differences in relationship satisfaction scores between the private and public sector were upheld. Within different stakeholder groups, these relationships appeared to be influenced by the intensity and regularity of interaction as well as by the aforementioned conflicts about vision implementation. As a result, a two-way arrow between relationships and the vision could be added to the interactions depicted in Figure 4.1. All other linkages between vision, image, reputation and stakeholder relationships appear to be justified by the research results.

As initially argued by the author, Figure 4.1's theoretical model can only be said to fit the corporation in this case study and different relationships and linkages may be found in other cases. Public interest in the airport corporation is primarily driven by issues related to its airport city vision at this time. In the current climate, the environment is ripe for stakeholders to have a strong view (either positive or negative) about that vision and the corporation's mode of operation. Thus, a contribution of this study has been its ability to observe stakeholder perceptions about vision, image, reputation and relationships at a time when the interplay between these constructs is most evident. Further research into how these findings can contribute to some consensus building about the 'brand' of the new airport city represents an opportunity to further reflect on how a model of 'corporate marketing' is operating in practice.

Research opportunities for other authors that arise from this work are diverse. To begin, the reputation-measurement instrument adapted for this airport research could be tested in other airport settings. However, similar studies of the four constructs in organizational environments where a highly publicized vision dominates business activities would be of interest. In particular, different methodological approaches could be explored. Where this study used qualitative research and quantitative indicators to jointly examine the constructs, some benefits could be obtained from developing a combined instrument to measure the strength and direction of views about a stated corporate vision, the operating style of executives (found to be important in this research), relationships and corporate reputation. The rich informational advantages of including qualitative methods in understanding image, reputation and relationships remain. However, an integrated survey instrument that measures attitudes towards corporate vision (including negotiating styles used to implement it), aspects of corporate reputation and the strength and direction of stakeholder relationships could be applied across several airports or different types of corporations by interested researchers. A comparison of the internal and external perceptions of the firm using a mirror-image survey instrument would also be useful to test for a co-orientation of views (Grunig, 2003). Limited comparative research work of this nature has been done on constructs across internal and external organizational contexts and it is widely accepted that the staff or people of an organization are among its most powerful ambassadors. In the intra-organizational setting, further work on how perceptions of the four constructs impact upon or relate to an overall concept of organizational identity would also be of interest to scholars of organizational behaviour and internal marketing.

For the airport corporation involved in this research, continued tracking of corporate image, reputation and relationships as the vision continues to unfold is critical. Since the implementation of this research, several major development projects within the vision have gained widespread publicity, and ongoing media interest in the corporation and its executive undoubtedly shapes and re-shapes the constructs in this study. Accordingly, the development of an instrument which studies the constructs in an integrated and consistent way over time could prove to be an important monitor to inform corporate communications at various stages of the implementation of the airport city vision. Further qualitative insights to the constructs and, in time, stakeholder input to the parallel development of the corporate and airport city brands will also be important inclusions in the research agenda of this airport corporation.

Appendix 4.1 Reputation measurement results

Reputation statements	Mean	SD
This is a well-managed corporation with excellent leadership	5.5	.83
Employees adopt high standards in dealing with external agencies/firms	5.3	.86
The corporation has a reputation for creativity, innovation and entrepreneurship	5.4	1.05
This corporation is seen as a trustworthy company to deal with	5.1	.99
This corporation is seen as a reliable partner among business and government agencies	5.4	1.07
This corporation holds external complaints in high regard and responds to those concerns	4.8	1.0
The corporation has a reputation for being transparent and forthright in sharing information	4.6	1.2
The corporation encourages stakeholder participation in its vision and strategies	4.5	1.3
The corporation is equitable in addressing the views of different stakeholders	4.2	1.1
The corporation is economically stable with good prospects for future growth	5.7	1.0
The corporation has a range of viable business opportunities for local and overseas firms	5.3	.93
The corporation's services reflect a good price/quality relationship	4.3	.93
The corporation is not just concerned with profits, but also manages other business impacts	4.2	1.2
The corporation is socially responsible and offers something of value to local communities	4.6	1.1
The corporation is environmentally responsible in its business and development activities	5.1	.94
Overall, the corporation has a very positive reputation among most businesses	5.4	.83
Overall, the corporation has a very positive reputation within state and local government	5.0	1.2

Appendix 4.2 Image descriptors from open-ended questions

Descriptor	Frequency
P – Progressive, cutting-edge, visionary risk takers	35 mentions
P – Dynamic, competitive and proactive marketers	20 mentions
P – Growing land and real estate developers beyond aviation	17 mentions
P – Leaders/top managers with an ability to achieve good solutions	17 mentions
P – Informative and consultative	15 mentions
P – Significant economic engine for the region	15 mentions
P – A positive, key partner for our organisation	13 mentions
P – Well-organised and efficient with a well-presented airport	11 mentions
P – Professional employees and operators	11 mentions
P – Growing as an air-transport service provider	11 mentions
P – Conscious of environmental issues	6 mentions
P – Safety conscious	4 mentions
P or N – Commercially oriented, but with some residual bureaucracy	20 mentions
P or N – Aggressive, determined, tough negotiators	19 mentions
N – Arrogant, difficult, unyielding, manipulators	22 mentions
N – Organisation with legal disputes and related negative images	14 mentions
N – Inflexible, non-responsive, lack of urgency in middle managers	13 mentions
N – Too expensive and dollar-driven	13 mentions
N – Lacking in strategic engagement beyond consultation	9 mentions
N – Monopolistic with some perceptions of elitism	8 mentions

Code: P = Positive descriptor, N = Negative descriptor.

References

Awuah, G. (2001) 'A Firm's Competence Development through Its Network of Exchange Relationships', *Journal of Business and Industrial Marketing*, 16, pp. 574–99.

Balmer, J. M. T. (1998) 'Corporate Identity and the Advent of Corporate Marketing', *Journal of Marketing Management*, 14, pp. 963–96.

Balmer, J. M. T. (2001) 'Corporate Identity, Corporate Branding and Corporate Marketing', *European Journal of Marketing*, 35, pp. 248–91.

Batonda, G. and C. Perry (2002) 'Approaches to Relationship Development Processes in Inter-firm Networks', *European Journal of Marketing*, 37, pp. 1457–84.

Beeby, M. and C. Booth (2000) 'Networks and Inter-organizational Learning: A Critical Review', *The Learning Organization*, 7, pp. 75–88.

Berens, G. and C. van Riel (2004) 'Corporate Associations in the Academic Literature: Three Main Streams of Thought in the Reputation Measurement Literature', *Corporate Reputation Review*, 7, pp. 161–78.

Bromley, D. B. (1993) *Reputation, Image and Impression Management* (London: Wiley).

Campbell, D. T. (1963) *Psychology: A Study of a Science* (New York: McGraw Hill).

Canaday, J. (2000) 'Planning the Aerotropolis', *Airport World*, 5, pp. 52–53.

Cravens C., E. Goad-Oliver and S. Ramamoorti (2003) 'The Reputation Index: Measuring and Managing Corporate Reputation', *European Management Journal*, 21, pp. 201–12.

Donaldson, T. and L. Preston (1995) 'The Stakeholder Theory of the Corporation: Concepts, Evidence and Implications', *Academy of Management Review*, 20, pp. 65–91.

El-Namaki, M. S. (1992) 'Creating a Corporate Vision', *Long Range Planning*, 25, pp. 25–9.

Ferrand, A. and M. Pages (1999) 'Image Management in Sports Organizations: The Creation of Value', *European Journal of Marketing*, 33, pp. 387–401.

Fillis, I. (2003) 'Image, Reputation and Identity Issues in the Arts and Crafts Organization', *Corporate Reputation Review*, 6, pp. 239–51.

Fombrun, C., N. Gardberg and J. Sever (2000) 'The Reputation Quotient: A Multi-Stakeholder Measure of Corporate Communication', *Journal of Brand Management*, 7, pp. 241–55.

Freeman, R. E. (1984) *Strategic Management: A Stakeholder Approach* (Boston: Pitman).

Friedman, A. and S. Miles (2002) 'Developing Stakeholder Theory', *Journal of Management Studies*, 39, pp. 1–21.

Grunig, J. (1993) 'Image and Substance: From Symbolic to Behavioral Relationships', *Public Relations Review*, 19, pp. 121–39.

Grunig, J. (2003) *Qualitative Methods for Assessing Relationships between Organisations and Publics* (Gainesville: Institute for Public Relations).

Hatch, M. J. and M. Schultz (1997) 'Relations between Organizational Culture, Identity and Image', *European Journal of Marketing*, 31, pp. 356–65.

Hatch, M. J. and M. Schultz (2003) 'Bringing the Organization into Corporate Branding', *European Journal of Marketing*, 37, pp. 1041–64.

Healy, M. and K. Hastings (2001) 'The Old, the New and the Complicated: A Trilogy of Marketing Relationships', *European Journal of Marketing*, 35, pp. 182–93.

Jarach, D. (2001) 'The Evolution of Airport Management Practices: Towards a Multi-point, Multi-service, Marketing-driven Firm', *Journal of Air Transport Management*, 7, pp. 119–25.

Kasarda, J. (2000/2001) 'Logistics and the Rise of the Aerotropolis', *Real Estate Issues*, Winter, pp. 43–8.

Knox, S. and D. Bickerton (2003) 'The Six Conventions of Corporate Branding', *European Journal of Marketing*, 37, pp. 998–1016.

Mahon, J. (2002) 'Corporation Reputation: A Research Agenda Using Strategy and Stakeholder Literature', *Business and Society*, 41, pp. 415–45.

Matt Zaid, A. (1994) 'Malaysia Airlines Corporate Vision and Service Quality Strategy', *Managing Service Quality*, 4, pp. 11–15.

Melewar, T. C. (2003) 'Determinants of the Corporate Identity Construct: A Review of the Literature', *Journal of Marketing Communications*, 9, pp. 195–220.

O'Brien, F. and M. Meadows (2003) 'Exploring the Current Practice of Visioning: Case Studies from the UK Financial Services Sector', *Management Decision*, 41, pp. 488–97.

Pesqueux, Y. and S. Damak-Ayadi (2005) 'Stakeholder Theory in Perspective', *Corporate Governance*, 5, 5–21.

Reputation Measurement (2004) *Reputex Report on 2004 Criteria Consultation Feedback* (Melbourne).

Rooijmans, K. (2003) 'Private Airports, Open Skies', *Australian Chief Executive*, July, pp. 44–6.

Schein, E. (1999) *The Corporate Culture Survival Guide* (San Francisco: Jossey Bass).

Schuler, M. (2004) 'Management of the Organizational Image: A Method for Organizational Image Configuration', *Corporate Reputation Review*, 7, pp. 37–53.

Schwalger, M. (2004) 'Components and Parameters of Corporate Reputation: An Empirical Study', *Schmalenbach Business Review*, 56, pp. 46–71.

Scott, S. and V. Lane (2000) 'A Stakeholder Approach to Organizational Identity', *Academy of Management Review*, 25, pp. 43–62.

Testa, M. (1999) 'Satisfaction with Organizational Vision, Job Satisfaction and Service Efforts: An Empirical Investigation', *Leadership and Organization Development Journal*, 20, pp. 154–61.

Wartick, S. (2002) 'Measuring Corporate Reputation, Definition and Data', *Business and Society*, 41, pp. 371–92.

Weigelt, K. and C. Camerer (1988) 'Reputation and Corporate Strategy: A Review of Recent Theory and Applications', *Strategic Management Journal*, 9, 443–54.

Yin, R. K. (1994) *Case Study Research: Design and Methods* (Thousand Oaks: Sage Publications).

5

Brand Identification: A Theory-based Construct for Conceptualizing Links between Corporate Branding, Identity and Communications

Sue Vaux Halliday and Sven Kuenzel

Abstract

This conceptual paper looks at 'brand identification'. It does this by providing an overview of social-identity theory as it illuminates marketing theories in customer relationships. We build on recent interest in the marketing literature in identity and develop a conceptual model of consumer brand identification in business relationships. Corporate identity has often been the entity that can be created/manipulated in design and marketing. Seen through the lens of organizational behaviour scholars this is perceived as organizational identity and in turn this is more focused on employee perceptions and responses. Brand identification links these two as it stresses the process by which individuals (customers and employees) may identify with the organization as a corporate brand. We offer this as providing theoretical foundations for a perspective integrating corporate branding, identity and communications. This is a timely contribution to issues of identity in marketing theory and practice.

Introduction

Brands are a most valuable, if intangible, asset for many companies (Lassar, Mittal and Sharma, 1995). Arnett, German and Hunt (2003) have criticized past literature regarding relationship marketing as having focused only on the economic nature of relationships and for being applied mostly in the business-to-business context. Key issues which have historically defined relationships – such as trust and commitment – have been investigated in some depth and the approach found insightful (Cornelissen, 2002; Morgan and Hunt, 1994). We believe that an overlooked but fruitful area of interest for relationship marketers is that of meaning for consumers via identification with their favourite brands (Aaker and Fournier, 1995; Fournier, 1998; Golder and Irwin, 2001). We add to the literature on identity the important company asset of current and potential customers by means of the construct 'brand identification'. This is the means by which many customers develop relationships with the brand and with the company and is nurtured by corporate branding communications. This is an important construct for understanding one further aspect of customer relationships.

Corporate identity has often been the entity that can be created/ manipulated in design and marketing. Seen through the lens of organizational behaviour scholars this is perceived as organizational identity and in turn this is more focused on employee perceptions and responses. The social-identity concept termed 'identification', now described as a key concept in organizational behaviour (Gioia, Shultz and Korley, 2000), has been investigated in the sociological and psychological disciplines and more recently in organization behaviour and human-resource management. However, a review of the literature has revealed that until very recently few studies seem to apply it in the context of marketing (Ahearne, Bhattacharya and Gruen, 2005). We follow Dutton, Dukerich and Harquail (1994), who define organizational identification as the cognitive connection made by the employee with an organization that preserves the continuity of their self-concept, enhances their self-esteem and provides distinctiveness. We substitute the word 'brand' for the word 'organizational' and 'customer' for the word 'employee'. We find this definition is most appropriate to marketing and corporate branding, where branding processes build valued differentiation into the company and its products to encourage increased custom and increased ability to obtain resources from stakeholders (Balmer and Gray, 2003) and where identity and values link at three levels – the customer, the brand and the organization (Urde, 2003). These processes need to be flexible and to adapt to changing competitive contexts. 'Identity' itself, once seen only as an enduring element of organizational life (Albert and Whetton, 1985), is more recently being understood to be a fluid, even evolving, and hence adaptable construct as it interacts with image (Balmer and Gray, 2003; Gioia et al., 2000). So our paper is based on the strong belief that this concept of identification is highly relevant to developing customer brand relationships, in some settings and with some customers, and so provides one point of connection between corporate branding, identity and communications. We will demonstrate from this literature how in business relationships customers identify with and associate themselves with brands, products or organizations that reflect and reinforce their self-identities (Bhattacharya and Sen, 2003). This matches Dutton et al.'s (1994) parallel observation of organizational identification that self-categorization is its foundation (Ashforth and Mael, 1989; Tajfel and Turner, 1985).

Since relationships are an important part of the individual's identity, it is not surprising that marketers looking to create long-term relationships have found that finding meaning in buying often makes a contribution to the construction of the individual (Fournier, 1995; Gruen, Summers and Acito, 2000). This search for personal meaning has tended to become inseparably linked to brands (Fournier, 1995; Holt, 2002; McAlexander, Schouten and Koenig, 2002), for brands have the potential to be designed around the need for belonging, and owning certain brands often affirms the consumer's sense of identity (Aaker, 1994; Aaker and Fournier, 1995; Fournier, 1998). It may be that this is a peculiarly American phenomenon, as Holt (2004) writes assuredly that customers of iconic brands such as Mountain Dew 'care about what the brand accomplishes for their identities'. His focus is the interesting area of cultural identity myths and he notes: 'Customers who make use of the brand's myth for their identities forge tight emotional connections to the brand' (p. 9). He introduces his subject by noting that 'identity brands create customer value differently than do other types of brands' (p. 4) and lists as examples Levi's, Chanel, Reebok, Pepsi, Saab and even IBM. However, in the UK Elliott and Wattanasuwan (1998) are of the view that 'it is essential for marketers to understand the concept and dynamics of self, the symbolic meaning of goods and the role played by brands' (p. 131). They therefore have researched how brands are used in the construction of identity. And in Denmark, Askegaard notes the broad cultural relevance of branding, since 'a brand is such a hegemonic vehicle of diversity, a widely intelligible way of communicating a potentially infinite number of corporate, product and consumer identities' (Askegaard, 2006, p. 97). Csaba and Bengtsson (2006), whose experiences span America and Europe, consider that issues of identity formation and brand identity merit further attention. In fact, in discussing brand identity as understood in the mainstream branding literature, these two authors consider the anthropomorphism of 'brand personality' to be 'highly contentious' (p. 124) and instead prefer to see the issue as brands being 'used by consumers in the process of identity formation and negotiation'. They acknowledge 'the need for 'conceptualizations that take into account the consumers' role in linking identity and brands' (p. 124). This breadth and depth of international scholarship drawing on social identity theory, current cultural anxieties about identity and the growth of branding supports our view that brand identification is a relevant construct to explore. Hall (1996) suggests that further attention be paid to this issue and that identification is a more appropriate term than identity. While we readily acknowledge that this is not the case for all goods, services, or even brands (see our later discussion of segments of consumers), where there is indeed an opportunity for consumers to identify with the corporate brand behind what they buy, identification is a powerful concept.

We conclude this paper by proposing a conceptual model and two relevant contexts for data collection to test the model and assess empirically the potential for such identification. We would expect analysis of this further research to confirm the finding of Arnett et al. (2003) that identification very often plays a very central role in successful marketing exchanges. Just recently the marketing discipline and its top journals have taken up customer/company identification (Ahearne et al., 2005; Algesheimer, Dholakia and Herman, 2005); therefore our study is a timely contribution to developing understanding of brand identification. This aspect of customer behaviour provides one possible explication of the links between the three areas brought together in this book.

Theoretical foundations

We wish to present an overview of how social-identity theory is relevant to marketing, providing a way of understanding how individuals identify with organizations, both as customers and employees. We see this identification as useful in illuminating the process by which there are interrelationships between corporate branding, identity and communications. Our focus is on the customer, proposing brand identification as a customer-relationship development process linking these three areas.

Social identity theory

Social identity theory has been used in a number of organizational studies (Bergami and Bagozzi, 2000; Kane, Argote and Levine, 2005; Smidts, Pruyn and van Riel, 2001). Social identification takes place when an individual identifies with a certain group. Consumers who share a joint identification will define themselves in relation to that group and in distinction from members of a rival social group (Tajfel and Turner, 1985). Social identity theory is useful for understanding consumer behaviour and underpins the practice of a segmentation strategy, as an individual consumer need not overtly act together with other consumers (nor even know them), but nevertheless does see his or her self as part of a social group, which can then be targeted. Organizational identity has been the subject of much research, mostly applied to the beliefs and attitudes of employees (Haslam, Postmes and Ellemes, 2003; Morgan, 1997; Whetten and Godfrey, 1998). This literature, based on social identity theory, provides a firm basis for focusing on the 'power of organizational identity to be both an externally shared... and an internalized aspect of the collective self' (Haslam, Postmes and Ellemes, 2003, p. 357). It provides a theory that explains the existence of 'collective products – plans and visions, goods and services' (Smidts et al., 2001).

Identity and identification

Social identification is essentially a perception of oneness with a group of persons (Ashforth and Mael, 1989). Our definition, given earlier, is of a self-concept. As we have noted, this does not need to result in overt group behaviour, but is powerful as a perception in driving other behaviour, such as choosing an employer and, we believe, in driving buying behaviour. It exists in individual's heads, or meaning-making processes, because it satisfies needs for social identity and self-definition; it is caused by the process of self-categorization (Dutton et al., 1994). In the organizational context, it has been defined as being 'the degree to which a member defines him- or herself by the same attributes that he or she believes define the organization' (p. 239). Marketing studies have already been carried out in organizations with memberships rather than with paying customers (Ahearne et al., 2005). We consider it timely to conceptualize it as relevant to the paying customer. Applying the identification concept in such a brand-customer context is justified as, according to Brewer (cited in Algesheimer et al., 2005) the notion of identification with an organization can also happen without a need to interact or to have formal ties with an organization. Scott and Lane (2000) support this view as they argue that people can seek identification even when they are not formal organizational members. They conclude that: 'To the extent that the group category is psychologically accepted as part of the self, an individual is said to be identified with the group' (p. 46). It can therefore be said that identification is but a 'perceptual constructive construct' (Ashforth and Mael, 1989) where the individual has an interior understanding and process of meaning creation that does not need to be overtly practised or demonstrated, where he/she is not compelled to expend effort towards group goals. For what determines identification is just a psychological perception on the part of an individual to consider him/herself as being intertwined with a particular group. Akerlof and

Kranton (2000) apply identity theory in an economics context and underline the importance of our focus in this paper, as they conclude that 'because identity is fundamental to behaviour, choice of identity may be the most important economic decision people make' (Akerlof and Kranton, 2000, p. 717).

An individual can have multiple identities: identification can be maintained through a variety of groups of people that he or she works, a department, and/or a union, and /or an age group and so on and not only from the overall organization itself (Ashforth and Mael, 1989; Ouwerkerk, Ellemers and Gilder, 1999). This multiplicity may often be matched by organizations (Pratt and Foreman, 2000). One influential view of organizational identification is that organizations have several identities (Bhattacharya, Rao and Glynn, 1995) and the development of identification can create complexities through the existence of competing organizational identity claims (Ashforth and Mael, 1989). Dutton et al. (1994) stress that the actual meaning of identification will vary with each individual, as it is *their* perception of the identity. And it is interesting to note how this connects with consumer-branding theory. For it has been suggested that the meaning of brands varies in each consumer's head (McAlexander et al., 2002). Practitioners are possibly ahead of academics in this area; Magnum advertising has stressed 'Me and my Magnum' across Europe for a number of years and the UK Marks and Spencer logo reads 'Your M&S' and is placed in their current advertising next to an individual well-known celebrity wearing Marks and Spencer products.

To summarize, all previous identified research suggests that individuals often actually identify with an organization when they share and receive the same attributes and also affiliate with the values and attitudes of that organization (Ahearne et al., 2005; Ashforth and Mael, 1989; Bhattacharya et al., 1995). Recently empirical studies in the marketing literature have confirmed this conceptual research. In contexts of membership, identification has been shown to be relevant (Arnett et al., 2003); in a commercial relationship between physicians and pharmaceutical companies identification has been shown to be important (Ahearne et al., 2005). A recent ethnographic study of responses made by international executives based in Australia to gaining and losing platinum air-traveller cards, and the deceits practised to retain the use of queues and facilities that bolstered their self-understanding of status benefits, suggests the power of identification in this segment of air-travel customers. As people of importance, their identity, and not merely the immediate benefits of platinum travel, has become linked with the perks;

for them longer queues were attractive, as long as they were for important customers (Black, 2006). Elliott and Davies (2006), working in a UK setting with consumers of fashion, music and club culture, draw on theories of identity and conclude that 'we so easily and readily view identity(ies) as in some way fixed or stable and coherent, rather than recognize what we view of self as merely a moment in time in a dynamic process of always becoming'. We believe that enough contexts, as noted above, have been researched to justify pursuing these connections between identification and some branded services and goods and associated firms by taking a closer look at the theory underpinning this. This theory suggests that statistically significant numbers of individuals categorize themselves and identify with the group with which they share similarities. Having established this, it is important to see that social classification of the self can predict the behaviours of the group members (Billig and Tajfel, 1973; Turner, 1975). This is of obvious relevance to brand managers. It is therefore of managerial interest and relevance to investigate the construct 'brand identification'.

Brand identification in our paper is different from what Algesheimer et al. (2005) called 'community identification'. Algesheimer et al. developed a new measurement instrument which is perhaps more about being included in a particular group. They have items related to friendship and the sharing of similar objectives with other group members. Our previous discussion emphasized the issue, in line with social-identity theory, that customers do not have to know or interact with other customers to identify with a brand. Also, the popular Mael and Ashforth (1992) measurement instrument has received some criticism (Askegaard, 2006). Therefore, in any future empirical work to measure brand identification, we would recommend using Bergami and Bagozzi's (2000) scale; this seems more appropriate for this particular perspective because of its oneness within Dutton et al.'s (1994) tripartite framework, as we mentioned where we gave our definition of brand identification.

Conceptual background and working hypotheses

We look at two concepts that contribute to brand identification, and at the role that corporate communications plays. What might cause customers (and indeed employees) to identify with a brand? From our reading of relevant literature we present an overview of the contribution to brand identification made by prestige, customer satisfaction and corporate communications, illuminated by social identity theory. From this we present three working hypotheses. We then turn to two possible consequences of brand identification, again using social-identity theory applied to two outcomes important in marketing. This leads to two further working hypotheses connecting word-of-mouth activity and repurchase intentions to brand identification. All our hypotheses are phrased very much in line with similar studies that permit quantitative methods to be used to test their model (Ahearne et al., 2005; Arnett et al., 2003; Morgan and Hunt, 1994). This phrasing allows researchers to test our proposed model in future studies.

The hypotheses indicate causal relationships but these are not perfect relationships and the strength of these relationships should be measured. Therefore, researchers should consider testing these relationships with multivariate methods such as regression analysis or structural equation modelling. Structural equation modelling seems especially useful since it permits the estimation of multiple and interrelated dependence relationships, and unobserved factors can be represented in these relationships. Additionally, measurement error in the estimation process can be accounted for (Hair et al., 1998).

Prestige

By prestige is meant the perceptions that other people, whose opinions are valued, believe that the organization or brand is well regarded – respected, admired, or well-known (Bergami and Bagozzi, 2000). Bergami and Bagozzi further add that to the extent that important others regard the brand that a person associates himself with as well-regarded, positive identification is generated, assuming other factors remain constant. The corporate reputation literature can also be helpful in this context because some previous studies have used prestige and reputation interchangeably (Fombrun, 1996; Fombrun and Shanley, 1990). The literature indicates that having a positive reputation means that customers also perceive the company and its brands more positively. According to Fombrun (1996) and Fombrun and Shanley (1990) a positive reputation may also make it possible to charge premium prices from customers.

Additionally, a positive reputation allows a company not only to keep its current customers, but also to attract new ones, which will increase the company's turnover. Nonetheless, establishing a good reputation takes time and resources and it would be unrealistic to anticipate that the price premium a company demands from its customers will pay off in the short term. A company has to take a long-term perspective, as revenues will only be transformed into profits over time (Fombrun and Shanley, 1990). In terms of measurement, previous studies have mainly used an index or parts of it to measure reputation or prestige based on *Fortune* magazine's 'Annual Survey of America's Most Admired Corporations' index (Carmeli, 2004; Carmeli and Tishler, 2005; Fombrun and Shanley, 1990). However, since this index has received a lot of criticism (Fombrun, 1996) we would suggest using Mael and Ashforth's (1992) organizational-prestige measure because it has shown very positive results (Bhattacharya et al., 1995; Smidts et al., 2001).

Prestige is sought after and leads people to associate themselves with prestigious organizations/brands to increase their self-esteem by 'basking in reflected glory' (BIRGing), a term coined by Cialdini and colleagues in 1976 (Campbell, Aiken and Kent, 2004). Most researchers therefore agree with the view that the prestige of the organization leads to the identification of individuals with it (Ahearne et al., 2005; Arnett et al., 2003; Bergami and Bagozzi, 2000; Bhattacharya and Sen, 2003; Bhattacharya et al., 1995). Ashforth and Mael (1989) note that 'individuals often cognitively identify themselves with a winner' (p. 24), which also satisfies their self-esteem. This view is also supported by the research of Arnett et al. (2003), where the researchers 'find that perceived organizational prestige is associated positively with organizational identification, which they define as a sense of oneness with or belongingness to an organization' (p. 94). Consumers will therefore want to maintain their self-enhancement and satisfy their self-esteem as they identify with prestigious organizations by purchasing from them (Bhattacharya and Sen, 2003).

In their research, Smidts et al. (2001) also concluded that 'prestige is strongly associated with identification' (p. 1058) whereby employees seem to identify more with organizations that are evaluated favourably by outsiders. The role of prestige is therefore closely connected to corporate identity concerns about reputation. According to Bhattacharya et al. (1995), because prestigious organizations are assumed to be successful, the prestige of an organization often serves as an indicator of organizational success. If the brand image is perceived as prestigious by consumers, this may also enhance their pride in identifying with a prestigious brand (Ahearne et al., 2005; Dutton et al., 1994). Therefore it is hypothesized that:

H_1:   A higher level of prestige will lead to a higher level of brand identification.

Customer satisfaction

Customer satisfaction theory is well known in the marketing literature and has been a subject of hot debate. However, in this paper we are using social identity theory to provide us with a framework for conceptualizing links between the three areas of corporate branding, identity and communications. Satisfaction has long been identified as being important for building relationships (Oliver and Swan, 1980). We take the core of the concept to be the emotional or cognitive response of the owner of a brand towards the customer after the latter has purchased and used the brand for some time. Arnett et al. (2003) found that the concept 'satisfaction' also plays an important role in identification, particularly in a university setting. Bhattacharya et al. (1995) also found, in their research on identification among art museum members, that satisfaction with the institution was related to identification. They hypothesized that 'the more satisfied a person is with an organization's offerings, the greater the identification' (p. 3). The level of satisfaction of the customers with goods and services leads to loyalty to the provider and affects their purchase intentions positively (Dowling and Uncles, 1997; Halliday, 1999; O'Malley and Tynan, 2000). Social identity theory researchers in organizational behaviour argue that satisfaction leads to organizational identification (Arnett and Hunt, 1994; Ashforth and Mael, 1989; Bhattacharya and Sen, 2003). Satisfaction is an antecedent of identification because satisfied customers are those who have fulfilled one of their self-definitional needs. Therefore, it is hypothesized that:

H_2:   A higher level of satisfaction will lead to a higher level of brand identification.

Corporate communications and branding

Communications is a very broad area of interest and, once again, our intention is to discuss it in the light of social identity theory as a contributor to the concept of brand identification. It has been claimed that corporate communication is a management instrument that can be used to engender identification (Smidts et al., 2001). According to Anderson and Narus (1990) communication refers to 'formal as well as informal sharing of information between firms' (p. 44) – often, however, it refers merely to the one-way traffic of organizations providing information to customers. Smidts et al. (2001), in their research on employee communication and organizational identification, tested the hypothesis that adequate information about an organization strengthens organizational identification. Their results revealed that 'providing relevant information appears to be the sine qua non for a communication climate and thus for identification (p. 1059). Beech and Huxham (2003), in the development of their collaboration theory, suggest that communication processes can indirectly affect the formation of identities. It is now timely to apply this work to corporate communications aimed at potential and current customers.

Bhattacharya et al. (1995), who researched consumers as formal members, claim that the greater the contact with an organization, the greater will be the strength of identification with that organization. They further add that greater exposure to an organization impacts positively on identification, building on Dutton et al.'s (1994) insights. This is further supported by Kleine III, Kleine and Kernan (1993) who propose that media connections are positively related to identification. One such exposure or media connection is likely to be communication messages sent from the supplier to the customer. Bhattacharya and Sen (2003) have further argued that customers are more likely to increase their knowledge about companies that actively engage in communicating with their stakeholders. This knowledge, once acquired, makes it more likely that they identify with these companies (Dutton and Harquail, 1994).

With positively valued information, members feel proud to be part of a well-respected company, as it strengthens their feelings of self-worth (Bhattacharya et al., 1995). This means that it serves the self-enhancement motive. As Bhattacharya and Sen (2003) point out, initiatives such as corporate advertising and public relations not only educate consumers about the company's identity but also make it more salient relative to other competing organizational identities. Moreover, it is suggested that salience is likely to be particularly high when in-group/out-group differences are heightened; think of Apple's 'Computers for Everyone Else' and 'Think Different' campaigns. In general, corporate communication is likely to increase perceptions of identification and contribute to the consumer's evolving construction of identity, because some of the strongest associations with corporate brands are intangible and identity-related (for example, innovative, a market leader, environmentally conscious). In fact, Scott and Lane (2000) assert that, over time, these factors increase an identity's share of mind and really help consumers internalize its relevance to their social identity, making it more salient and accessible.

Scott and Lane (2000) also point out that when stakeholders encounter an advertisement that represents a desired organizational image or when they read a news article that addresses organizational actions, they are encouraged to reconsider their role as stakeholders and to reflect on the fit of the organizational image with their own identity. Indeed, as pointed out by Dutton et al. (1994) in organizations that are perceived favourably by their members, organizational identification is more likely to occur because it enhances members' feelings of self-worth. Social identity theory suggests that one of the most relevant functions of organizational communication for brand identification is the reduction of uncertainty for customers. Uncertainty in terms of psychology can be defined as 'the motivation of people to reduce uncertainty by seeking information (information dependence) from physical or social environments' (McGarty et al., 1993, p. 18).

Corporate branding processes are not merely an overarching brand-management activity. For the corporate brand has been defined as 'the visual, verbal and behavioural expression of an organization's unique business model' (Knox and Bickerton, 2003, p. 1023). Balmer (2001) highlights five key aspects of these processes: corporate brands are cultural, intricate, demand total commitment from the management and appeal to the emotions. We know that relationship theory shows that emotional as well as cognitive elements lead to a mutually satisfying relationship, notes the necessity for commitment from both parties and requires a relational culture and skill-set within the organization. We find, then, that brand identification is closely linked to corporate branding and the communication of values and culture in brand values. Therefore, in conjunction with our discussion of the importance of satisfaction, it is hypothesized that:

H_3:   A higher level of corporate communication will lead to a higher level of brand identification.

Word of mouth

Equally, the role of informal communications between customers is important. The increasing phenomenon of communities of consumers on the web, communicating unofficially and outside the power and control of the firm, can be underpinned theoretically using identity theory as an approach, because individuals who share a common social identity would want to communicate in order to reduce uncertainty and to affiliate (Haslam, 2001). Successful relationships are ones in which organizations encourage certain cooperative behaviours in their partners (Morgan and Hunt, 1994). Cornelissen (2002) notes that the metaphor of relationships has shed new light on marketing practices. His emphasis on the role of social structures is highly relevant to considering identification through word of mouth. Marketing enables organizations to provide benefits that customers will pay for, and satisfied customers want to talk about these benefits to others. It has been shown in past studies that identification may have favourable impacts on loyalty and citizenship behaviours (word of mouth) (Ahearne et al., 2005; Bergami and Bagozzi, 2000; Bhattacharya and Sen, 2003; Mael and Ashforth, 1992). In relationship marketing, customers can be promoters of a company's products, services and brands and can display loyalty behaviours (Bhattacharya et al., 1995; Dowling and Uncles, 1997). Aaker (1994) has claimed that 'over 95 per cent of Saturn buyers said they would enthusiastically recommend the car and the retailer to others' (p. 116). Organizational identification research suggests that when customers identify with a company they 'tend to purchase more and recommend the company's products more often' (Ahearne et al., 2005, p. 5). Again, Algesheimer et al. (2005) has found that customers identifying with a brand and the brand's community tend to be supportive and make positive recommendations about the brand. This is also supported by previous research in which university students were found to enact supportive behaviours towards the organization with which they identify and then provide positive word of mouth (Arnett et al., 2003).

According to Bhattacharya and Sen (2003), 'consumers become champions of the companies with whom they identify' (pp. 76–7). Such championing behaviours may vary depending on the context. In the not-for-profit higher-education sector, which was the main focus of Arnett et al.'s (2003) research, desired outcomes were experienced through more donations, volunteerism and positive word of mouth/promotion. However, in the for-profit sector the outcomes would more likely to be purchases, positive word of mouth and referrals, or they may include, as indicated by Bhattacharya and Sen (2003), company loyalty, customer recruitment, promotion, and resilience to negative information on the brand. Therefore, it is hypothesized that:

H$_4$:   A higher level of brand identification will lead to a higher level of word of mouth.

Repurchase

Finally, marketing theory in general, and relationship-marketing theory in particular, aims to encourage repeat purchase of goods and services, as bundles of customer benefits. Customer retention is of key importance in markets where supply threatens to outstrip demand. Retention is a strategy for long-term survival and profitability is dictated by the relationship-marketing paradigm (Bhattacharya and Sen, 2003). Various studies have shown that retaining customers and reducing defections

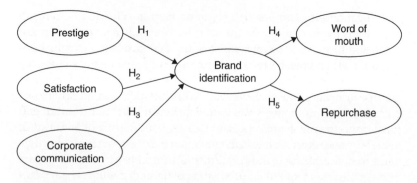

Figure 5.1 Model of brand identification

lead to higher profitability (Reichheld and Sasser, 1990). 'Brand and service loyalty is indicated by repeat purchase or repurchase intentions'
(Bettencourt, 1997, p. 384). Brand loyalty can be defined as the tendency
of customers to purchase a brand (Reichheld and Sasser, 1990). In the
consumer context, Bhattacharya et al. (1995) have suggested that identification may have positive consequences on brand repurchase. They
take an example from Peter and Olson (1993) to demonstrate that 94
per cent of Harley-Davidson buyers would buy a Harley again. Ahearne
et al. (2005) add that in terms of customer-company identification, the
more the customers identify with a company the greater the impact on
purchasing behaviour. Hence we deduce our fifth and final hypothesis:

H_5: A higher level of brand identification will lead to a higher level
of brand re-purchase.

We have presented our five hypotheses in a model, depicted in
Figure 5.1.

Segmentation

As noted earlier, and as common sense suggests, neither all brands
nor all customers are susceptible to identification. Therefore customer
segmentation, which is a very popular and powerful technique in a
marketer's toolkit, is most useful. Segmentation is regarded by some
experts as the panacea of modern marketing management because it
permits managers to satisfy the heterogeneity of consumer needs in
a resource-effective approach (Dibb and Simkin, 1996; Wind, 1978).
It can be a compelling tool for a marketer especially if transactional
data from a customer relationship-management database is available as

well (Grapentine and Boomgaarden, 2003). Marketing practitioners and academics are well aware of the potential positive outcomes of using segmentation (Doyle, 1995; Piercy, 1997; Wedel and Kamakura, 2000; Yankelovich and Meer, 2006).

Despite this consensus, there is no best way to segment the customers. Marketing managers should try different combinations of variables to find the most effective way of grouping customers for their organization. The discussion that follows outlines just one possible approach that could be used. Certain popular demographic variables that have been used extensively in the past for customer segmentation have been criticized for not being very useful as predictors (Hooley and Saunders, 1993). This is particularly so for predicting and responding to customer responses to identity branding (Elliott and Wattanasuwan, 1998). Consequently, it could be helpful to isolate the customers who are prone to identify with their brand because that would allow marketers to focus their resources on those customers. Particular stories in the culture may resonate for a period and a place for the relevant participants in the story (Elliott and Wattanasuwan, 1998). Certain personality traits may influence consumer attitudes and behaviour (McClelland, 1987; Mowen, 2000).

One possible trait may be the customer's choice of level of involvement with a particular product category. Involvement is a key construct of the consumer behaviour literature and has been extensively researched. There is agreement in the literature on the broad definition of involvement based around the ideas of personal interest and relevance (Beatty and Smith, 1987; Celsi and Olson, 1988; Zaichkowsky, 1985).

Therefore, involvement can be seen as the extent to which the product category is of personal relevance and interest to the individual and the degree to which it fulfils his/her needs. This focus on needs and benefits has also received a lot of attention in the segmentation literature. In their award-winning article Ter Hofstede, Steenkamp and Wedel (1999) use the relations consumers have with certain products as a basis for segmentation because it is widely acknowledged that consumers buy products not for their physical attributes per se but rather for how they contribute to achieving desired ends. Some customers may be quite prone to identify with certain brands because these brands fulfill certain needs. For example, we earlier discussed the human tendency to form groups with others and how owning a certain brand can perhaps, at least partially, fulfill the need to do so. Equally, some other customers are reluctant to get involved with the product category, and any relationship marketing initiative to increase the level of brand identification would be wasted

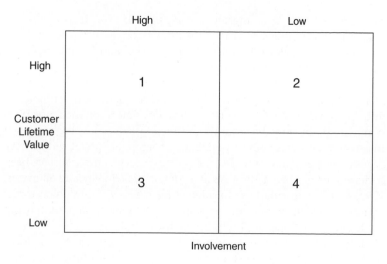

Figure 5.2   The segment evaluation matrix

on these customers. Consequently, marketers could try to segment their customers by their level of involvement with the product category. To segment these customers, cluster analysis could be used. A more detailed discussion of different methods that can be used to categorize different segments can be found in ter Hofstede et al. (1999).

Since Fournier's research (Fournier, 1998) was based on a very small sample it remains unclear how many customers are actually willing to form strong relationships with brands. In order to help managerial practice we suggest a matrix that could be used to classify and identify which customers should be targeted. Customer lifetime value (CLV) has been suggested recently as a very important variable for segmenting customers (Lemon and Mark, 2006). Therefore, we are considering using CLV in our classification, because it may help to select customer segments that allow the strongest growth potential compared to customer segments that might well not achieve a high level of CLV.

Figure 5.2 shows four different segments. Segment 1 is a highly lucrative segment for an organization. Due to its high CLV it can be assumed that competitors are also very interested in this segment. Therefore, an organization should think carefully about using appropriate marketing programmes. This would be the segment on which to focus relationship-marketing activities in order to increase the level of brand identification. The customers that Fournier (1998) investigated most likely fall into Segment 1 or Segment 3. Segment 2 also achieves a high CLV but these customers do not reach a high level of involvement. These are very important customers for the organization because they help to increase revenue. Most brand-identification programmes for these customers would be a waste of resources since they are not receptive towards such initiatives. These customers are clearly not interested in any kind of relationship with the company. More traditional marketing programmes are possibly more appropriate for this segment. Segment 3 ranks high on involvement but low on CLV. These are customers who perhaps buy products from the company on a regular basis but not in large volumes.

This argument is supported by previous large-scale studies of brand loyalty. Uncles et al. (1995) showed that across different product categories only about 10 per cent of buyers are 100 per cent loyal. It seems reasonable to assume that quite a few of these customers may be highly involved since they achieve such a high level of brand loyalty. The problem for managerial practice, however, is that these 100 per cent brand loyal customers are only light buyers (Uncles et al., 1995) which, according to our classification, achieve a low CLV. The researchers pointed out that this is particularly problematic for smaller brands (Uncles et al., 1995). Based on our comments the customers of Segment 3 are also not appropriate candidates for relationship-marketing tactics. Segment 4 seems unattractive for any marketing initiative.

Since this is a conceptual paper, the suggested classification remains to be evaluated. It should be used in different industries. Industries that tend to consist of high-involvement products such as cars, motorcycles and speedboats may achieve a larger percentage of customers for segment 1 compared to low-involvement industries such as petrol, supermarkets and gas suppliers. However, even within the car industry it depends on the product category; for sports cars involvement may be higher compared to family cars. A company has to decide if the potential and size of segment 1 is large enough to justify relationship marketing focusing on brand-identification strategy. As we have pointed out, in a lot of industries this may not be the most appropriate strategy.

Contexts and constructs for further research

As mentioned in the discussion above, one context might well be the global car market. Car purchasing provides ample opportunities for self-categorization of consumers, and so social identity theory should be relevant. Earlier studies have looked at car ownership and empirical work in this context would therefore contribute to developing understanding of this important sector of the global economy (Algesheimer et al., 2005; Lambert-Pandraud et al., 2005; Sismero and Bucklin, 2004). Characterized by relentless competition, product proliferation, communication clutter and buyer disenchantment, it is surely in the interest of car manufacturers to establish deep, meaningful relationships and maintain long-term bonds with customers. Similarly, financial industries in the UK constitute a highly competitive marketplace and services branding is an under-developed area (De Chernatony and Segal-Horn, 2001). Customer satisfaction and trust are critical and contentious issues in this sector. Where these issues have been satisfactorily addressed in the reputation of the firm, there may well be segments of customers for whom brand identification would prove relevant. In fact, there we would expect to find an even closer fit with issues of identification because services branding involves internal branding as much as external branding, given the importance of the service encounter to much services purchasing. Work developing links between corporate branding processes and services branding and relationships will contribute to work identified as necessary in Balmer and Gray's (2003) comments about marketers failing to take seriously corporate branding issues.

Conclusions and management implications

We believe that marketers will benefit from strengthening identification. Such a focus offers one way of integrating the latest scholarship in corporate branding, identity management and communications. It represents a relevant offering from the relationship-marketing field to these brand-management concerns. The use of marketing theory and application has also been enriched by recent discussion of social identity theory. We present our overview as a contribution to this discussion. We believe our discussion of brand identification can also encourage managers to move on from mere analysis and recording of customer satisfaction levels to devise a process linking them with brand values and corporate communications as they build on the dynamics of brand identification. Managers may want to devise a process linking satisfaction to brand values and corporate communications as they build on the dynamics of brand identification. Also, managers may want to try to increase the satisfaction levels of customers with their brands. Quick customer-complaint handling, customer care lines, quick response to customer queries, and fast order systems may be some of the measures that can be used to promote satisfaction, which can then reinforce identification with the corporate brand.

We also suggest that managers should think beyond the traditional brand when considering their allocation of total promotion resources. The object of brand identification should eventually be the corporate brand rather than just individual brands. The reason for that is that companies with a focused product mix targeted to a focused segment are likely to see the benefit of customer-company identification with the corporate brand and consequently across its various brands (Ahearne et al., 2005).

Additionally, marketers would most likely benefit from strengthening identification by enhancing the level of prestige associated with their brand. Focusing on the visibility and reputation via external communication may positively impact on the prestige of a corporate brand. Such efforts are likely to increase the level of identification that brand owners feel about their brand by making them 'bask in reflected glory'. Nevertheless, prestige is not solely affected by a company's communication efforts towards various stakeholder groups. Some information sources are obviously outside a company's influence. These sources could be quite influential in shaping the perceived prestige of an organization. Such sources could be widely read consumer magazines such as *Which?* Previous research has shown that independent external information sources have an even bigger influence on prestige than company-controlled communication efforts do (Smidts et al., 2001). For that reason, managers have to be realistic about the likely influence of communication efforts. Also, in times of a product recall (which have become more common in recent years) the prestige of a corporate brand is likely to suffer. Public-relations strategies can certainly increase visibility and broaden corporate brand credibility in such difficult circumstances. Marketing managers are encouraged to develop contingency plans so that measures are in place for dealing with such occurrences to limit possible negative consequences on the perceived prestige of corporate brands.

Our previous discussion has highlighted the importance of corporate communication and showed that customers are more likely to identify with organizations that provide relevant information and communicate well with them. Hence, managers may find it useful to keep in touch with their customers through regular contact. To do this most effectively managers have to investigate which communications medium – mail, phone or e-mail – customers prefer and how often they would like to receive information. Also, customer clubs could be used to increase the level of relevant information for the customers. Additionally, communication between customers could be encouraged via websites to exchange ideas about product usage. This is not about one-way management-directed communication. Somehow, the communications need to foster closeness. As Drucker writes: 'for communications to be effective, there has to be both information and meaning. And meaning requires communion' (Drucker, 2001, p. 341). And we caution that in the realm of communication, and indeed of branding, in order to learn and change it is necessary to listen and not just speak. Duncan and Moriarty (1998) discussed the parallels between communications management and marketing management; they emphasized the need for marketing to move on from aiming to persuade, to communicating with customers via a two-way dialogue. So much so, that Prahalad and Ramaswamy (2002) wrote:

> The market has become a forum in which consumers play an active role in creating and competing for value. The distinguishing feature of this new marketplace is that consumers become a new source of competence for the corporation (p. 2).

We have put the customer at the core of our aim to use relationship marketing practice and social identity theory to contribute to the discussion of corporate branding, identity and communications. We believe that the dynamics of brand identification, supported by social identity theory, can be one innovative way of conceptualizing links between these the three areas discussed in this book. We have conceptualized one link between corporate branding, identity and communications as the process by which individuals (customers and employees) can identify with the organization as corporate brand.

References

Aaker, D. (1994) 'Building a Brand: The Saturn Story', *California Management Review*, 36 (2), pp. 114–33.

Aaker, D. and S. Fournier (1995) 'A Brand as a Character, a Partner and a Person: Three Perspectives on the Question of Brand Personality', *Advances in Consumer Research*, 22, pp. 391–92.

Ahearne, M., C. B. Bhattacharya and T. Gruen (2005) 'Antecedents and Consequences of Customer–Company Identification: Expanding the Role of Relationship Marketing', *Journal of Applied Psychology*, 90 (3), pp. 574–85.

Akerlof, G. A. and R. E. Kranton (2000) 'Economics and Identity', *Quarterly Journal of Economics*, 115 (3), pp. 715–53.

Albert, S. and D. A. Whetten (1985) 'Organizational Identity', in L. L. Cummings (ed.) *Research Organizational Behavior* (Connecticut: JAI Press).

Algesheimer, R., U. M. Dholakia and A. Herrmann (2005) 'The Social Influence of Brand Community: Evidence from European Car Clubs', *Journal of Marketing*, 69 (3), pp. 19–34.

Anderson, J. A. and J. C. Narus (1990) 'A Model of Distributor Firm and Manufacturer Firm Working Partnerships', *Journal of Marketing*, 54, January, pp. 42–58.

Arnett, D. B., S. D. German and S. D. Hunt (2003) 'The Identity Salience Model of Relationship Marketing Success: The Case of Nonprofit Marketing', *Journal of Marketing*, 67, April, pp. 89–105.

Ashforth, B. E. and F. Mael (1989) 'Social Identity Theory and the Organization', *Academy of Management Review*, 14, pp. 20–39.

Askegaard, S. (2006) 'Brands as Global Ideoscope', in J. E. Schroeder and M. Salzer-Mörling (eds) *Brand Culture* (London: Routledge) pp. 91–102.

Balmer, J. M. T. (2001) 'The Three Virtues and Seven Deadly Sins of Corporate Branding', *Journal of General Management*, 27 (1), pp. 1–17.

Balmer, J. M. T. and E. R. Gray (2003) 'Corporate Brands: What Are They? What of Them?', *European Journal of Marketing*, 37 (7/8), pp. 972–97.

Beatty, E. S. and M. S. Smith (1987) 'External Search Effort: An Investigation across Several Product Categories', *Journal of Consumer Research*, 14, pp. 83–95.

Beech, N. and C. Huxham (2003) 'Cycles of Identity Formation in Interorganizational Collaborations', *International Studies of Management & Organization*, 33 (3), pp. 28–52.

Bergami, M. and R. P. Bagozzi (2000) 'Self-categorization, Affective Commitment and Group Self-esteem as Distinct Aspects of Social Identity in the Organization', *British Journal of Social Psychology*, 39 (4), p. 555–77.

Bettencourt, L. A. (1997) 'Customer Voluntary Performance: Customers as Partners in Service Delivery', *Journal of Retailing*, 73 (3), p. 383–406.

Bhattacharya, C. B. and S. Sen (2003) 'Consumer–Company Identification: A Framework for Understanding Consumers' Relationships with Companies', *Journal of Marketing*, 67 (2), pp. 76–88.

Bhattacharya, C. B., H. Rao and M. Glynn (1995) 'Understanding the Bond of Identification: an Investigation of Its Correlates among Art Museum Members', *Journal of Marketing*, 59 (4), pp. 46–57.

Billig, M. and H. Tajfel (1973) 'Social Categorization and Similarity in Intergroup Behavior', *European Journal of Social Psychology*, 3 (1), pp. 27–52.

Black, I. (2006) 'Who Are You Trying to Fool? Customer Reactions to Withdrawal Services', in 9th International Research Seminar in Service Management, LaLonde Institut d'Administration des Enterprises, Universite Paul Cezanne, France, May/June.

Campbell, Jr., R. M., D. Aiken and A. Kent (2004) 'Beyond BIRGing and CORFing: Continuing the Exploration of Fan Behavior', *Sport Marketing Quarterly*, 13 (3), pp. 151–58.

Carmeli, A. (2004) 'The Link between Organizational Elements, Perceived External Prestige and Performance', *Corporate Reputation Review*, 6 (4), pp. 314–31.

Carmeli, A. and A. Tishler (2005) 'Perceived Organizational Reputation and Organizational Performance: An Empirical Investigation of Industrial Enterprises', *Corporate Reputation Review*, 8 (1), pp. 13–30.

Celsi, L. R. and C. J. Olson (1988) 'The Role of Involvement in Attention and Comprehension Processes', *Journal of Consumer Research*, 15, pp. 210–24.

Cornelissen, J. (2002) 'On the 'Organizational Identity' Metaphor', *British Journal of Management*, 15, pp. 159–268.

Csaba, F. F. and A. Bengtsson (2006) 'Rethinking Identity and Management', in J. E. Schroeder and M. Salzer-Mörling (eds) *Brand Culture* (London: Routledge) pp. 118–32.

de Chernatony, L. and S. Segal-Horn (2001) 'Building on Services' Characteristics to Develop Successful Services Brands', *Journal of Marketing Management*, 17, pp. 645–69.

Dibb, S. and L. Simkin (1996) *The Market Segmentation Workbook* (London: ITBP)

Dowling, G. R. and M. Uncles (1997) 'Do Customer Loyalty Programs Really Work?', *Sloan Management Review*, 38 (4), pp. 71–82.

Doyle, P. (1995) 'Marketing in the New Millennium', *European Journal of Marketing*, 29 (13), pp. 23–41.

Drucker, P. (2001) *The Essential Drucker* (New York: Harper Business).

Duncan, T. and S. E. Moriarty (1998) 'A Communication-based Marketing Model for Managing Relationships', *Journal of Marketing*, 62, April, pp. 1–13.

Dutton, J. E., J. M. Dukerich and C. V. Harquail (1994) 'Organizational Images and Member Identification', *Administrative Science Quarterly*, 39 (2), pp. 239–63.

Elliott, R. and A. Davies (2006) 'Symbolic Brands and Identity Performance', in J. E. Schroeder and M. Salzer-Mörling (eds) *Brand Culture* (London: Routledge) pp. 155–70.

Elliott, R. and K. Wattanasuwan (1998) 'Brand as Symbolic Resources for the Construction of Identity', *International Journal of Advertising*, 17 (2), pp. 131–44.

Fombrun, C. J. (1996) *Reputation, Realizing Value from the Corporate Image* (Boston: Harvard Business School Press).

Fombrun, C. J. and M. Shanley (1990) 'What's in a Corporate Name? Reputation Building and Corporate Strategy', *Academy of Management Journal*, 33 (2), pp. 233–58.

Fournier, S. (1995) 'The Brand as Relationship Partner', *Advances in Consumer Research*, 22, p. 393.

Fournier, S. (1998) 'Consumers and Their Brands: Developing Relationship Theory in Consumer Research', *Journal of Consumer Research*, 24, March, pp. 343–73.

Gioia, D. A., M. Schultz and K. G. Corley (2000) 'Organizational Identity, Image and Adaptive Instability', *Academy of Management Review*, 25 (1), pp. 63–81.

Golder, P. and J. Irwin (2001) ' "If They Could See Us Now": a Look at How Consumers Relate to Their Products and How These Relationships Explain Why Leading Brands Succeed or Fail', *Advances in Consumer Research*, 28, p. 42.

Grapentine, T. and R. Boomgaarden (2003) 'Maladies of Market Segmentation', *Marketing Management*, 15 (1), pp. 27–30.

Gruen, T. W., J. O. Summers and F. Acito (2000) 'Relationship Marketing Activities, Commitment, and Membership Behaviors in Professional Associations', *Journal of Marketing*, 64, July, pp. 34–49.

Hair, J. F., R. E. Anderson, R. L. Tatham, and W. C. Black (1998) *Multivariate Data Analysis*, Fifth Edition (New Jersey: Prentice-Hall).

Hall, S. (1996) 'Introduction: Who Needs Identity?' in Stuart Hall and Paul du Gay (eds) *Questions of Cultural Identity* (London: Sage) pp. 1–17.

Halliday, S. V. (1999) *Perceptions of Service Quality*, PhD thesis (University of Bradford Press).

Haslam, S. A. (2001) *Psychology in Organizations: The Social Identity Approach* (London: Sage).

Haslam, S. A., T. Postmes and N. Ellemers (2003) 'More than a Metaphor: Organizational Identity Makes Organizational Life Possible', *British Journal of Management*, 14, pp. 357–69.

Holt, D. B. (2002) 'Why Do Brands Cause Trouble? A Dialectical Theory of Consumer Culture and Branding', *Journal of Consumer Research*, 29, June, pp. 70–90.

Holt, D. B. (2004) *How Brands Become Icons* (Boston: Harvard Business Press) p. 111.

Hooley, G. J. and J. Saunders (1993) *Competitive Positioning: the Key to Market Success* (London: Prentice-Hall).

Kane, A. A., L. Argote and J. M. Levine (2005) 'Knowledge Transfer between Groups via Personnel Rotation: Effects of Social Identity and Knowledge Quality', *Organizational Behavior and Human Decision Processes*, 96, pp. 56–71.

Kleine III, R. E., S. Schultz Kleine and J. B. Kernan (1993) 'Mundane Consumption and the Self: A Social-identity Perspective', *Journal of Consumer Psychology*, 2 (3) pp. 209–36.

Knox, S. and D. Bickerton (2003) 'The Six Conventions of Corporate Branding', *European Journal of Marketing*, 37 (7/8) pp. 998–1016.

Lambert-Pandraud, R., G. Laurent and E. Lapersonne (2005 'Repeat Purchasing of New Automobiles by Older Consumers: Empirical Evidence and Interpretations', *Journal of Marketing*, 69, April, pp. 97–113.

Lassar, W., B. Mittal, and A. Sharma (1995) 'Measuring Customer-based Brand Equity', *Journal of Consumer Marketing*, 12 (4) pp. 11–19.

Lemon, K. and T. Mark (2006) 'Customer Lifetime Value as the Basis of Customer Segmentation: Issues and Challenges', *Journal of Relationship Marketing*. 5 (2/3), pp. 55–69.

Mael, F. and B. E. Ashforth (1992) 'Alumni and their Alma Mater: A Partial Test of the Reformulated Model of Organizational Identification', *Journal of Organizational Behavior*, 13 (2), pp. 103–23.

McAlexander, J. H., J. W. Schouten, and H. F. Koenig (2002) 'Building a Brand Community', *Journal of Consumer Research*, 66 (1), pp. 38–54.

McClelland, D. (1987) *Human Motivation* (Cambridge: Cambridge University Press).

McGarty, C., J. C. Turner, P. J. Oakes and S. A. Haslam (1993) 'The Creation of Uncertainty in the Influence Process: The Roles of Stimulus Information and Disagreement with Similar Others', *European Journal of Social Psychology*, 23, pp. 17–38.

Morgan, G. (1997) *Images of Organization* (London: Sage).

Morgan, R. A. and S. D. Hunt (1994) 'The Commitment–Trust Theory of Relationship Marketing', *Journal of Marketing*, 58, July, pp. 20–38.

Mowen, J. C. (2000) *The 3M Model of Motivation and Personality: Theory and Empirical Applications to Consumer Behavior* (Norwell: Kluwer Academic Press).

Oliver, R. L. and J. E. Swan (1980) 'A Cognitive Model of the Antecedents and Consequences of Satisfaction Decisions', *Journal of Marketing Research*, 17, pp. 460–69.

O'Malley, L. and C. Tynan (2000) 'Relationship Marketing in Consumer Markets Rhetoric or Reality?', *European Journal of Marketing*, 34 (7), pp. 797–815.

Ouwerkerk, J. W., N. Ellemers and D. de Gilder (1999) 'Group Commitment and Individual Effort in Experimental and Organizational Contexts', in N. Ellemers, R. Spears, and B. Doosje (eds) *Social Identity* (Oxford: Blackwell) pp. 184–204.

Peter, J. P. and J. C. Olson (1993) *Consumer Behavior and Marketing Strategy* (Irwin: Homwood).

Piercy, N. (1997) *Market-led Strategic Change* (Oxford: Butterworth-Heinemann).

Prahalad, C. K. and V. Ramaswamy (2002) 'Co-opting Customer Competence', *Harvard Business Review*, 78 (1) pp. 1–10.

Pratt, M. G. and P. O. Foreman (2000) 'Classifying Managerial Responses to Multiple Organizational Identities', *Academy of Management Review*, 25 (1), pp. 18–42.

Reichheld, F. F. and W. E. Sasser, Jr. (1990) 'Zero Defections: Quality Comes to Services', *Harvard Business Review*, 68 (5), pp. 105–11.

Scott, S. and V. Lane (2000) 'A Stakeholder Approach to Organizational Identity,' *Academy of Management Review*, 25 (1), pp. 43–62.

Sismero, C. and R. E. Bucklin (2004) 'Modeling Purchase Behavior at an E-commerce Website: A Task-completion Approach', *Journal of Marketing Research*, XLI, August, pp. 306–23.

Smidts, A., A. T. H. Pruyn and C. B. M. van Riel (2001) 'The Impact of Employee Communication and Perceived External Prestige on Organizational Identification', *Academy of Management Journal*, 49 (5), pp. 1051–62.

Tajfel, H. and J. C. Turner (1985) 'The Social Identity Theory of Intergroup Behavior', in S. Worchel and W. G. Austin (eds) *Psychology of Intergroup Relations* (Chicago: Nelson-Hall, 1985) pp. 6–24.

Ter Hofstede, F., J. B. E. M. Steenkamp and M. Wedel (1999) 'International Market Segmentation Based on Consumer-product Relations', *Journal of Marketing Research*, 36, February, pp. 1–17.

Turner, J. C. (1975) 'Social Comparison and Social Identity: Some Prospects for Intergroup Behavior', *European Journal of Social Psychology*, 5 (1), pp. 5–34.

Uncles, M., A. Ehrenberg and K. Hammond (1995) 'Patterns of Buyer Behavior: Regularities, Models and Extensions', *Marketing Science*, 14 (3) pp. G71–G78.

Urde, M. (2003) 'Core Value-based Corporate Brand Building', *European Journal of Marketing*, 37 (7/8) pp. 1017–40.

Wedel, M. and W. Kamakura (2000) *Market Segmentation: Conceptual and Methodological Foundations* (Boston: Kluwer).

Whetten, D. and P. Godfrey (1998) *Identity in Organizations: Developing Theory through Conversations* (Thousand Oaks: Sage).

Wind, Y. (1978) 'Issues and Advances in Segmentation Research', *Journal of Marketing Research*, 15, pp. 317–37.

Yankelovich, D. and D. Meer (2006) 'Rediscovering Market Segmentation', *Harvard Business Review*, 82, February, pp. 122–31.

Zaichkowsky, L. J. (1985) 'Measuring the Involvement Construct', *Journal of Consumer Research*, 12, pp. 341–52.

6
Organizational Branding within Creative SMEs

Shaun M. Powell

Abstract

Creative organizations mainly rely on their own employees and internal processes for enhancing creativity in their work, which in turn enhances their creative reputation and strengthens their organizational brand. This research uses an inductive approach based upon thematic network analysis to explore organizational creativity and identity. Its aim is to uncover their relationship with the brand, within a business-to-business context. It asks 'what issues and complexities might be uncovered when taking a mainly internal, employee perspective to organizational creativity, identity and the brand?'.

Introduction

It has been acknowledged that creativity is an important source of competitive strength, and is a key element for developing a good reputation for organizations within the creative industries (Andriopoulos and Gotsi, 2000; Cook, 1998; Sutton and Kelly, 1997). Creative organizations often differentiate themselves through the proactive and successful use of ambiguous operating conditions, often relying upon word of mouth and referrals from previous and current clients, as well as media publicity and industry awards, to gain future work. Here the extent that the employees identify with the desired organizational identity leads to an impact on the image that they will potentially project to clients and other stakeholders (Andriopoulos and Gotsi, 2001; Kennedy, 1977; Post and Griffin, 1997; Saxton, 1998). Thus the behaviour of the employees within the organization, their creative output and the way they interface with their clients become a key component of the brand. Within this context, investigations into the impact of an employee's identity construction process on the organizational brand have been called for (Andriopoulos and Gotsi, 2001; Balmer and Soenen, 1998; Balmer, 2001; Balmer and Greyser, 2003; Sveningsson and Alvesson, 2003). In addition, to date, much of the developments relating to the management and building of a strong identity and brand have occurred within business-to-consumer rather than business-to-business contexts (Ensor, Cottam and Band, 2001). The limited literature that has tackled the business-to-business perspective has also tended to discuss ambiguity as a state that a firm passes through, rather than an environment it constantly has to operate in. Others have highlighted that this does not seem to apply to the environment faced by most knowledge-intensive organizations (Robertson and Swan, 2003), and in particular those based around creativity.

This paper therefore explores and integrates business-to-business literature relating to organizational creativity and identity within the context of the creative brand for small and medium-sized enterprises (SMEs). It also presents the findings from exploratory empirical research undertaken within three case-study creative organizations, driven by the following research question:

What issues and complexities might be uncovered when taking a mainly internal, employee perspective to organizational creativity, identity and the brand?

Creative industries and workers

The UK government has defined creative industries as comprising 'activities which have their origin in individual creativity, skill and talent, and which have the potential for wealth and job creation through the generation and exploitation of intellectual property' (DCMS, 1998, p. 10). The UK creative industries accounted for 8.2 per cent of Gross Value Added (GVA) during 2001 and grew by an average of six per cent per annum between 1997 and 2001, compared to three per cent for the economy as a whole. They also contributed £11.4 billion to the balance of trade in 2002. Between 1997 and 2003 creative employment within the creative industries increased by three per cent per annum compared to one per cent for the economy as a whole and by 2003 totalled at least 1.1 million jobs within approximately 122,000 companies (DCMS, 2004). Hence creative industries are significant both in terms of revenue generation, exports and employment within the UK.

Individual qualities of creative workers, the philosophy and/or approach used by owners and managers, as well as the environment around them, have been reported as significant elements for the creative process and output. Therefore, organizational-creativity models need to uncover and investigate the influence of organizational factors on individual creativity, as well as incorporate extra-organizational aspects that influence creative ideas or processes. Many influencing sources, for example, come from far beyond the organization; these include clients (Amabile, 1988). The small- to medium-sized nature of many creative organizations also leads to the issue of the evolving nature of the organizational identity and the brand as the company grows, where both are often seen to be in a state of ongoing flux.

Cultural-ideological control within the context of knowledge work

The need for a sensitive and distinctive approach to the way expert workforces are managed has also been dominant in the literature, often through the development of a culture of 'responsible autonomy' (Robertson and Swan, 2003). Others have suggested the increased relevance of 'cultural-ideological' forms of control rather than normative or prescriptive forms of control for knowledge-based workers through, for example, the targeting of the values, ideas, beliefs, emotions and identifications of employees (Alvesson, 1995a). Thus, under the conditions of creative process and outcome, ambiguity, identity and organizational identification become significant, since it is argued by some that these could be used as the means for management control and/or regulation within knowledge-intensive creative organizations. Indeed some authors have postulated that control of this type could help to accomplish the right kind of employee action in various situations and contexts, matching the desired organizational image and helping to create or sustain the desired organizational image or brand (Alvesson, 2000).

A number of authors have also stated the need for an expansion of the limited nature of empirical work that has been conducted to date in the context of knowledge work, identity, and normative and non-normative control (Alvesson, 1995b; Balmer, 1996; Wilson, 1995), with calls for more substantive empirical support and analysis in the relevant organizations (Robertson and Swan, 2003). Further, those empirical studies that have looked at the processes of identification within organizations and the impact upon the organizational brand have often used

such a broad-brush approach that the subtleties and complexities of the dynamics which underlie these processes have rarely been adequately revealed (Brown, 2001).

Organizational identity and creativity

Organizational identity has been defined as that which is central, enduring and distinctive about an organization (Albert and Whetten, 1985); within the literature this definition has been seen as a main point of departure for further exploration and debate of the concept. More recently, a postmodern view has been applied to the terminology and concepts involved, leading, in some views, to identity having a more fluid nature than in earlier conceptualizations (Alvesson, 1995b; Filby and Willmott, 1988; Kunda, 1992; Martin and Meyerson, 1988; Meek, 1988; Starbuck, 1992; Willmott, 1993). Culture from this standpoint is not a 'variable' but is something an organization 'is' rather than 'has' (Robertson and Swan, 2003; Smircich, 1983). This perspective allows that an individual's interpretation of any event or situation does not necessarily mean it is shared with others, and thus this perspective has a pluralist view on culture. Importantly, this challenges the ability of management to actively create or sustain a culture shared by all employees, one which will then generate, through normative or prescriptive control, workers who naturally or automatically work in ways that interest and benefit the firm (Robertson and Swan, 2003).

Gioia, Shultz and Corley (2000) have also highlighted that identity is essentially a social construction, which is drawn from repeated interactions with others, where identity is partly based on how others see us. Those identities are often different depending on the roles or the situation faced. If this view of identity and identity construction is accepted, then the interaction between those outside, such as customers, media groups, competitors, investors and regulators, must also be taken into account, especially in relation to the organizational brand (Ashforth and Mael, 1996; Balmer, 1996, 2001; Balmer and Soenen, 1998; Berg and Gagliardi, 1985; Fombrun, 1996; Gioia, 1998; van Riel and Balmer, 1997). Creative employees often have their identity bound closely with the work or process they are involved with (Rostan, 1998), and evaluation for creative employees has often been reported to be more important if carried out by their peers and/or profession than by their organization. Creative employees often exhibit a need for achievement and autonomy and often show an associated lack of concern for power and organizational affiliation; this may frequently lead to creatives being seen

as 'out of kilter' in some knowledge-based organizations and therefore potentially difficult to manage (Mumford et al., 2002).

Creativity has often been modelled as a discrete task, which is conducted by individuals who form part of a small group and are sometimes seen as somewhat isolated from the broader environment (e.g. a department or project team) (Drazin, Glynn and Kazanjian, 1999). However, project-based creative work, often having long time frames, means that such self-contained groups are relatively uncommon. The complexity of the task means that multifunctional, interdependent teams engaging with others beyond the team, whose memberships naturally grow and shrink over time, are more likely to be the norm. Hence, employees who have only partial inclusion in a group will probably occupy many organizational roles and memberships, and are thus influenced by each of these. In addition, for these employees, particular situational or contextual circumstances within the organization, perhaps relating to the project stage, can make a particular group more relevant, and lead to the exclusion of other groups (Ashforth and Mael, 1996; Drazin et al., 1999). In addition to internal memberships, any employee may also have an external occupational identity, and perhaps even a professional identity as well, along with other external identities (Drazin et al., 1999; Trice, 1993). Acknowledging that employees may occupy many organizational roles and internal and external group memberships, due to the evolving nature of creative processes, naturally complicates such organizational identity research. Effects can no longer be simply attributed to membership in a single group or category, but to involvement in multiple groups and categories, adding complexity and potential confusion to the concepts being investigated. This may explain why a great deal of previous research in the area of organizational identity has tended to stay focused at one particular level or on a limited number of levels or membership categories. Nevertheless, it needs to be acknowledged that for organizational identity and branding research to be relevant, especially within the context of creative organizations, which operate within perpetual ambiguous operating conditions, it needs to accept and address these multi-level, multi-category and internal/external influences (Ashforth and Mael, 1996; Drazin et al., 1999).

By taking an alternative, 'cross-level perspective' within creative organizations, by ensuring all levels of employees are included from all applicable divisions, research can open up relatively newer avenues for sense-making within a creative context (Drazin et al., 1999). The extent to which this is relevant is, in most cases, probably directly related to the size of the projects and/or the size of the creative organization and/or client. In the case of SMEs, small group settings are more likely to be characterized by a higher degree of employee inclusiveness, internally as well as externally.

More research is also needed on identity processes, focused upon individuals and organizations *becoming* identified rather than *being* identified (Sveningsson and Alvesson, 2003) where people often 'engage in forming, repairing, maintaining, strengthening or revising the constructions that help them to produce a sense of coherence and distinctiveness' (Sveningsson and Alvesson, 2003, p. 1165). Although there are some at the conceptual level, there are relatively few empirical studies that address processes of identity construction at the personal level, particularly within a creative context.

Previous creative brand research

Although limited to date, the topic of creative employees and their behaviour, as a component of the organizational brand, has started to become an area of focus since the turn of this century (cf. Andriopoulos and Gotsi, 2000). This research is an early attempt to outline some of the complex interrelationships between creative employee management practices, individual/team creativity, and the brand. For example, Andriopoulos and Gotsi (2000) have introduced the concept of bonding, which refers to employees associating with others whom they identify as sharing similarities. A creative organization that encourages bonding processes helps to signal that the company values its employees and the encouragement of discussions between employees. This in turn may lead to a heightened sense of belonging, thus also helping to shift employees from the individual to the collective level in their working lives. However, employees are likely to still need encouragement and guidance in order to align with the key values of the organization. In the case of the research reported by Andriopoulos and Gotsi (2000), this is aided by providing differing forms of inspiration, indicated by a belief in the power of creativity, alongside role modelling by more senior members of the organization. A final level of bond strengthening can be seen via the creation of a reputation for breaking new ground, thus promoting a positive image of the company as being at the forefront of creativity rather than being a follower. To achieve this, relevant and adequate encouragement and resourcing are seen as vital, alongside the need to create a sense of ownership in the overall creative process and outcome. Ensor et al. (2001) have also taken some preliminary looks at the creative work environment within a knowledge and branding context. Their research has revealed that employees may have only a vague understanding of a creative organization's vision due to frequent changes in ownership and structure in periods of rapid growth.

Methodology

A qualitative case-study approach was deemed the most appropriate because 'a "how" or "why" question is being asked about a contemporary set of events over which the investigator has little or no control ... allowing the development of a rich explanation for the complex pattern of outcomes' (Yin, 1994, p. 115). In addition, the case-study design is seen as useful where the researcher is aiming to gain an in-depth understanding of a situation and where the study is one more of discovery than confirmation, and of process and context, than any outcomes. In addition, using a qualitative paradigm allowed for the research to be focused on 'discovery, insight, and understanding from the perspectives of those being studied' (Merriam, 1988, p. 3).

Selection criteria and approach for case studies

The three organizations subjected to case study were all located within central London, England. London was selected due to its relative high density of creative organizations within the UK and its dominant role in the creative industries, both as a location for enterprises and as a major cultural influence (DCMS, 2000; Drake, 2003). The specific type of case study organizations were chosen for their ability to demonstrate that their competitive strategy was based upon a highly customized service to clients in the form of a creative solution, which primarily relied upon the employees' own knowledge and skills base.

Data collection

The primary field research was conducted in three phases over approximately seven months with a total of 36 interviews. The first phase consisted of several weeks of visits to the three case-study creative organizations to conduct initial exploratory interviews. These were an architectural practice, a design consultancy and a branding consultancy. The interviewees occupied various senior and junior levels of each case study organization. The second phase occurred several months after the first phase of interviews had been transcribed and analysed. These interviews included the same members as those initially interviewed wherever possible. Observation of the working environment was also reported. The third phase of interviews occurred several months after the second. These interviews were directed at those within the client organization responsible for, and interfacing with, the creative supplier-client relationships. The clients included well-known names within the UK such as British Airways, Slazenger/Dunlop, Abbey National and Diageo.

In an attempt to limit possible misunderstandings, errors of fact, omissions or interpretation, the full verbatim transcription was undertaken without third-party assistance. Once transcribed, the interview transcripts were transferred into computer software for text storage and as an aid to (not replacement for) the analysis of the data.

Coding and thematic discourse analysis

QSR NVivo, a Qualitative Data Analysis (QDA) software package, was used to aid the process of analysis through coding and thematic network analysis, and as the main methodological aid in the analysis of the collected and transcribed data.

During the first stage of the analysis, the data produced from transcription was broadly coded both factually and heuristically. Using the capabilities within NVivo, the transcribed interviews were coded to produce inductively generated concepts, leading eventually to key themes which highlight specific aspects relating to that piece of text (Silverman, 2000).

Hence codes were created 'up' from the data early in the coding process, as ideas emerged from the data, rather than 'down' from prior ideas, project designs or theories (QSR, 2001; Richards, 2005). The process ultimately led to the initial creation of 262 codes and concepts emerging from the corpus of the collected material. The more frequently occurring of these – those that appeared as common within a minimum of four or more individual interviews from across the three case studies – were then selected for further analysis. This led to 58 codes and concepts being identified as worthy of further investigation and analysis. Ten of these codes, grouped under the main theme of 'identification' are discussed below.

Inter-reliability judgment checks

Two independent and qualified research academics, unrelated to the project, checked and judged the relevance of the codes generated against a percentage of the transcripts on which the interpretations discussed shortly were based. NVivo, as used to aid the bulk of the analysis of the data, does not allow for inter-reliability checks to be conducted from within the program. Thus an alternative was used, namely 'QDA Miner' from Provalis Software (Provalis, 2004). Within qualitative research, and specifically with exploratory research, where the codes are inductively generated along with their descriptions and not taken from pre-existing literature or hypothesis, a figure of greater than 70 per cent is normally acceptable. In addition, in relation to the free marginal figure, a figure of greater than 0.7 is seen as significant for such research. The inter-reliability rating outcomes for this research, following the above procedure, led to agreement of 86.4 per cent using a simple percentage rating, and 0.73 using the adjusted free marginal calculation.

Findings

Within smaller creative organizations there are often no dedicated units or sections tasked with interfacing with the clients. As a result, various individuals may interface with a client at any one time, often from all levels within the organization. It emerged that this often created multiple images of the way the organization was perceived in relation to its brand.

This organizing theme encompasses these multiple images and the reasons underpinning them, as discussed below. This theme captures various forms of identification apparent within the data, each with implications for creative organizations and their brand. Ten identified sub-themes of the organizing theme termed 'Identification' are shown in Figure 6.1 and Table 6.1 and discussed below.

Expert egos, creative egos and individual identification

Egos, particularly the expert ego, and individual identification issues were often evident during the interviews. Whenever the clients attempted to control the creative process, friction would be evident between the creatives and the clients, with the creative 'expert' ego seemingly feeling under direct threat. In addition, a more specific 'creative' ego was evident within the data; this was characterized by a desire to create something new and different, and to leave a personal mark on whatever creative product was being worked upon. For example, one of the architect directors stated:

> you start somewhere small and eventually expand into something wide ... and all the young guys and girls aspire to have their own

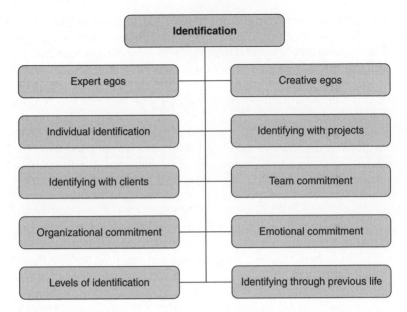

Figure 6.1   Inductively generated identification theme and sub-themes

project to run... that's what they all want so that they can make their mark if you like... it's part of the ego-centred sort of feeling that we all have as creative people I guess... if you can create something of your own you can say that's mine... it sounds almost like a selfish thing but it is ego.

Despite their own egos, creatives indicated that they like to encourage creative input from many of the clients, as long as this does not threaten the creatives' own position or ego; this was often a difficult balancing act. Due to these expert and creative egos, the organization was also often thought to be seen as a mixture of individuals with many single visions. One of the supervisors within the design agency highlighted this aspect of the creative brand:

I think you have all sorts of different characters and personalities... the way 'Employee x' deals with a client is totally different from the way I deal with a client so I don't think there is a common view of [the design agency]... the company is full of a lot of single visions.

Single visions could sit at any level within the organization and were even apparent at the senior layers of the case-studies' guiding coalitions.

Table 6.1 Code descriptors for identification theme

Expert egos, creative egos and individual identification

Expert ego: refers to instances where the expert ego is evident. For example, attempts by clients to overly control the creative process would lead to friction due to the challenge the experts perceive

Creative ego: refers to excerpts where a creative ego is evident, meaning the need to feed a desire to create something, something new, something different, something that leaves a personal mark on the world

Individual identification: refers to excerpts which indicate some form of identification is taking place focused mainly on an individual level rather than a wider organizational level

Identifying with projects and clients

Identifying with projects: refers to excerpts indicating that the creatives identify with specific projects more than their own employer

Identifying with clients: refers to excerpts indicating that the creatives identify externally with the client more than their own employer

Team commitment, organization commitment and emotional commitment

Team commitment: refers to excerpts indicating a higher level of commitment to the team than the organization as a whole

Organization commitment: refers to excerpts discussing individual commitment to the organization and its mission and/or vision

Emotional commitment: refers to instances of an expressed emotional form of commitment to the creative organization. This was linked into the way individuals seemed to relate with others and their work in general

Levels of identification and identifying through previous life

Levels of identification: refers to excerpts where a distinction was evident between differing levels of identification

Identifying through previous life: refers to excerpts where employees indicated that their experience of life before joining the creative organization has a bearing upon the way they currently relate with the organization and their peers

---

More importantly, these single visions risked being perceived directly by the clients externally, creating, in effect, multiple identities and images of the organization's brand. The control of such single visions within a creative environment was also an issue within the interviews, leading to the important question of: 'What is control in a creative environment?'. Furthermore, should this control be 'autonomous' or 'internally' generated, a point made by one of the creative branding directors:

> there are bounds between control and creativity, if you like, and you can say those are not opposites anyway but... we are trying to get to this thing which is the sort of very essence of what we are what we can do and what makes us different what excites us... that should be sufficient to condition expectations as to what is and isn't right for us but allow a great deal of leeway of people to express that in a way that is precisely right for them... right for the occasion or right for the client.

Interestingly, linking to the discussion above on creativity, identity and control, many of the creatives indicated they avoided any attempts made by management to make them formally identify with the creative organization; they were more comfortable within organizations that avoided forcing such identification management upon its employees. For example, one of the junior architects stated:

> we are a big firm and there is no sort of forced attempt to make everyone feel like one big family or one big team and I think I quite like that, you know, because it is just... we are not you know... that is contrary to Company X [which was another big firm]... they were very American about trying to get everyone you know... get a real sort of you know... we are great, we are marvellous, we are all one big family or one big team... and you thought, well, no, we are not frankly [laugh] and that sort of annoyed me.

Identifying with projects and clients

In addition to 'identifying with the clients', as will be discussed shortly, some creatives indicated they often 'identify more with the project' they are working on than their employing creative organization. This is particularly relevant in relation to organizational brand management, because many of the projects within creatively based organizations can last many months or even years, with multiple and varying levels of team members involved throughout.

Under such time-frames, managers frequently highlighted that family/team relationships built up, and were often actively encouraged. However, this also led to a downside in that conflicts often occurred if those allegiances became threatened through enforced project change, as indicated clearly by one of the architect directors:

> a team can last anything from between a year and three years depend-ing on the scale of the project...people might transfer from group to group to make things happen but the general idea is to try and keep the core of people together so that a certain...family or team relationship builds up...now within that then you get some sort of allegiances being created and people like working for you as a director and therefore sometimes [laugh] quite an interesting conflict comes up, er, when you transfer somebody out of the team.

Junior members, in particular, preferred the more interesting projects and a lack of access to such projects sometimes led to frustration and the employee leaving. This was driven by the need to be doing more than they were currently doing, being challenged. Senior management were clearly aware of this dynamic occurring, as indicated by one of the architect directors:

> some projects that we are doing...people will be very fulfilled because they are great projects to work on and there are others which are more mundane...all the young guys will want to do more than they are actually doing...they want to be running a project, they want to be designing the building and when they come in here they often don't do that...everyone has to learn...well some people will leave, they get sufficiently frustrated that they leave and they go somewhere else.

At times, the creatives indicated that they found themselves iden-tifying externally with the client organization more than anything else (sub-theme: identifying with clients), causing a potential conflict between differing values within the client organization and the employ-ing creative organization. Some of the directors believed that by selecting and employing people with client-side experience, they could help such employees in their intended boundary-spanning role, interfacing within the client-supplier relationship. Interestingly, the collected data also indicated that this increased the likelihood of such creatives also identi-fying externally rather than internally with their own creative brand, a likelihood that the directors had not detected. This is seen, for example, below, with a senior branding consultant, who often identified with the client more than her own organization due to her falling back to her prior knowledge and experience of living in the client world in general.

> Do I feel closer to the project than the client or do I feel closer to the project than [brand consultancy]? I am not sure which...I think it does phase and I think it is almost a case of if you are working on a part of a project that gets very involved with the clients I find myself starting to feel close...you know part of the client world...which is probably also me falling back into my old world as well and trying to think of it from their point of view, and I probably almost pull myself back out of it at times...

It was also noted in the data that one way that project identification and client identification appear to be managed in relation to the creative organizations' own brand is through regular internal meetings as well as by utilizing open-plan and informal office layouts and informal team structures, as indicated by one of the junior branding consultants:

> I wouldn't consciously say I have ever thought 'I am so focused on this project that the rest of the business is meaningless'... not meaning-less but taking a second role to my immediate project objectives ... I think that is largely because we meet fortnightly, sometimes on a weekly basis, so we are always aware of everyone's issues involving their work and the possibility that I will have to move perhaps some-where else and someone else will move over to help me out so we are always aware of the fluidity within the office.

Team commitment, organizational commitment and emotional commitment

The creatives often felt commitment at work, to either their immediate team or their organization, and at times the commitment was expressed as an emotional one. Creative employees also often indicated a higher level of commitment to the team than the organization as a whole, espe-cially teams where all individuals were seen to be equal in some ways. For example, one of the junior architects stated:

> in a way architecture is also...it's group work, it's teamwork, it is never individual work unless you have got your own practice...in a way a successful company always has successful teams behind them...successful teams that work together because that's a very important part of the whole company's identity and success, and therefore in a very good architectural practice you don't have a hierar-chy, you don't have a director and you don't have the summer trainee when it comes to design...everybody is on an equal level.

It was also apparent that within these SME case-study organizations, commitment to the organization and its vision rather than just the team was a primary requirement expressed by senior management. Commitment was also often qualified as an emotional form of commitment to the organization, and this linked into the way that individuals seemed to relate with others and to their work in general. For example, one of the branding directors stated:

> I think there is a very, very strong level of commitment to [branding consultancy] ... that is a common theme around here and if it wasn't ... if that commitment wasn't there I don't think individuals would find us a very comfortable place because it's kind of ... it's expected ... and people that don't look as though they are going to evince that are screened out during the recruitment process ... basically we want a high level of commitment ... emotional commitment.

Equally, as will be seen below, the junior members of the organizations also indicated that their commitment could sometimes be seen in emotional terms, although this also linked to the way an employee tends to think in general:

> I think there is an emotional bond ... I think probably the emotional bond is stronger and more important to some members of the staff compared to others but that's ... you know, they are all different characters so I don't think that's necessarily that surprising ... I think there is definitely ... I think it depends on the way they think.

Levels of identification and identifying through previous life

A distinction was evident in the data between differing levels of identification, as outlined by this quote from the one of the branding directors. Here the concept of identifying in a mainly 'exchange'-based way through more immediate 'situational' factors, such as increased effort for immediate financial compensation or additional time off, is compared with the perception that there is an alternative, more abstract, long-term and 'intrinsically rewarding' way of identifying with work and the organization through, for example, its values, mission and vision:

> that it is sort of hygiene factors vs. motivation factors and the like ... the situational level is the easiest one to describe and to embrace the deep structural ... I mean, that is where the magic lies, in the deep structural identification and how you get to it ... and that is

very complicated... I don't want to be part of something where it is about a transactional relationship which ends up in pounds, shillings and pence...working hours...holiday days and stuff like that... I don't really want to be part of an organization where that...all the primary motivation...that sort of stuff...that is all necessary but not sufficient to me.

However, it was also apparent that some creative organizations are set up specifically to react to external situational factors, and this is likely to impact on the way that employees identify with the organization. For example, this may also lead to multiple identities and images being perceived by the clients. As an architect director reflected:

Yeah, I find it difficult to think we are a deep-structure organization... I think that's inward looking ... whereas I don't think we are ... I think we are outward looking ... that's just as a gut reaction to that so therefore it's situational ... it is related to people ... clients ... situations ... places ... projects ... it is all those things that are the influences and the structure ... the organization is structured to meet those.

It was also noted that even within creative organizations that have been set up and structured to encourage more situational identification, others within the organizations have usually been tasked or feel the need to consider the issues relating to deeper levels of identification, particularly within any guiding coalition. This is outlined in the following excerpt from one of the architect divisional directors, discussing the board of directors that sit above him. One implication of this is a heightened risk of a disconnect from a organizational branding perspective, between those client-facing employees who are more situation-driven, and those offstage senior management and owners who may be identifying with more long-term and deep-structural aspects of the organization and its future:

People like me are more situational, I guess, because we are more driven to client requirements, project requirements, without thinking necessarily about the whole thing behind me, the whole structure behind me...there are other people who are thinking on a different...on a wider scale maybe...that's not the right words...but a more cultural level to try and generate the best from within.

Previous life, for example through work, education and career experience, often lead to common ways of thinking amongst the creative employees, and this impacted upon the way they also identified with one another. One of the branding directors highlighted this when discussing the mixture of employees in the organization:

> It is interesting that there is a mix of largely biology... geography and media studies employees... it's all about the context and networks and relationships... things with bigger things if you like and I think in some way that might help... I mean a lot of the metaphors that we are using in our branding work and our organizational development work would be evolutionary metaphors... ecological metaphors.

Discussion

As outlined earlier, the literature on knowledge-worker identity and creativity makes some initial links between creativity, identity and the brand. (Andriopoulos and Gotsi, 2000, 2001; Andriopoulos and Lowe, 2000; Ensor et al., 2001; Fisher, 1997; Rostan, 1998; Alvesson, 2000; Mumford et al., 2002; Robertson and Swan, 2003; Brown, 2001; Albert and Whetten, 1985; Gioia, 1998; Sveningsson and Alvesson, 2003). A number of additional themes emerged from this research.

Due to their SME status, these smaller organizations were found to be more likely to be seen as a mixture of individuals with many single visions than a unified whole or brand; this was often driven by individual creative egos within them. Multiple-level employee identification also emerged within the data, with owners, managers and other employees indicating that they identified on a number of levels, often linked to situational or non-situational motivators. Some of the creative organizations had been specifically set up to react and flex to situational factors driven by the client, and this was seen to impact on the way that employees were likely to identify with the organization. This also often led to multiple identities and images being perceived by the clients. The findings also demonstrated that these single visions could sit at any level of the organization and were apparent even at senior levels within some of the case studies' guiding coalitions. Hence, for these reasons, creative organizations were often seen by the clients more as a collection of individuals than a firm with a common identity; if sustained, this could create significant problems for the formation of a consistent organizational brand in the medium to long term. Interestingly, however, for some clients, rather than being viewed as a problem, this multiple identity and non-consistent brand was appealing, because in some circumstances it added to the client's perception of the creative firm's greater organizational creativity.

Identifying with projects was also a common theme within the data. In particular, junior creative members preferred the more exciting or high-profile projects; in some cases this led to a lowering of organizational loyalty and an intention to quit if denied access to them. Owners and managers seemed aware of this potential problem, but it was not clear from the data what, if any, steps were taken to try and avoid its occurrence. Many of the projects within creatively based organizations could also last many years, and often had multiple and varying levels of team members throughout their lifespan. Managers frequently highlighted that family/team relationships were thus built up, and if those allegiances were threatened through enforced project or team change, conflict sometimes ensued. It was also noted that some of the creatives had worked within the client-side world before joining the creative organization. Employees who had done so indicated that they tended to fall back on their prior knowledge and experience of the client world and thus start to overly identify with the project and client, rather than their own employing organization.

Creatives also clearly indicated that they often avoided any attempts to make them formally identify with their employing organization. It should therefore be observed that these types of employees may not in fact be ideally suited to be managed through 'cultural-ideological control', via, for example the targeting of the identifications of employees, as has been suggested by some researchers for other forms of knowledge-based organizations (see Alvesson, 1995a). In addition, the relevance and impact of the internal single visions often related to the size of the client or project/account, with smaller clients more likely to become exposed to the creative organization's multiple identities. Consequently, smaller clients were more likely to notice any fragmented and non-uniform identities in their supplying creative organization; creative owners and managers should be aware of this and consider taking steps to reduce any impact.

The interrelationships between all of these factors with organizational creativity management and the brand are summarized in Figure 6.2 below.

Conclusion

Creative organizations rely heavily on their own employees and internal processes for enhancing creativity, which in turn enhances their creative

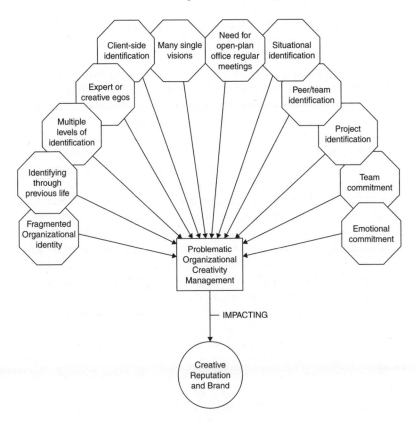

Figure 6.2   Factors contributing to problematic creativity management in relation to the brand

reputation and strengthens their organizational brand. This chapter, by following an exploratory and inductive approach, uncovered and presented more subtle and often interrelating issues than can be found in previous studies relating to organizational creativity, identity and the brand. It therefore responded to calls within the literature to broaden the contours of research in these areas (Andriopoulos and Gotsi, 2000; Ensor et al., 2001). It also raised a number of implications for the academic and creative communities in relation to organizational creativity and identity management in relation to the creative brand:

- employing creatives with previous client-side experience, with the intention of aiding the creative-supplier boundary-spanning role, may also lead to an unintended lowering of identification with the employing creative organization, with an associated impact on the creative brand

- there is a potential for a disconnect between client-facing creative employees, who are more situationally driven, and non-client-facing (off-stage) senior management or owners who may identify with more long-term and deep-structural aspects of the organization and its future
- in the area of control of single visions, many of the creatives clearly indicated that they avoided any attempts to make them formally identify with their employing organization. Hence, employees within creative organizations may not be ideally suited for being managed through 'cultural-ideological control', via, for example, the targeting of the identifications of employees, as has been suggested by some researchers as being suitable for other forms of knowledge-based organizations
- multiple organizational identities generated by the dis-identification behaviour of some employees, rather than being seen as a problem, actually appealed to some clients, as it ultimately led to the perception that the organization's brand was more creative
- the relevance and impact of the internal single visions often related to the size of the client or project/account, with smaller clients more likely to become exposed to the creative organization's multiple identities than larger clients. Consequently, smaller clients are more likely to notice any fragmented and non-uniform identities in their supplying creative organization
- management of employees identified as 'mavericks' within a creative team or organization may present additional issues in relation to the management of the organizational brand. This is worthy of future empirical investigation.

References

Albert, S. and D. Whetten (1985) 'Organizational Identity', *Research in Organizational Behavior*, 7, pp. 263–95.

Alvesson, M. (1995a) *Cultural Perspectives on Organizations* (Cambridge: Cambridge University Press).

Alvesson, M. (1995b) *Management of Knowledge-intensive Companies* (Berlin: de Gruyter).

Alvesson, M. (2000) 'Knowledge Work: Ambiguity, Image and Identity', Working paper series 2000/6, Institute of Economic Research, University of Lund, Sweden, pp. 1–25.

Amabile, T. M. (1988) 'A Model of Creativity and Innovation in Organizations', *Research in Organizational Behavior*, 10, pp. 123–167.

Andriopoulos, C. and M. Gotsi (2000) 'Benchmarking Brand Management in the Creative Industry', *Benchmarking: An International Journal*, 7 (5), pp. 360–72.

Andriopoulos, C. and M. Gotsi (2001) 'Living the Corporate Identity: Case Studies from the Creative Industries', *Corporate Reputation Review*, 4 (2), pp. 144–54.

Andriopoulos, C. and A. Lowe (2000) 'Enhancing Organizational Creativity: The Process of Perpetual Challenging', *Management Decision*, 38, p. 474.

Ashforth, B. and F. Mael (1996) 'Organizational Identity and Strategy as a Context for the Individual', *Advances in Strategic Management*, 13, pp. 17–72.

Balmer, J. M. T. (1996) 'The Nature of Corporate Identity: An Explanation Study Undertaken within BBC Scotland', Unpublished PhD, Department of Marketing, University of Strathclyde.

Balmer, J. M. T. (2001) 'Corporate Identity, Corporate Branding and Corporate Marketing: Seeing through the Fog', *European Journal of Marketing*, 35 (3/4), pp. 248–91.

Balmer, J. M. T. and S. A. Greyser (2003) *Revealing the Corporation: Perspectives on Identity, Image, Reputation, Corporate Branding, and Corporate-level Marketing* (London: Routledge).

Balmer, J. M. T. and G. B. Soenen (1998) 'A New Approach to Corporate Identity Management', Working Paper Series 1998/5, University of Strathclyde.

Berg, P. O. and P. Gagliardi (1985) 'Corporate Images: A Symbolic Perspective of the Organization-environment Interface', Paper presented at the SCOS conference on Corporate Images, Antibes.

Brown, A. D. (2001) 'Organization Studies and Identity: Towards a Research Agenda', *Human Relations*, 54 (1), pp. 113–21.

Cook, P. (1998) 'The Creativity Advantage – Is Your Organization the Leader of the Pack ?', *Industrial and Commercial Training*, 30 (5), pp. 179–84.

DCMS (1998) Department for Culture, Media and Sport (UK) *Creative Industries (1st) Mapping Document* (London: HMSO).

DCMS (2000) Department for Culture, Media and Sport (UK) *Creative Industries, Report of the Regional Issues Working Group* (London: HMSO).

DCMS (2004) Department for Culture, Media and Sport (UK), *Creative Industries Economic Estimates* (London: HMSO).

Drake, G. (2003) 'This Place Gives Me Space: Place and Creativity in the Creative Industries', *Geoforum*, 34 (4), pp. 511–24.

Drazin, R., M. A. Glynn and R. K. Kazanjian (1999) 'Multilevel Theorizing about Creativity in Organizations: A Sense Making Perspective', *Academy of Management Review*, 24 (2), pp. 286–307.

Ensor, J., A. Cottam and C. Band (2001) 'Fostering Knowledge Management through the Creative Work Environment: A Portable Model from the Advertising Industry', *Journal of Information Science*, 27 (3), pp. 147–55.

Filby, I. and H. Willmott (1988) 'Ideologies and Contradictions in a Public Relations Department: The Seduction and Impotence of Living Myth', *Organization Studies*, 9, pp. 335–49.

Fisher, T. (1997) 'The Designer's Self Identity – Myths of Creativity and the Management of Teams', *Creativity and Innovation Management*, 6 (1), pp. 10–18.

Fombrun, C. (1996) *Reputation, Realizing Value from the Corporate Image* (Boston: Harvard Business School Press).

Fombrun, C. (1998) 'From Individual to Organizational Identity', in D. A. Whetten and P. Godfrey (eds) *Identity in Organizations* (Thousand Oaks: Sage), pp. 17–31.

Gioia, D. A., M. Shultz and K. G. Corley (2000) 'Organizational Identity, Image, and Adaptive Instability', *The Academy of Management Review*, 25 (1), pp. 63–81.

Kennedy, S. H. (1977) 'Nurturing Corporate Images – Total Communication or Ego Trip?', *European Journal of Marketing*, 11, pp. 120–64.

Kunda, G. (1992) *Engineering Culture* (Philadelphia: Temple University Press).

Martin, J. and D. Meyerson (1998) 'Organization Cultures and the Denial, Challenging and Acknowledgment of Ambiguity,' in L. R. Pondy, J. R. Boland and H. Thomas (eds) *Managing Ambiguity and Change* (New York: Wiley), pp. 93–125.

Meek, V.L. (1988) 'Organizational Culture: Origins and Weaknesses', *Organization Studies*, 9, pp. 453–74.

Merriam, S. B. (1988) *Case Study Research in Education* (London: Jossey-Bass).

Mumford, M. D., G. M. Scott, B. Gaddis and J. M. Strange (2002) 'Leading Creative People: Orchestrating Expertise and Relationships', *The Leadership Quarterly*, 13, pp. 705–50.

Post, J. E. and J. J. Griffin (1997) 'Corporate Reputation and External Affairs Management', *Corporate Reputation Review*, 1 (1–2), pp. 165–71.

Provalis (2004) 'QDA Miner – Software Programs Help File: Accessing Inter-coders Agreement', at www.simstat.com

QSR (2001) 'Using NVivo: Instruction Manual', at www.qsrinternational.com

Richards, L. (2005) *Handling Qualitative Data: A Practical Guide* (London: Sage).

Robertson, M. and J. Swan (2003) 'Control – What Control – Culture and Ambiguity within a Knowledge Intensive Firm', *Journal of Management Studies*, 40 (4), pp. 831–58.

Rostan, S. M. (1998) 'A Study of Young Artists: The Emergence of Artistic and Creative Identity', *Journal of Creative Behavior*, 32, pp. 278–301.

Saxton, K. (1998) 'Where Do Reputations Come From?', *Corporate Reputation Review*, 1 (4), pp. 393–99.

Silverman, D. (2000) *Doing Qualitative Research: A Practical Handbook* (London: Sage).

Smircich, L. (1983) 'Concepts of Culture and Organizational Analysis', *Administrative Science Quarterly*, 28, pp. 339–59.

Starbuck, W. H. (1992) 'Learning by Knowledge-intensive Firms', *Journal of Management Studies*, 29 (6), pp. 713–40.

Sutton, R. I. and T. A. Kelly (1997) 'Creativity Doesn't Require Isolation: Why Product Designers Bring Visitors Backstage', *California Management Review*, 40 (1), pp. 75–91.

Sveningsson, A. and M. Alvesson (2003) 'Managing Managerial Identities: Organizational Fragmentation, Discourse and Identity Struggle', *Human Relations*, 56 (10), pp. 1163–93.

Trice, H. M. (1993) *Occupational Subcultures in the Workplace* (New York: Cornell University, ILR Press).

van Riel, C. M. B. and J. M. T. Balmer (1997) 'Corporate Identity: The Concept, Its Measurement and Management', *European Journal of Marketing*, 31 (5/6), pp. 340–55.

Willmott, H. (1993) 'Strength Is Ignorance; Slavery Is Freedom: Managing Culture in Modern Organizations', *Journal of Management Studies*, 30, pp. 515–52.

Wilson, A. M. (1995) 'The Role and Importance of Corporate Culture in the Delivery of a Service', Unpublished PhD Thesis, Department of Marketing, University of Strathclyde.

Yin, R. K. (1994) *Case Study Research* (London: Sage).

7

Corporate Identity as Strategic Management Communication: A Working Framework

Lee Chun Wah

Abstract

There has been a lack of systematic conceptual and empirical research on the term 'corporate identity'. This paper is an attempt to synthesize some of the key prior research on the concept and posit an integrative working framework of the dimensions and determinants of corporate identity. The framework incorporates the original constructs of strategy, structure and culture as well as a set of additional constructs related to management processes and environmental characteristics. For a managerial audience, this analysis helps managers to identify a broad range of issues to consider, including corporate artifacts, symbolism, shared values, the nature of employee relationships and mental schemata. There is no 'fixed' solution to corporate-identity management as such, but there is a framework that fosters flexible positioning when executing the associated corporate identity mix. The process is an important management communication issue.

Introduction

Few issues in the communications and public relations literature have been subjected to as much theoretical imprecision as corporate-identity management (Grunig, 1993). Fuelled by the metaphorical qualities of the term, which conjures varying interpretations (Cornelissen and Harris, 2001), the subject has made little theoretical headway. The lack of systematic conceptual and empirical work on the issue is particularly urgent in light of the continuing interest in corporate identity in both academia and industry. In an attempt to understand this problematic state, it is necessary to review prior research and posit an integrative conceptual framework of the dimensions and determinants of corporate identity that defines the subject and enables systematic empirical research. Before outlining the framework, the next section provides a brief overview of previous writings on corporate identity.

Corporate identity: an overview

The repeated use of the term 'corporate identity' within academic and practitioner writings is a complex phenomenon involving many cross-currents, but a few broad patterns do present themselves. A first pattern, from a public-relations and communications industry perspective, emerges with the corporate design specialists Lippincott and Margulies (1957) who coined the term 'corporate identity' in relation to an organization's logos and symbols, because these were seen as 'identifying' the organization to external parties. Ever since, fuelled by the dramatic growth of the graphic design industry, with companies investing in product and graphic design for logos, corporate styles and other publicity collaterals, design and image consultancies have continued to endorse the label of 'corporate identity' when emphasizing the importance of visual 'identity' systems (Olins, 1978, 1989). Recent years have seen a further extension of the meaning and use of corporate identity within the design and public-relations industry, where the term has come to incorporate all communication techniques and even the behaviour with which organizations communicate with key publics and stakeholders in promoting corporate branding (Birkigt and Stadler, 1986; van Riel and Balmer, 1997). A second pattern, arising from the public-policy and legal sphere, is the use of the term 'corporate identity' as a result of the perceived need to personify organizations to embody the necessity of accountability (Czarniawska-Joerges, 1994). As Christensen and Cheney (1994, p. 224) explain in this regard: 'firms have gradually attained the status of juristic, artificial, or legal persons. Thus that which was originally thought to be explicitly collective in nature has come to be treated as individual: in the language of advanced capitalism, the corporation is a person with attendant rights and to a lesser extent ascribed responsibilities'. A third pattern of the use of 'corporate identity' is located in the academic organizational behaviour and management literature, and emerged with the coining of analogies, symbols and metaphors by academics as a means to understand organizational reality. Perceiving

organizations as organisms was a particularly popular analogy: '... organizations were anthropomorphized as organic, corporeal entities, and
terms such as "corporate identity", "organizational identity" and "corporate personality" have ever since the 1980s found continuing use in this
regard' (Albert and Whetten, 1985; Cornelissen and Harris, 2001, p. 51).

Notably, while the term 'corporate identity' had been used by public
relations and marketing academics and practitioners as referring to the
symbolic outward presentation of a company, within the organizational behaviour and management literature, the term has rather been
reserved for the distinctive features and core activities of an organization.
Informed by the metaphor that an organization is an actual organism
similar to a person, writers such as Larçon and Reitter (1979) have argued
in this regard that 'corporate identity' refers to a set of intrinsic characteristics or 'traits' (for example, strategy, culture, core competencies) that
give the organization its specificity, stability and coherence.

Corporate identity: some theoretical issues

The preceding section briefly outlined the complexity of forces that
appear to have drawn out the repeated use and salience of 'corporate
identity' in academic and practitioner writings. Although there has been
little commentary so far on the obvious differences for research and
understanding that these perspectives of corporate identity imply, their
diverging accounts of the nature of corporate identity are bound to unset-
tle the field and could have hampered theoretical progress. In effect, the
generic term 'corporate identity' now 'includes both the strict sense of an
organization's name or identifying emblems (e.g. logos) and the much
broader sense of a system's representations by/to itself and by/to others'
(Christensen and Cheney, 1994, pp. 223–4). Such a stretched definition, together with the undifferentiated use of the corporate identity
construct, concealing its diffused meanings, has already led to ambiguity in theory and research. Such ambiguity or openness of meaning of
the construct has in turn expanded the variety of operationalizations that
have been included within the theory's encompassing frame of reference
(Cornelissen and Harris, 2001; van Riel and Balmer, 1997). The problem
from an academic stance is that this flexibility of meaning continues to
permit researchers to apply the concept to qualitatively different types
of public relations and organizational phenomena located at different
levels of analysis, in turn increasing the potential number of empirical tests conducted on the theory, but effectively reducing the chance
that those tests can amount to a refutation of the theory. In effect, the

corporate identity construct is, through its stretched meaning and undifferentiated use, so general in scope, and so ambiguous in meaning, that it is almost unbounded in its potential range of applications; it is therefore difficult to refute.

It follows that there is a need for a further specification of the corporate identity construct through an examination of the social construction of the term 'corporate identity' and its derivatives. It is, however, not an objective of this study to provide a fully fledged account of the genesis and mutation of the term 'corporate identity'. Rather, it sets out to: demonstrate the previously implicit multiple constructions of the term as a vital means of deciphering the varieties of academic use that have arisen as a result; and to heed the problems associated with theoretical imprecision mentioned above, and thus to enable theoretical progress and aid empirical research. It advances a definition of corporate identity in communications management and public-relations theory that enables an operationalization of the construct into measurable variables. From such a communications-management and public-relations perspective, corporate-identity management can be defined as the strategic development of a distinct and coherent brand image of an organization that is consistently communicated to stakeholders through strategic intent, symbolism, planned communications and strategic branding.

Notably, as mentioned, the corporate identity mix is thus considerably broader in scope than just conventional planned communications and public-relations programmes, that include symbolism (logos, house style) and representational forms of behaviour (e.g. behaviour of store employees, sales representatives, receptionists) alongside planned forms of publicity and advertising under the adage that everything a company 'says, makes or does' in some way 'communicates' (Balmer, 1998). Next to these three types of media (symbolism, brand communication and behaviour), another dimension that has been considered as pertinent to corporate-identity management is a thematic and visual consistency across 'messages' carried by these media (Birkigt and Stadler, 1986; van Riel and Balmer, 1997).

To structure future enquiry, this set of discernible dimensions (the coordinated use of symbolism and branding, communication, behaviour, the thematic and visually consistency of messages) within the public relations definition of corporate identity have subsequently been related to organizational and environmental conditions and drawn into a conceptual framework (see Figure 7.1), as there has been an enduring gap between theoretical literature on corporate identity management and descriptive accounts of how companies actually construct an image

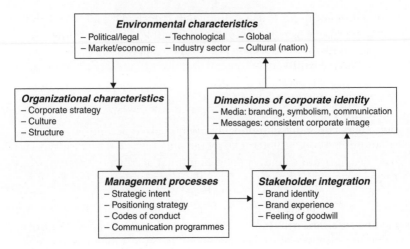

Figure 7.1 Conceptual framework for the study of corporate identity management

of themselves for representation to third parties (Grunig, 1993). Therefore, one of the primary objectives of this chapter is the development of a conceptual framework that identifies key dependent and independent variables whose relationship can be examined.

Overview of working framework

In this section, a conceptual framework is introduced that links dimensions of corporate-identity management to situational and contextual factors (see Figure 7.1). This will review and integrate prior literature, provide a systematic perspective on the topic, and identify the types of factors that may be relevant. The framework, based on structurational and open-systems precepts (Botan, 1993), helps to focus future enquiry on the topic. For the sake of clarity, it is not feasible to provide a comprehensive list of every construct that may be relevant in a specific context. Rather, the framework should be seen as delineating the most important constructs in relation to corporate identity management. The next few paragraphs provide an overview of the framework and its key constructs.

The conceptual framework presented in Figure 7.1 incorporates the original constructs of strategy, structure and culture that have been posited in prior work as determinants of corporate-identity management, as well as a set of additional constructs under the headings of management processes, environmental characteristics and stakeholder integration. The addition of these sets of constructs is needed because previous research has found little relationship between the original constructs of strategy, structure and culture on the one hand and dimensions of corporate identity management on the other. The present paper highlights these issues and the potential interconnectedness among the various constructs, adding to the theoretical base for future construct specification, modelling and testing. The remainder of this section is organized around outlining each of these constructs and their relationship to dimensions of corporate-identity management.

Strategy

The corporate positioning of an organization through the corporate identity mix has, in much previous work, been considered as a direct function of the strategy of an organization as captured in its corporate mission and vision. The concerted interest in the construct of strategy, and the allocation of predictive value to the construct in relation to corporate-identity management, is then primarily based on the belief that mission and vision statements provide an overall unifying theme for both motivating and focusing all employees, and for creating a coherent corporate image in advertising that differentiates the organization from its competitors (Balmer, 1995; Hatch and Schultz, 1997). Christensen and Cheney (2000) refer in this regard to 'essentializing' the strategy of the organization, its products and its history through immediately recognizable symbols. However, as the paper argues, there is little in the way of systematic research that identifies a direct relationship between strategy and dimensions of the corporate identity mix. Thus leading writers such as Alvesson (1993) claim that, although corporate identity might be influenced and motivated by the mission of an organization, it is not wholly or, more importantly, directly determined by it: '... corporate identity as something which naturally and spontaneously is developed as an undifferentiated part of the basic activities of the corporation probably does not often characterize the modern sectors of the economy' (p. 375).

As shown in Figure 7.1, rather than considering strategy as a direct antecedent of corporate identity, there is likely to be an intermediary phase, where strategy as captured in the mission and vision of an organization becomes translated into a positioning strategy, communication programmes and codes of conduct that, in turn, give rise to corporate imagery. These constructs in this 'management processes' phase are discussed in more detail below.

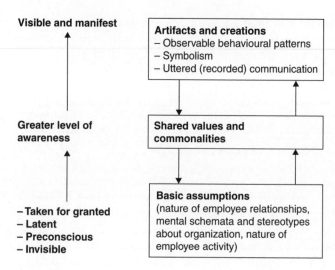

Figure 7.2 Levels of culture in relation to corporate identity (adapted from Schein, 1985)

Culture

Previous work has also shown a preoccupation with the construct of culture, variously labelled 'corporate culture', 'corporate personality' and 'organizational identity', as an antecedent of corporate-identity management (Balmer, 1995; Hatch and Schultz, 1997; van Riel and Balmer, 1997). The prevailing idea is that an integrated, strong culture (with shared meanings, ideologies and commonalities that are homogeneous, monolithic and organization-wide) gives rise to symbolization of the organization not only internally, but also externally in its representation to stakeholders and publics through the corporate identity mix. Such an idea is, as Figure 7.2 outlines, motivated by the view that visual manifestations through behaviour and communication are derived from and grounded in the collective psychological attributes of an organized group (see Schein, 1985), and that there should be a concordance strong enough to avoid outward manifestations that are not 'factually' based within the corporate culture, because these would then come to be considered as a false front (Cornelissen and Harris, 2001; Kennedy, 1977).

More importantly, however, previous empirical research has found little evidence of a strong correlation between culture and corporate-identity management (Balmer and Wilson, 1998). Explanations for the breakdown of a direct relationship then include the observation in previous research that the notion of a single, monolithic corporate culture is precarious because employees are subject to a complex set of identifications, which at times result in differentiated subcultures (van Maanen, 1991). It has also been observed that the role of cultural values and sense-making in corporate-identity management is mediated, in a managerial sense, by codes of conduct and prescribed communication programmes: 'If culture is thought to consist of beliefs and values that make sense in a company – to help employees serve the organization – that alone does not give a sense of the structure and principles of the organization, or the activities that are performed by each employee' (Heath, 1994, p. 88).

Rather than considering culture as a direct antecedent of behavioural and communication manifestations within the corporate identity mix, this study argues that, while the core credo, values and beliefs held by members of an organization might influence the content of representations to stakeholders and publics, such symbolic representations are, because of managerial mediation, not directly determined by it. This observation is supported by Olasky (1987) who, reviewing the extant historical evidence on corporate communications, argued that there is no such thing as an antecedent 'organizational reality' determining corporate communications. The creation of a corporate image is a largely subjective management affair; as a result, an image is something to be used as an enabler within the context of market and societal conditions facing an organization.

Structure

The overall structure of an organization, in the form of the relationship between the corporate parent and its divisions, has also been considered as a factor of importance in determining corporate imagery that may be presented through the corporate identity mix to stakeholders and publics (Olins, 1989; Balmer, 1998; van Riel and Balmer, 1997). Again, in a similar way to the strategy and culture constructs detailed above, the construct of structure (e.g. division, geographic, hybrid) per se does not have a direct and immediate effect on corporate-identity management. This is because senior managers of large organizations have a choice in deciding not only how divisions and the corporate group are managed, but also how these are presented outwardly. In particular, senior managers can decide whether separate divisions and products should be endorsed by and associated with a larger group or corporate brand (Hatch and Schultz, 2001) by opting for one of three general positioning strategies:

1. 'uniformity' (monolithic position: corporate profile analogous to business-unit and product-level) (e.g. Sony, BMW, Philips);

2. 'variety' or a 'branded' approach (diversified: two or three different levels) (e.g. product brands of Procter and Gamble and Unilever); or
3. 'endorsement' (brand with corporate image recognizable in the background) – a mixture of the previous two (e.g. GM, Kellogg, Nestlé) (Olins, 1978, 1989).

Management processes

The preceding sections have already started to articulate that while there might be a relationship between the original constructs of strategy, culture and structure, and dimensions of corporate identity management, such a relationship is ultimately modified by and hence subject to managerial interpretation of the organization and how it should be represented through the corporate identity mix. Such managerial interpretation and decision-making on the corporate image that is to be presented to stakeholders and key publics then involves a choice regarding the positioning strategy (monolithic, endorsed or branded), as mentioned above, and a specification of codes of conduct for employees and communication plans and programmes which, in turn, guide the media and the messages employed within the corporate identity mix. In addition, as Figure 7.1 outlines, these managerial processes of deciding on a positioning strategy and of organizing relevant communications and behaviour are also influenced by conditions in the environment inhabited by an organization. The corporate image and positioning of direct competitors of an organization, for instance, may influence the adoption of a corporate image that is sufficiently distinct to differentiate the organization from this competition (Cornelissen and Harris, 2001). Equally important, the type of industry sector may drive an organization towards a particular image, branding and positioning strategy, as evidenced by the widespread use of a monolithic positioning strategy in the financial and banking industry (Morison, 1997).

The concept of a contingency perspective, where managerial decisions regarding the positioning strategy and corporate identity mix are influenced by organizational and environmental characteristics, has emerged at various points in the above analysis. This viewpoint is valid in view of the empirical support presented and it is also timely to assert that there are no universal answers to practising managers' questions regarding corporate-identity management. Hence, as argued in this chapter, there is value in laying out the types of contingencies that may be important. In consideration of the little progress made so far in identifying the determinants of corporate-identity management, the conceptual framework

The concepts of brand equity and brand identification are intertwined and connected with both advertising and public relations. Wood (2000) indicates that there are several different meanings associated with brand equity. First, it may be interpreted as the total value of a brand as a differentiated asset – in other words, when the brand is actually sold in the marketplace or included on a financial balance sheet. Second, brand equity may be construed as the strength of attachment that consumers have to particular brands. Finally, it may describe the associations and beliefs that consumers have in relation to particular brand names. The distinctions in these definitions have their origin in the disciplines of accounting and marketing.

In many cases, financial accountants (with the first definition) will use the term brand value rather than brand equity. The brand's value, as a factor in the overall marketplace, emerges as the primary consideration. Public relations and advertising professionals acknowledge this first definition, but they place special emphasis on customer–brand relationships and associations. These practitioners have further refined the concept with ideas such as brand identity or brand image.

Brand image is associated with the needs and desires of a target market by using the four 'Ps' of marketing (product, price, place and promotion). The strategic implementation of these factors determines brand strength, that is, the degree of loyalty or attachment that customers feel towards a brand. With the number of related conceptual ideas, Blackston (2000) argues that brand equity is the critical factor. A brand is associated with a product in the marketplace, but the value of consumer investment changes over time.

Brand equity consists of the incremental, added-value qualities that synergistically combine in consumers' mindsets. The idea of added value is particularly important in this discussion. Even though usage of the brand may not be overly complex from the consumer stakeholder's point of view, the ongoing use of the brand demonstrates that it has added value in that person's life. Blackston (2000) posits that some of this utilization may be quite automatic (reaching for a glass of milk) but continuous usage indicates that some measure of significance has been associated with the brand by the consumer. A brand may be a product, but it may also represent the 'heart' of an organization through the creation of a unique identity (Knapp, 1999).

Blackston (2000) argues that fundamental marketing variables, such as product and price, are essential ideas but the added-value concept is where the ultimate success of branding is realized. However, added value is not always easy to define. Generally, this idea is indirectly measured or inferred in terms of consumers' brand ideas. Even though such inferences remain, Blackston (2000) suggests that greater understanding of brand equity may be achieved by acknowledging that brand relationships are occurring, interactive processes involving both the brand and the consumer. The essence of relationships is communication, the process which constructs and provides meaning to the relationships. The organization is projecting an image, and consumers are providing meaning to the messages. Thus, a relationship between the brand and the consumer develops or disintegrates. These brand relationships include two factors that are essential for added value; trust in the brand and customer satisfaction. In short, added value is achieved when these factors are maximized.

The brand's success depends on the development of a personal link with each consumer. According to Blackston (2000), when an organization moves from a self-centred to a more customer-focused stance, success in these relationships may be eventually realized. Blackston indicates that the brand-relationship concept has been applied to the development of advertising campaigns, but it can be extended to all areas of integrated marketing communication, including public relations. The overarching objective of a desired relationship with the consumer stakeholders may provide a guide for the brand's 'communication' with each individual. Since behavioural continuity is essential for long-term relational success, the sales promotion, packaging and public relations that are associated with a brand must be consistent and continuously leveraged.

However, are public relations and brand identification becoming so closely linked so as to obscure the communicative essence of relationships? Can we really have a communicative transaction with a brand name?

According to Blackston (2000), if the consumer is satisfied, he/she is likely to continue the brand relationship and, thus, added value may be maximized over time. Corporate branding is the 'mark' of a product or organization. In other words, it can be interpreted as a unique declaration of identity, quality, trust and value with the final judgment on those aspects resting with the individual consumer.

The branding concept in public relations is often associated with four process areas: 1) creating; 2) maintaining; 3) damaging; and 4) repairing. Creating unique identities for brand names can be difficult, considering the vast array of information in the marketplace. Consumers are exposed to a large amount of data regarding brand names and complete mental processing/comprehension of some brand names and their associated applications is virtually impossible. Wells, Burnett and

Moriarty (2003) provide the following recommendations for advertising and public relations professionals as they create messages about brands:

1. Make the brand distinctive by drawing attention to its qualities/ strengths.
2. Utilize a design that aligns with the brand image that you wish to project and send public relations and advertising messages that are generally consistent with other mass-media messages.
3. Make the packaging as functional as possible.
4. Product packaging, advertising, and public relations should dovetail. In other words, consistency is repeatedly emphasized.

Organizations need to ensure that human and material resources are committed to brands that offer the greatest potential for success. As Sackett and Kefallonitis (2003) argue, creating a differentiated brand experience can reflect the organization's advantages over its competitors. Thus, the organization can provide reinforcing messages to its existing customer base and also attract other consumers.

Sackett and Kefallonitis (2003) emphasize the importance of aligning the consistency, originality and relevance of the brand experience to a core brand value, an essential quality that is worth communicating about (for example, quality or durability). If this alignment does not occur, organizations will struggle to differentiate their brands in the vast consumer pool of information. They posit that creating brands involves attention to consumer stakeholders' perceptions of similar brands in the marketplace. Subsequently, the organization must design product features that are not only unique but add value. Thus, added value is created and potentially maintained.

In many cases, organizations will conduct research (such as interviews and surveys) to determine the likely importance of various brand characteristics in selection processes. For example, potential customers may be asked to rank attributes from lowest to highest or vice versa. Consumers may also be interviewed with these types of questions: 1) What is missing in the marketplace? (in a particular product category); and 2) What would you like to see to fill that void? Subsequently, a brand is developed that addresses these needs and perceptions, and this information is synthesized with data about the target market. It should be noted that not all organizations follow these guidelines in brand creation but, in general, many companies in the 21st-century business environment engage in these rigorous market research activities.

Wansink (1997) provides some additional thoughts on the brand-creation discussion by talking about 'brand re-creation', in other words, providing a revised brand perspective for consumers. Many integrated marketing communication professionals believe that brands, as with natural life cycles, observe the law of positive entropy; they are created, they grow, they mature, they decline and they die. In some instances, brand sales and market share decline because customers have lost interest due to changing conditions in the marketplace (typewriters and the advent of word processing) or because another brand becomes more salient (Apple Computers lost its edge in the late 1980s/early 1990s to Microsoft, a company which was able to provide more tools for software customers). Even though brand creation and re-creation are distinct in the actual product life-cycle, the same idea guides the success of these processes, addressing the needs of consumers and their perceptions of a product and/or market niche.

Brand re-creation can also be considered a natural maintenance activity in the overall brand-identification process. In order to maintain a successful brand relationship, some modifications may need to occur. Of course, there are examples of limited brand maintenance because the product continues to address the needs of consumers in its market niche. However, ongoing communication processes are always recommended so that consumers are reminded about the characteristics and strengths of the organization or product. But can we really claim that we have relationships with brands?

In the process of brand identification, organizations have different maintenance strategies and tactics. Corporate brands are used when a company operates in a tightly defined market (Kellogg's with breakfast cereal), and promoting related products is a brand-maintenance strategy for the company. Standardization strategies may also be used when companies choose to associate related products or names at the international level. In this sense, company executives make a 'non-adaptation' choice in the various global markets where they are operating. Additionally, corporate history can be a primary factor when brands are leveraged or extended. With this approach, a brand name is maintained by associations with new products. In other words, the brand name is revitalized by these connections.

With the immense amount of information directed towards consumers, dynamic brand-maintenance strategies are essential. Creativity is helpful and, in some cases, maintaining an information-based context may also be useful. Through a medium such as a website, people consume, communicate and transact with the organization or corporate brand. With regular website maintenance, brand identity may be preserved in the minds of consumer stakeholders. Even though some changes may occur, the brand is still important because a personal link to the consumer has been maintained. However, the organization needs to remember that personal links, outside of brand-identification strategies and website development, are just as important for the health of public relationships as they were 30 years ago.

The importance of personal connections is emphasized when damage to a brand name's reputation occurs. Management indiscretions (such as covering up information about products or financial misinformation) or the mishandling of crisis situations may cause the damage. Since organizations have distinct brand identities, there are numerous examples of brands enduring painful circumstances in the public sphere. The debacles that have plagued corporations such as Exxon (1989) and Enron (2001–2003) have been extensively documented in the popular media. These events create an excellent environment for brand damage, especially when stakeholders perceive that the organization does not care and/or is mishandling the situation.

In most cases, however, brand names decline as perceptions change in the marketplace. Over the course of time, without proper maintenance, brand damage is likely to occur and the brand's image cannot be restored to a positive state. Corporate brand names can also be damaged by claims from internal and external stakeholders, such as the media, that are inconsistent with organizational narratives. These claims may eventually lead to brand damage. However, if the organization can distance itself from the claims and provide evidence of accountability, brand damage may be significantly reduced. On the other hand, social legitimacy and financial stability may be permanently harmed but if the organization is committed to strong public relationships, organizational brand identity may weather the storm.

Image-restoration strategies employed by various companies provide some insight into brand rejuvenation after damage occurs (Benoit, 1995, 1997, 2000). This author provides the following typology of brand-repair and image-restoration strategies: 1) denying; 2) evading responsibility; 3) reducing offensiveness; 4) taking corrective action; and 5) mortification. Each of these strategies may be effective in particular cases. With the first two approaches, if the organization can legitimately deny or not take responsibility for a potentially damaging situation (someone else takes the blame), these communicative responses may be appropriate.

However, in most instances, denying and evading are not helpful in the overall brand-rejuvenation process. Reducing offensiveness can involve lessening or minimizing the apparent damage with rhetoric ('it's not as bad as we thought') as well as a couple of other responses; differentiation (not as negative as another company's situation) and transcendence, which involves placing the event and the organization in a different context (communicating to stakeholders about the 'bigger picture'). In other words, the details of a particular negative situation may be presented as being not as important as a view of the organization and its associated brands at a more holistic level. Corrective action is fairly straightforward; the organization takes steps to remedy the problem with the objective of returning to the previous, positive state of affairs. Finally, mortification is a completely apologetic stance; wrongdoing is admitted and the organization asks stakeholders for forgiveness.

Benoit (1995) also provides the following suggestions for image-restoration discourse:

1. Avoid making false claims for brands and provide adequate support.
2. If your organization is responsible, admit this fact immediately.
3. Communicate plans to correct and prevent recurrence of the problem.

The final point might be classified as goodwill, if such actions are designed to appeal to a group of stakeholders beyond merely repairing particular brand damage. If customers perceive that the organization is truly acting in their best interests, the brand image(s) may begin to recover. Additionally, restoration tactics may not need to take place over a long period of time, if the organization is straightforward with its stakeholders about issues and claims. In such cases, brand damage is limited because the company assumes responsibility and provides appropriate evidence related to the claims.

Audience perceptions are critical to brand image restoration. If the organization reminds stakeholders of past good deeds and positive relationships through bolstering communication strategies (boosting morale/perceptions by deflecting attention) without addressing the critical brand damaging issue(s), brand repair may not even occur. Customers may quickly reject the brand, or it may gradually fade from the marketplace. Corporate credibility plays a significant role in customers' attitudes towards corporate brands (Goldsmith, Lafferty and Newell, 2000). The research evidence for the influence of such credibility on purchase intentions has been noted by Winters (1988), who argues that as the perceived credibility of a company increased, sales also moved in a positive direction.

In terms of advertising/marketing in relation to branding, Aaker (1996) also indicates that the influence of brand names on consumer stakeholders is significant. According to Aaker, corporate brand names identify the corporation behind the products or services offered, performing an 'endorser' role. The corporate brand name reassures customers that the product will deliver the promised benefits because the company behind the brand is a substantial, successful organization that is associated only with strong products. If customers' perceptions are aligned with this corporate reassurance, the marketplace should be a favourable venue for the product(s). A key point to emphasize at this juncture is that it is representatives of the organization who are providing the reassurance, and not the brand name.

Several different brand strategies are associated with integrated marketing communication: 1) brand-user strategies; 2) brand image strategies; 3) brand-usage strategies; and 4) corporate advertising. Brand-user strategies focus on the types of individuals that use certain brands. Celebrity endorsements are common examples of this type of strategy (Goldsmith et al., 2000). When celebrities are present in the advertisements, there is a tendency to show the user of the brand more than the brand itself. The relationship is not with the brand, but with the person, even if that person is inaccessible from the buyer's private sphere. The idea is simple; consumers who like the celebrity will transfer that attraction to the brand. Thus, golfers who like Tiger Woods will use the Nike brand, action-movie fans who like Chuck Norris will purchase exercise equipment, and so forth.

A brand-image strategy works toward the development of a brand 'personality'. In this type of marketing communication, the focus is on the brand as an object of choice rather than the user. If a person appears in the advertisement, it is a typical person rather than a celebrity. The importance of a strong brand in the business environment has led many companies to devote more money to brand-image advertising and associated sales promotions and public relations campaigns. In addition to developing the brand image for various specialty audiences in trade journals (for example, suppliers), businesses use broadcast media, print media and online sources. Increasingly, organizations are realizing that having a strong brand name gives the company a better opportunity to bid on business contracts and enhances the public relationships that organizations have with their stakeholders.

Brand-usage strategies emphasize different uses for the brand while corporate advertising promotes the corporate name and image rather than the individual brand. Increasingly, organizations are interfacing with their stakeholders in the realm of social responsibility. Thus, corporate advertising is an essential communication strategy. Garbett (1981, p. 13) defines corporate image advertising by emphasizing its potential outcomes:

1. To educate, inform or impress the public with regard to the company's policies, functions, facilities, objectives, ideals and standards.
2. To build favourable opinion about the company by stressing the competence of the company's management, its scientific knowhow, manufacturing skills, technological progress, product improvements and contribution to social advancement and public welfare; and on the other hand, to offset unfavourable publicity and negative attitudes.
3. To build up the investment qualities of the company's securities or to improve its financial structure.
4. To sell the company as a good place in which to work, often in a way designed to appeal to college graduates or to people with certain skills.

The primary goal of each brand strategy approach is brand development, including image, brand awareness, positive perceptions of the brand, and 'interaction' (that is, purchase) with the brand. The nature of the communicative strategy should incorporate the advertising messages conveyed with the overall integrated theme, so that a relatively consistent message is disseminated to stakeholders. The message and its subsequent effect on stakeholders is the overriding consideration. Public-relations efforts are primarily focused on making sure that every possible contact delivers a positive and unified message about the company.

In general, an integrated marketing communication programme involves all the messages that an organization delivers to both internal and external stakeholders. Every contact point provides an opportunity for a message to be sent about the organization and its associated brands. The essential argument in this discussion is that messages about corporate identity and brand identification are delivered by individuals in the organization as they interact with stakeholders. A brand, in and of itself, cannot create a relationship with a customer. The public-relations department is involved with these various contact points, whether these encounters are planned or unplanned. An unanticipated negative situation is an opportunity to place the brand image in the spotlight, to show that the organization is committed to its stakeholder relationships.

According to Dean (2004), corporate crisis is defined as a chaotic event that creates uncertainty and threatens an organization's goals. Public expectations are higher for an organization that is highly respected compared with organizations that are less well-regarded or less well-known. In other words, when crises happen, stakeholders expect the organization to uphold its brand image. A good reputation can be a double-edged sword. A solid reputation benefits the company with positive public attitudes and potential financial success, but it also means that consumers will have high expectations for the company when crises happen and the brand is truly tested. Fulfilling these expectations enhances integrated marketing communication efforts. Gildea (1994–1995) argues that a company's social (public relationship) performance affects decisions by customers, employees and investors. Gildea provides the following recommendations:

1. Study the scope of your corporate responsibility.
2. Closely analyse your reputation and those of your competitors.
3. Measure and manage what 'drives' the perceptions of those reputations.
4. Put the findings to work for you in the marketplace (p. 21).

Additionally, Sethi (1979) argues that while corporate communicative responses and public relationships are certainly involved with problems/issues, there should be an overriding concern with solutions. For businesses to successfully operate in the marketplace, solutions in stakeholder relationships are paramount.

Heath (1997) outlines a couple of additional image-advertising tactics, designed to enhance brand reputations. First, direct image advertisements differentiate the sponsor, its brand names or services from its competitors. In this process, the company may appeal to common sense and/or human compassion. These corporate-image ads are designed to cast the organization in a positive light for taking a particular position on an issue. The organization and its associated products are considered to be 'good' because the issue is thought to be of general concern/interest. Direct ads, according to Heath, can be taken at face value because they demonstrate admirable characteristics which have not only social value but commercial value as well. As Heath (1997, pp. 200–1) further observes about this type of communication:

1. It directly affects image through a favourable description of the company's products or services that are not the subject of public debate.

2. It directly affects image by providing facts about the organization's operations or activities.
3. It directly affects image through a description of how well an organization's activities and policies agree with values that meet key publics' expectations of appropriate corporate behaviour.
4. It directly affects image through a description of the organization's support of charitable community-service activities and expected and appropriate community relations.

On the other hand, indirect image advertising asks stakeholders to assign positive attributes to the organization, based on the positions it takes on issues; the image of the company can therefore be enhanced by associations with values and attributes that are held in high regard.

For example, valuing the environment is viewed positively by many stakeholders and could lead to more sales. Increasingly, companies are being evaluated on social criteria (Waddock, 2000). Heath (1997) argues that these image advertising types are, essentially, attitudes that stakeholders hold regarding the company. An attitude is an expression of the belief that an object is associated with key traits and favourable or unfavourable dispositions toward those traits and, ultimately, towards the object itself (Fishbein and Ajzen, 1975). In short, people can have attitudes towards brands but can they really have relationships with brand names? According to Sternthal, Phillips and Dholakia (1978), expertise and trustworthiness are influential in persuading consumers, lending credence to the argument that the human dimension plays a major role in the integrated marketing communication process. However, Chaiken (1980) indicates that a relationship exists between attitude towards the ad (object) and purchase intentions. This relationship appears to exist under conditions of low involvement. Chaiken's conclusion is significant at this point in the essay; low-involvement relationships are more concerned with attitude than consumption.

In terms of the ramifications for relationships with internal and external stakeholders, a key argument in this discussion is that people cannot have strong relationships with brands per se. Although consumers and other stakeholders can interact with brands, Blackston (2000) argues that this relationship tends to be automatic and marked by low involvement. So, what does this mean for branding? Increasingly, the power of branding is evident in society. For example, sporting contests with corporate names and stadiums with corporate identities in everything from sporting events and venues (the O_2 Arena, formerly the Millennium Dome, in London) to sponsorship liaisons with nonprofit or charity initiatives.

Knapp, D. (1999) 'Brand Equity', *Risk Management*, 46, pp. 71–4.

Sackett, P. J. and E. G. Kefallonitis (2003) 'Using Feature Design to Showcase the Corporate Brand', *Design Management Journal*, 14, pp. 62–7.

Sethi, S. P. (1979) 'Institutional/image Advertising and Idea/issue Advertising as Marketing Tools: Some Public Policy Issues', *Journal of Marketing*, 43, pp. 63–78.

Sternthal, B., L. W. Phillip and R. Dholakia (1978) 'The Persuasive Effect of Source Credibility: A Situational Analysis', *Public Opinion Quarterly*, 42, pp. 285–314.

Travis, D. (2000) *Emotional Branding: How Successful Brands Gain the Irrational Edge* (Roseville: Prima Venture).

Waddock, S. (2000) 'The Multiple Bottom Lines of Corporate Citizenship: Social Investing, Reputation, and Responsibility Audits', *Business and Society Review*, 105 (3), pp. 323–45.

Wansink, B. (1997) 'Making Old Brands New', *American Demographics*, 19, pp. 53–8.

Wells, W., J. Burnett and S. Moriarty (2003) *Advertising Principles and Practice* (Upper Saddle River: Prentice-Hall).

Winters, L. C. (1988) 'Does It Pay to Advertise to Hostile Audiences with Corporate Advertising?', *Journal of Advertising Research*, 28, pp. 11–18.

Wood, L. (2000) 'Brands and Brand Equity: Definition and Management', *Management Decision*, 38, pp. 662–69.

9
Strategic Corporate Re-branding

Patrick Cettier and Bernd Schmitt

Abstract

Corporate re-branding – a change of a corporate brand with the goal of improving perception of the company by customers, employees and investors – is a widespread activity. However, from 1995 to 2004 only about half of all re-branding activities were successful. In this article, we focus on strategic corporate re-branding and provide a conceptual framework for managing it. We identify seven key factors that contribute to success, and present both failures and best-practice cases to illustrate the seven success factors. We conclude with a model that presents strategic corporate re-branding as a dynamic process.

Introduction

From 1995 to 2004, numerous prominent companies re-branded themselves. Philip Morris became the Altria Group. British Steel turned into Corus. Andersen Consulting changed its name to Accenture. The consulting division of KPMG became Bearing Point. Daimler-Benz, after merging with Chrysler, became Daimler-Chrysler. The UK Post Office switched (briefly) to Consignia and then again to Royal Mail. Paine Webber now operates under the UBS brand. There are numerous others: AOL-Time Warner, Vodafone-Mannesmann, Exxon-Mobil, Deutsche Telekom-Voicestream.

Corporate re-branding, which is usually expressed in a corporate name change, is not simply a tactical change in a name or logo. It is an important corporate strategy decision, undertaken as a result of a change in the customer or employee base, new products and services, or a revised strategic position and value proposition. This decision impacts how a firm's

166

constituents (customers, employees and investors) view the company's mission, vision and values. Moreover, corporate re-branding results in a broad-based perception and image change. As a result, a well managed re-branding initiative provides many opportunities for the corporation. Yet, corporate re-branding also entails risk. The new brand may fail to attract new customers and potentially alienate existing ones. Employees may be attached to the old brand. From a shareholder perspective, returns of the new corporate brand may disappoint. It is therefore pertinent to ask why corporations engage in re-branding in the first place. Moreover, to mitigate risks, it is key to develop an organizational model of the process of corporate re-branding and identify key success factors.

The vast literature on brand management has largely ignored corporate re-branding. The focus has been on how to build and manage brand equity, incorporating concepts such as brand core, brand personality and brand values; brand identity; brand architecture; and brand leverage and extensions (Aaker, 1991, 1996; Aaker and Joachimsthaler, 2000; de Chernatony, 2001; Gregory, 2004; Hatch and Schultz, 2001; Keller, 1998). While some have acknowledged the importance of corporate re-branding as well as its complexities and risks (Keller, 1998; Kapferer, 2004), concepts and frameworks for handling this challenge have not been forthcoming.

In this paper, we present a conceptual and empirical analysis of strategic corporate re-branding. We first perform an empirical analysis of the corporate re-branding landscape in the United States, the UK and Germany from 1995 to 2004 to see how common corporate re-branding is. In addition, we analyse the reasons why corporate re-branding was pursued in order to identify how often re-branding initiatives are motivated by strategic factors. We then present a general model of the strategic process of corporate re-branding from an organizational perspective. We identify seven specific key success factors of strategic corporate re-branding and illustrate them with short case examples. Finally, we present cases of failed re-branding initiatives and, as a best-practice case, the re-branding initiative undertaken by UBS, the Swiss financial corporation.

An empirical analysis of corporate re-branding (1995–2004)

In the beginning of this study, we provided several examples of corporate re-branding initiatives that attracted attention in business circles and in the press. Yet, how common is corporate re-branding, and specifically, strategic corporate re-branding?

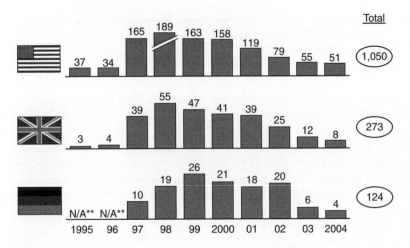

Figure 9.1 Number of corporate re-brandings*, 1995–2004
Notes: *Publicly traded companies with name change and with revenue exceeding USD/EUR 100 million.
**No data available in Bloomberg database.
Source: Bloomberg, own analysis.

To address this question, we examined publicly traded companies with revenues exceeding $100 million using the Bloomberg database. We used name change as the key indicator of corporate re-branding. While this indicator may not be entirely unproblematic (for example, corporations do not have to change their names to engage in corporate re-branding and, vice versa, there may be name changes that are not followed by corporate re-branding initiatives), we believe that name changes are nonetheless the best single indicator of corporate re-branding. As a reasonable time period for our analysis, we chose a ten-year period (1995-2004). For an international perspective, we included three leading industrialized nations: the US, the UK and Germany (note that the Bloomberg database does not contain data for Germany for 1995/1996).

As Figure 9.1 shows, with 1050 cases, the largest total number of corporate re-branding cases occurred in the US, followed by 273 cases in the UK and 124 cases in Germany. In all three countries, corporate re-branding was most frequent in three consecutive years toward the middle of the time period analysed, signalling a trend in corporate re-branding at that time. This three-year period accounted for approximately 50 per cent of all re-branding in each country (49 per cent in the US; 52 per cent in the UK; and 53 per cent in Germany). In the US, this time period was the years 1997–1999; in the UK and Germany it was

1998–2000. If we add the one year with the next highest incidence of re-branding, it was a year adjacent to the three-year time period in each case (2000 for the US, 1997 or 2001 in the UK, and 2000 for Germany); approximately 65 per cent of all cases then fall within this four-year period, offering further empirical support that re-branding was a trend in the corporate world. This trend may be explained by the 'new economy' as well as by market deregulation in the energy and banking industries in the US and UK.

Why did companies re-brand? Specifically, how many companies re-branded for strategic reasons? To answer this question, we closely analysed the reasons for the re-branding efforts on a randomly chosen subset of the data set (260 in the US, 102 in the UK, and 90 in Germany), examining public sources as well as information provided by the company and experts. In this analysis three key categories emerged:

1. *Strategic*: Corporate re-branding here occurs because of changes in the marketplace (for example, customers and competition), new positioning or value propositions, innovation, expansions into new business fields, or a drive for globalization – and the name no longer fits the strategy. The purpose of the re-branding is to present the changed strategic conditions more accurately to external constituents. The Altria Group and Corus, mentioned earlier, fall into this category.
2. *Mergers and Acquisitions (M&As)*: Corporate re-branding here occurs because two companies have merged or one company has acquired the other. The reasons for M&A may differ (and may include some strategic considerations). However, the prime trigger for the re-branding is the M&A, and corporate re-branding is done specifically to reflect the new reality after the merger. Daimler-Chrysler is an example.
3. *Miscellaneous*: If a particular case did not clearly fall into the strategic or M&A category, it was put into a miscellaneous category. Examples of cases within this category include: companies that are forced to change their name for legal reasons (for example, Andersen Consulting's change to Accenture), companies simply changing their names to an acronym, companies launching a new business (e.g., Hutchison with Orange, HP with deepcanyon), and others.

As Figure 9.2 shows, strategic considerations are the most common reason for corporate re-branding in the US and the UK (accounting for 43 per cent and 39 per cent of cases respectively). In Germany, M&As and

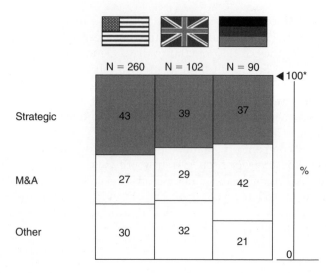

Figure 9.2   Main reasons for corporate re-branding, 1995–2005
Note: *Data basis: randomly chosen sample of total re-branding database.
Source: Bloomberg, own analysis.

strategic reasons are of roughly equal importance (42 per cent and 37 per cent respectively).

Finally, how successful is corporate re-branding? We answered this question by focusing on corporate re-branding done for strategic considerations. Strategic considerations are an active decision by a company's management. Corporate re-branding is done to build value and viewed as a key aspect of success for the company. In contrast, re-branding after M&As, is usually done out of necessity to reach a compromise between two merging companies. Moreover, M&A-related re-brandings are confounded by numerous merger-related aspects that could distort conclusions.

What could be an appropriate measure of re-branding success for our strategic re-branding cases? Since it was practically impossible to get detailed awareness and image data on most re-branding initiatives directly from the companies, we focused on the shareholder's perspective and analysed the total return to shareholders (TRS) for each company. While other factors besides re-branding may also affect TRS, a re-branding initiative can be considered to have been successful only if TRS increased over time. In fact, even if a re-branding initiative increased a company's awareness and image but failed to positively impact TRS, a re-branding initiative would not be considered to be fully successful.

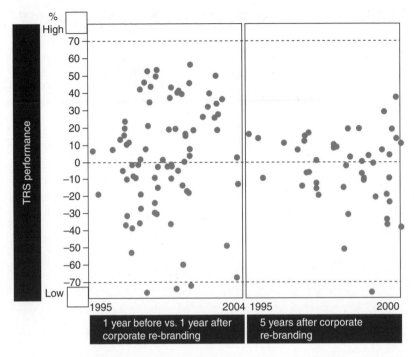

Figure 9.3 TRS performance after re-branding
Source: Bloomberg, own analysis.

Figure 9.3 shows the results. Interestingly enough, there is no clear pattern and no correlation between corporate re-branding initiatives in different years with TRS performance. Roughly 50 per cent of the companies in scope had a negative TRS performance. On average, the analysis of the TRS performance one year before vs. one year after corporate re-branding resulted in a minus-22 per cent net TRS. This negative number is due, in part, to extreme outliers. Excluding outliers with TRS of more or less than 100 per cent in the one year before vs. one year after analysis still results in a value of minus-3 per cent. The analysis of the performance five years after corporate re-branding resulted in minus-14 per cent net TRS. Interestingly enough, this analysis does not contain extreme outliers, perhaps because the underperforming companies went out of business.

With half of corporate re-brandings failing, it is important to find out how corporate re-branding can be effective and what guarantees success.

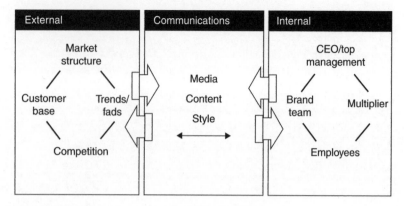

Figure 9.4   A model of strategic corporate re-branding
Source: Own analysis.

To do so, we took a close look at dozens of cases and, on the basis of these cases, developed a simple organizational model of corporate re-branding.

A model of strategic corporate re-branding

As Figure 9.4 shows, we view strategic corporate re-branding as an organizational process that must include analyses of both the external and internal corporate domains and provide communications that bridge the two domains. As we will see, a corporate re-branding initiative is successful only if all three domains are well managed.

External domain: Because corporate re-branding will result in a new perception of the company and its competitive position, the key concern for a company as part of the re-branding process needs to be a consideration of how a corporate re-branding will affect its customer base and other key constituents (such as employees and investors). Moreover, a company needs to consider market structure, current and future industry trends/fads and potential competitive moves.

Internal domain: Because corporate re-branding also results in change within the organization, re-branding needs favourable starting conditions and employee buy-in. The organization must be ready for change and understand the necessity for it. This requires input from top management as the leaders of the organization, the brand team as the natural owner of the re-branding initiative, key employees who can act as multipliers for the initiative, and the overall workforce who must accept it.

Communications domain: Finally, only the right media and right communication content and style will ensure success of the re-branding initiative. Communications must target all the constituents involved – both outside and inside the organization.

This general conceptual model can help us to identify specific key requirements that need to be met to make re-branding a success: First, re-branding must be sensitive to external triggers and pressures. Since all the external factors in the model (market structure, customer base, competition and trends/fads) are dynamic factors that are in constant flux, it is key to engage in strategic corporate re-branding for the right reasons (based on an analysis of these factors) and at the right time. Second, corporate re-branding must be managed well internally. Senior management must support the effort; employee-buy-in is key, and a brand team must manage the process. Also, as we will see, research must be commissioned and the organization must grasp the opportunities that re-branding provides. Finally, starting with the right name, communications must be executed well, both externally and internally, in terms of media, content and style. By looking at a range of cases where these requirements of the model were met, we have identified in more detail seven key success factors for corporate re-branding. As we will see later on, these factors are usually not present or even deliberately ignored when re-branding initiatives fail.

The seven success factors of strategic corporate re-branding

The seven key success factors were developed initially as hypotheses based on a dozen successful case studies. The remainder of the successful case studies then served as a validation check of the initially developed hypotheses. Subsequently, we contrasted the success stories with cases of failure (based on public information) to make sure that the success factors were not present in the failure cases.

Key success factor 1: Right reason

Corporate re-branding has to link soundly with corporate strategy and be motivated by the right reasons. The right reasons and a persuasive rationale must be found through an analysis of the company's current competitive position and business model, market structure, current and future industry trends, as well as current and future target segments. Most importantly, corporate re-branding should only be done if the company's objectives cannot be achieved with the current brand.

How can a company assess whether the timing is right? We suggest that a company use a variety of methodologies and tools. For example, a fit-analysis between current and future brand images as well as emotional and functional benefits is pivotal to decide if adjustments to the current brand are sufficient or a corporate re-branding is necessary.

A re-branding decision that seemed to be based solidly on the right reasons was the pharmaceutical company Novartis Generics' change to Sandoz. In 2003, Novartis Generics, formed in 1996 as part of the Ciba and Sandoz merger, consisted of 14 brands with no unifying identity and no integrated operations. As stated in Sandoz's annual report of 2003, the objective of the corporate re-branding for Sandoz was 'to consolidate our overall leadership position by joining forces and speaking with one unique and strong voice'. This was necessary because the large number of generic products made it difficult for distributors (such as physicians and pharmacists) and patients to remember each product brand. Moreover, global companies were leveraging their corporate brand across all stake-holder groups. Finally, the weak performance of Novartis Generics' 14 brands and high costs for production and distribution were weakening the market position and profits. Therefore, Novartis Generics' decision to re-brand was based firmly in its corporate strategy and analysis of current and future target segments.

Key success factor 2: Right timing

An analysis of whether the time is right includes both internal and external considerations. The key internal question to ask is whether the corporation is ready for change (for example, is re-branding a natural activity after a M&A, is there a positive organizational climate, is the orga-nization excited about entering new markets?). This can be done through internal research, such as by using employee surveys and by work-shops with key employees. If the organization is ready for re-branding, then external timing factors such as market dynamics, trends and the competitive landscape should be considered as well. Through external research, projections can be made about market dynamics, customer developments, trends and competitors' intentions and likely actions.

The re-branding of Dynagen to Able Laboratories (2001) seemed to occur at the right time. Both the organization and the market were ready. As C. Robert Cusick, chairman and CEO of Able Laboratories, Inc., stated, 'We are positioning Able to capitalize on the expected growth in the generic market'. As part of the company's new strategy, Able invested significant resources in research and development and in upgrading its facilities and equipment in order to position itself early on in the US generics market, which had an estimated potential value of US$84 billion between 2002 and 2008. In sum, the timing was right for Dynagen both in terms of external (market) and internal (R&D and investment) factors.

Key success factor 3: Senior management backing

Senior management must be the sponsor of the initiative right from the start. This will convey how important the initiative will be and put re-branding on everybody's agenda. On an operational level, the brand team will drive the initiative, and key employees will be involved to secure buy-in throughout the organization.

The move from SBC Communications to AT&T (2005) was strongly supported by Edward E. Whitacre, chairman and CEO of SBC Communications Inc. His public statements and the associated new brand promise were passionately communicated: 'No name is better-suited than AT&T to represent the new company's passion to deliver innovation, reliability, quality, integrity and unsurpassed customer care.' Or: 'The combination of SBC and AT&T will bring together the right assets and the right strategy to be a very strong competitor in this new IP-based services market, and we fully intend to make the most of this once-in-a-century opportunity.'

Key success factor 4: Thorough research

Understanding the image of the brand in the mind of customers and employees is pivotal when changing a corporate brand. The re-branding effort as a whole must be sensitive to the levels of brand awareness, existing associated attributes and the level of attachment. A mix of quantitative and qualitative research should be used to provide a holistic picture.

When Philips and Whirlpool joined forces in the household appliance business in 1989, Whirlpool had extremely low awareness in Europe. In contrast, the Philips brand was known all over the Continent. Moreover, Whirlpool was associated with change and dynamism whereas Philips stood for reliability and quality. The new brand (Philips-Whirlpool) secured awareness for Whirlpool and combined the positive characteristics (change/dynamism and reliability/quality) of the two original brands (Kapferer, 2004). In 1996, after a seven-year transition period, Philips-Whirlpool became Whirlpool.

Key success factor 5: Organizational grasp

Organizational grasp refers to the sense of internal direction that must be part of a re-branding initiative. Implementation only makes sense if everyone in the organization understands where the initiative is heading. All product and service changes need to be clearly defined. Project management is key to execute the planned re-branding.

The re-branding of DHL in Europe in 2003 was a massive undertaking that involved 150,000 employees. Superb project management was instrumental in creating the world's largest logistics company. In addition to a signage change on thousands of vehicles and aircraft and on packaging, DHL also had to coordinate its various distribution centres, fleets and IT systems.

Key success factor 6: The right name

The name development must follow from the procedures outlined thus far: it must be chosen based on an understanding of strategy, the organization and the unique perceptual factors of the situation. Researching different name options provides key input, and the name must be acceptable to employees. In fact, if possible, employees should be involved in the name-creation process. Again, employee surveys, pilots and consultations with opinion leaders in the organization can give indications of the likelihood that the new name will be accepted.

This was the case in the re-branding of Andersen Consulting to Accenture in 2000. To create a new name in only 147 days (due to legal requirements) was a tremendous challenge. Nonetheless, Andersen Consulting decided to involve all its 75,000 employees. Employees were encouraged under a company-wide programme (called 'brandstorming') to submit name suggestions. After one employee's suggestion was selected, top management gradually introduced the name, continuing to keep all employees abreast of the process.

Key success factor 7: Communication sensitivity

After the name and identity change, tailored external marketing campaigns need to reflect the company's new positioning. Training sessions of key employees are critical to turn them into ambassadors of the brand. The roll-out of the corporate re-branding may be accompanied by a culture-change programme and a redesign of the incentive structure to ensure desired behaviour.

In 2000, France Télécom (the formerly state-owned telecom monopoly) bought Orange, a UK mobile phone operator, as part of its international expansion strategy. Two very different company cultures

	Success factors	Short description
External	Right reason	• Consistent and convincing rationale for re-branding
	Right timing	• Leading industry trends • Favourable market environment • Organizational readiness for transformation
Internal	Senior management backing	• Strong top management support
	Thorough research	• Deep understanding of current brand positioning • True insights into customer and employee experience • Clear strategic direction for brand with focus on customer touch points/proof points
	Organizational grasp	• Clear idea of necessary changes accompanying re-branding • Excellence in execution
Communications	Right name	• Meaningful name (with context to business, tradition)
	Communication sensitivity	• Internal and external communication sensitivity • Tight management of customer and employee experience (information training, learning-on-the-job)

Figure 9.5   The seven success factors
Source: Own analysis.

had to be united. This was done in a coordinated effort that involved each employee in an in-depth immersion in the new values, both individually and within their functional teams. Employee focus groups, internal meetings and global sessions helped in building a common understanding of the brand over the period of one year. Externally, communications were personal as well: key existing clients were contacted individually to inform them of the name change and to explain what it meant for them.

The seven key success factors and corresponding principles are summarized in Figure 9.5.

Cases of failure

As stated earlier, in our analysis we contrasted successful cases of re-branding with unsuccessful ones and found that in the case of failures several of the seven success factors were usually not met.

The British Post Office's change to Consignia in 2001 provides an example. Wrong reasons, wrong timing and lack of communication sensitivity stand out as core reasons for the failure. Management changed the well-known and trusted name of the Post Office into Consignia, in part because other UK companies had dropped traditional names associated with an earlier, nationalized, era (for example, National Power had changed to Innogy and British Steel to Corus); this was hardly a strong reason for corporate re-branding. Moreover, the timing was poor: in 2001 the Post Office was in the midst of a heavy restructuring programme and was under immense competitive pressure from new entrants into the market. Finally, instead of designing a sensitive communication strategy, CEO John Roberts publicly admitted in a TV interview that the name had no meaning. In 2002, after heavy customer and employee opposition, the company was 're-re-branded' to Royal Mail.

There are numerous other cases that indicate that the key success factors are missing when re-branding efforts fail. For example, Condor, a successful German charter airline, changed its name to Thomas Cook in 2002 as part of the group's strategy to use Thomas Cook as the international leisure and travel brand across all business units. The name was changed back to Condor in 2004 after facing customer criticism and a significant slowdown in business. Management underestimated customers' attachment to the brand (thus disregarding success factor 4, thorough research). Also, there was no convincing reason (other than internal efficiency and the notion that a single brand is always better) for the re-branding of a well-established charter airline; management thus also disregarded success factor 1, right reason.

Another striking example of re-branding failure occurred in the US after the acquisition of the bank First Interstate by Wells Fargo in 1996. As some commentators put it: 'Wells Fargo's executives were so eager to quickly complete the re-branding and integration of the two banks that they failed to properly anticipate, strategize, and prepare for the immense amount of work required to integrate First Interstate's operational systems, management style and employee culture [...]'. In 1998, Wells Fargo was acquired by Norwest Corporation for a bargain price. Wells Fargo especially disregarded success factor 5, organizational grasp, and success factor 7, communication sensitivity.

A final example is Windscale, the British nuclear power station that re-branded itself as Sellafield after a history of safety hazard incidents. This was a weak attempt to disguise a tarnished reputation with a simple re-branding. The re-branding was not successful in diverting public opinion. Management disregarded success factor 1, right reason, as well as success factor 7, communication sensitivity.

While there may be many reasons for a re-branding failure, in each case several of the success factors were usually violated. Next, we present a case that illustrates successful management across all seven criteria and shows how the success factors are interrelated. The case may be used as a best-practice case study for corporate re-branding.

Its advertising campaign, based on the slogan 'U and US', was very successful. The campaign reflected UBS's brand positioning; for example, one of the ads stated: 'We take time to understand our clients' needs and goals.' Internally, communications included middle-management training with a strategic focus on branding, as well as 'brand influencer training' featuring hands-on branding discussions on how to convey the branding message appropriately to target audiences. By June 2005, about 1000 key marketing and communications staff had taken part in 30 brand-influencer workshops. The so-called Communication Specialist Database keeps track of all employees involved in brand communications. Finally, changes were made in the four-step UBS client-advisory process (understand; propose; agree and implement; review and monitor). The process was altered from a product-oriented selling approach to a needs-oriented advisory approach. Much more time is now spent on understanding clients' needs (step 1) and reviewing/monitoring its suitability and impact (step 4).

In sum, each decision and direction taken by UBS during its corporate re-branding was well thought through and well planned. All the different pieces of the corporate re-branding initiative fitted together. UBS excelled at internal and external change operations and bridged them through a powerful communications programme.

Strategic corporate re-branding: a model for other branding activities

Companies engage in corporate re-branding for several reasons. The most important motivations seem to be strategic changes in the customer and employee base, different organizational structures and processes, new products and services, or a revised strategic position and value proposition. Any of these changes can be the impetus for re-branding and necessitate a change in name, logo, slogan and communications. Often, these reasons co-occur: changes in customers or employees result in new organizational structures and processes, and new products and services, which in turn require new positionings and value propositions. Then, even more, corporate re-branding is needed, and needs to be undertaken in a strategic way.

Once a corporate re-branding initiative has started, the re-branding will result in a change in the perception of the corporation, including its products and service offers, in the minds of customers and employees. This is because the name, logo, slogan and communication changes are a signal for a corporation's new strategic positioning, value proposition

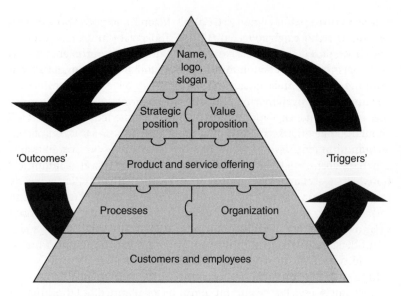

Figure 9.8 A strategic model of corporate re-branding
Source: Own analysis.

and direction. Once the re-branding addresses organizational alignment, the initiative will produce additional outcomes; for example., by
affecting organizational structures and processes and thereby affecting
customers and employees more deeply.

As Figure 9.8 shows, corporate re-branding is a dynamic process
involving external factors (such as customer perceptions) as well as
internal factors (employees and organizational structures and processes).
Moreover, changes in the same factors may be viewed as antecedents
('triggers') or as consequences ('outcomes') of corporate re-branding.

The seven success factors discussed here, and illustrated by the UBS
case study, may be viewed as 'trigger' or 'outcome' factors, respectively.
Right reason, right timing and thorough research are 'trigger' success factors. Senior management backing, organizational grasp, right name and
communication sensitivity may be viewed as 'outcome' success factors.

Our Complete Model of Strategic Corporate Re-branding may be an
apt model for other branding activities as well. Brand repositioning
at the product rather than company level, new brand development,
and launching brands in new markets share similarities with corporate
re-branding. They all require a consideration of external, internal and

communication factors. Moreover, they all require triggers as well as outcome success processes.

Future research should examine to what degree new brand initiatives are strategically similar and dissimilar to re-branding situations and what specific success factors and benchmarks are useful for understanding them. In addition, future research should examine what makes the other major reason for corporate re-branding, namely mergers and acquisitions, most successful from a branding point of view.

References

Aaker, D. (1991) *Managing Brand Equity* (New York: The Free Press).

Aaker, D. (1996) *Building Strong Brands* (New York: The Free Press).

Aaker, D. and E. Joachimsthaler (2000) 'The Brand Relationship Spectrum: The Key to the Brand Architecture Challenge', *California Management Review*, 42 (4), pp. 8–23.

Berner, R. and D. Kiley (2005) 'Global Brands', *Business Week*, July, pp. 86–94.

Bruce, M. and S. A. Greyser (1994) *Changing Corporate Identity: The Case of a Regional Hospital* (Boston: Design Management Institute).

De Chernatony, L. (2001) *From Brand Vision to Brand Evaluation: Strategically Building and Sustaining Brands* (Oxford: Oxford University Press).

Gloger, A. (2004) 'Markenartikler Statt Graue Maus', *Handelszeitung*, 3 March.

Gregory, J. R. (2004) *The Best of Branding: Best Practices in Corporate Branding* (New York: McGraw Hill).

Hatch, M. J. and M. Schlutz (2001) 'Are the Strategic Stars Aligned for Your Corporate Brand?', *Harvard Business Review*, 79 (2) pp. 128–34.

Kaikati, J. G. (2003) 'Lessons from Accenture's 3Rs: Re-branding, Restructuring and Repositioning', *Journal of Product and Brand Management*, 12 (7), pp. 477–90.

Kapferer, J. *The New Strategic Brand Management: Creating and Sustaining Brand Equity Long Term* (London: Kogan Page).

Keller, K. L. (1998) *Strategic Brand Management. Building, Measuring, and Managing Brand Equity* (Upper Saddle River: Prentice-Hall).

Nicholson, D. (2001) 'Accenture: A Brand New Adventure', *Computing*, 30 May.

Sources of and further information on some of the examples of re-branding mentioned in this chapter can be found on the following websites:

Condor/ThomasCook
www.1.thomascook.de/tck/6172.html

DHL
www.dhl.com/publish/g0/en/press/release/2003/250303.low.html

Dynagen/Able Labs
www.ablelabs.com/investors/press/pr051701.html

First National/Wells Fargo
www.en.wikipedia.org/wiki/Wells_Fargo_Corp

Novartis/Sandoz
www.novartis.com/investors/en/financial_reports.shtml

Post Office/Consignia
www.brandchannel.com/features_profile.asp?pr_id=76

SBC/AT&T
www.attalascom.com/press/sbcattname.html

Windscale/Sellafield
www.iknow-lakedistrict.co.uk/tourist_information/cumbria_coast/seascale_
   millom/rebranding_sellafield.htm

10

Renault-Nissan: A Study into the Advantages of a Prior Strategic Alliance in the Development of a Post-merger Corporate Identity

T. C. Melewar, David Stark and Elif Karaosmanoğlu

Abstract

This paper highlights the role corporate identity plays in merger and acquisition activity and examines the advantages of a prior strategic alliance in the development of a new corporate identity post-merger. This paper considers whether a prior strategic alliance could be of benefit in developing and installing a new post-merger corporate identity. In order to do this the framework that is suggested by Melewar and Jenkins (2000) is applied to the Renault-Nissan strategic alliance to analyse which areas in the formation of a new corporate identity are directly aided by the alliance. The potential success of a Renault-Nissan merger on corporate identity grounds is also considered.

Introduction

Corporate identity is an important area of business that has many different definitions. It can be linked with both marketing (externally projecting an image of a company) and organizational behaviour (simply from the word 'identity'). One definition that is widely accepted is 'the Strathclyde statement' (See Appendix 10.1, p. 203). This states that corporate identity creates cohesion between a company's corporate ethos, its activities and its corporate communication, in order to build understanding and commitment amongst its stakeholders (ranging from customers to employees). It enables companies to differentiate themselves from their competitors.

Van Riel and Balmer (1997) suggest that corporate identity is determined by factors including cultural history, corporate strategy, the

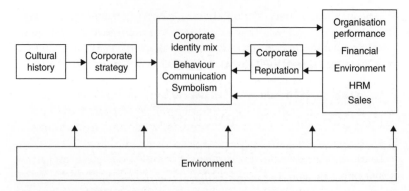

Figure 10.1   Factors determining corporate identity
Source: van Riel and Balmer, 1997.

corporate identity mix, corporate reputation and organizational performance, and that the environment in which the firm operates affects all
of these (Figure 10.1). It is obvious, therefore, that corporate identity
plays an important role in all parts of an organization.

The objective of this paper is to illustrate how prior consideration for
post-merger corporate identity can help avoid many of the 'soft' integration issues of a merger. Primarily, information was obtained from Renault
and Nissan published materials and documents, and from the Renault
website. In the next section we discuss the background to mergers,
acquisitions and strategic alliances. Next, we present the Renault-Nissan
alliance. We then apply the framework in relation to Renault-Nissan and
finally we present the conclusion.

Background to mergers, acquisitions and strategic alliances

The large number of mergers and acquisitions that have taken place in
international business over the past decade is well documented. They
have both accelerated the internationalization of industry and reshaped
industrial structure on the global level. Initially, these mergers were
concentrated in the United States. However, the adoption of the Anglo-
Saxon approach to business, including aggressive and hostile takeovers
such as TotalFinaElf (*The Economist*, 1999b) by many continental European firms has led to a dramatic increase in merger and acquisition
activity in Europe. This trend is highlighted by the fact that in 1999
the volume of European merger and acquisition (M&A) deals worth over
$1.5 trillion was greater than that of the United States for the first time
(*The Economist*, 2000a).

Nissan Almera. Ten common platforms are planned to be in use by 2010.

3. Powertrains – the joint use (and streamlining) of engines and gearboxes already has started. Renault is using Nissan's existing 3.5 litre V6 engine and its four-wheel drive transmission system. Nissan uses manual gearboxes and 1.5 and 1.9 dCi engines in their vehicles. By 2010, eight engine families and seven transmission families are planned to be shared.

4. Information systems – a joint Renault-Nissan Information Services was established in 2002 to enable efficient and reliable communications between the allies, especially to support convergence of information technology and systems to research and development processes.

5. Purchasing – the Renault-Nissan Purchasing Organization was created in April 2001 to put the joint purchasing policy in action in order to create savings of 70 per cent in the long term. A supplier quality-assurance program (Alliance New Product Quality Procedure) has been put into action.

6. Distribution – an aim of jointly taking 10 per cent of the world automobile market by 2010 has been made by harmonizing the two companies' distribution networks. This harmonization has already been achieved in seven western European markets (France, the United Kingdom, Germany, Spain, Italy, the Netherlands and Switzerland). The allies are also cooperating in the packaging and containers areas.

7. Research and advanced engineering - the allies jointly work on vehicle weight reduction, emission control, hybrid drive units, fuel cells and on-board telematics.

Through the alliance, Renault and Nissan have benefited from many of the hard aspects of a merger (as shown above) without having the difficulties of creating a new corporate identity or dealing with other soft issues, which so many mergers have struggled with in the past (for example, DaimlerChrysler). It is intended that within a few years the majority of the hard aspects between the two firms will be merged even further.

An outline of the likely corporate brand structure of Renault-Nissan, post-merger

The success of the strategic alliance between Renault and Nissan has suggested that a merger will certainly result in the near future. 'The executive boards of both companies have considered merging and decided that it must be the eventual goal, even though nobody talks publicly about it' (*The Economist*, 2000b). The likely structure of the merged company can be drawn from the existing alliance.

The head of the merged organization is predicted to be Carlos Ghosn, who has played key roles in both companies. It is likely to be a relative 'marriage of equals', perhaps with Renault playing the role of the slightly more dominant member given its status as such in the alliance. However, the group's strong brands (Renault and Nissan) would be kept separate at customer level, each with different car models (although based on the same platforms). They would, therefore, have a 'branded' corporate image as opposed to a 'monolithic' or 'endorsed' one, following Olins's (1995) categorization of corporate brands.

Applying the framework for corporate identity analysis to Renault-Nissan

As stated earlier, the strategic alliance between Renault and Nissan has meant that many of the hard issues of a merger have already been covered successfully; many aspects of design and production are already well integrated and joint information systems and a purchasing organization have already been established. This should bode well for all further aspects of hard integration when the merger takes place.

The Renault-Nissan strategic alliance did not necessitate addressing many soft issues; however, a full merger would require full cultural integration and, therefore, more consideration of these soft issues. As Melewar and Harrold (2000) have argued, corporate identity is a 'soft issue' that plays a vital role in merger and acquisition activity. They suggest that many soft merger issues could be identified and avoided by employing Melewar and Jenkins's (2000) model for corporate identity (Figure 10.4) to the firm and establishing a clear, new corporate identity that creates a strong sense of purpose for all stakeholders of the Renault-Nissan group.

In terms of the formation of a new corporate identity, the Renault-Nissan merger will clearly benefit from the pre-existing corporate relationship established through the alliance because the teams and departments from both firms have been working alongside each other since the turn of the millennium. The application of Melewar and Jenkins's (2000) framework to the group may illustrate the areas in which these benefits may be most apparent.

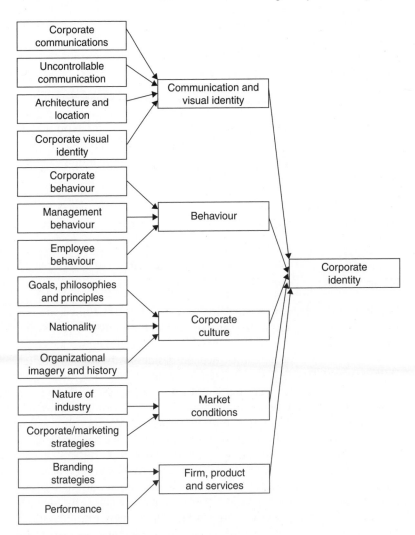

Figure 10.4 Framework for corporate identity analysis
Source: Melewar and Jenkins, 2000.

Corporate culture

Melewar and Jenkins (2000) suggest that culture is formed through a combination of the organization's goals, nationality and history. Ostensibly, it would seem that two companies from France and Japan would struggle to find similarities between cultures; however, as shown below, this is not the case.

Goals, philosophies and principles

Renault and Nissan are both based in the family-car market (saloons, hatchbacks, superminis) and have a certain pedigree. Their pricing policies are also similar, although Renault focuses slightly more on design and styling than Nissan. As the firms share the same product market, their brands are not necessarily complementary; however, they are well matched in terms of the location of their markets, as Nissan primarily operates in Asia and has a strong foothold in North America, while Renault operates almost entirely in Europe. Both firms have goals to spread internationally, as shown by their strategic alliance and are, therefore, ideally suited in this way.

Nationality

Despite being on separate sides of the world, the two firms' national differences are not substantial. Indeed, both nations are heavily bureaucratic and their governments are heavily protective of their workers. The strategic alliance will have provided both sides with a much greater appreciation for the other's differences, which will make integration far easier. One troublesome trait is both nations' resistance to change; however, this has caused no immediate problems for the alliance to date.

In terms of organizational culture, the firms are also surprisingly similar, as 'heavily bureaucratic, they were both staffed by former civil servants, long on sophistication and short on hard-nosed knowledge about how to make cars efficiently, and how to sell them' (*The Economist*, 2000b). Both firms have close relations with their governments [the French government retains a 25.9 per cent stake in Renault (Renault, 2003b)] and with unions, while remaining slightly distant to investors. Although they match, these traits are not all necessarily constructive in terms of running an efficient and successful business. Both firms have had significant financial trouble in the past. However, the conservative and bureaucratic attitude of both firms has been changed greatly by Carlos Ghosn, who is in charge of cross-company integration. His influence is an invaluable link between the firms because he has applied similar reforms to both companies' structures. Cross-company teams and departments have meant that both firms' structures have been aligned a great deal.

History

Renault was founded slightly earlier than Nissan (1898 as opposed to 1914), and both firms have varying histories with some common trends. Throughout its history Nissan has been based around family cars (small or large) and, although also centred on such production, Renault has also produced tanks (during the First and Second World Wars), heavy trucks and farm machinery. However, both companies have a strong racing heritage: Nissan primarily in American touring car racing and Renault in Formula 1 with the teams Williams-Renault and Renault F1. Neither firm has a history of luxury car production and both have always concentrated on automobiles for the mass market, with their brands representing reliability and value for money.

Behaviour

Corporate behaviour is, perhaps, less tangible and more difficult to measure than management and employee behaviour. However, they all derive from the aspects of culture explored above (Melewar and Harrold, 2000). As the cultures of the two car manufacturers were not as different as may have been expected, the firms' behavioural traits should converge with relative ease. This is supported by the notoriously strong leadership of Carlos Ghosn, the likely head of a merged Renault-Nissan organization. The dominant culture will more than likely be that of Renault, however, as the two cultures are so similar and Ghosn's influence has standardized the companies somewhat (with both companies now operating predominantly in English, for example). Any behavioural problems should therefore be minimized. As long as the dominant culture is decided upon early, Renault-Nissan should avoid the problems discovered by DaimlerChrysler which led the latter to a loss of key talent and morale.

Market conditions

Nature of the industry

The structure of the industry would not be overly affected by a Renault-Nissan merger as, although their products are complementary, the two companies predominantly operate in different geographical markets and would keep their separate brands. The evidence from the strategic alliance, which has not impacted the industry structure, supports this. However, the strong branding and marketing of the firms will have to be continued in order to avoid affecting customers and dealers.

Corporate and marketing strategy

Both brands are very strong due to reputations developed over many years. Maintaining the individual brands at dealership level and pursuing marketing plans segmented by brand should enable the brands to remain strong; this is supported by the fact that the two makes' markets are segmented geographically, if not necessarily in terms of product.

Communication and visual identity

Corporate visual identity

It is likely that the French and Japanese automobile companies will follow the example of DaimlerChrysler and become the Renault-Nissan group, forgoing their corporate logos. Corporate name, logotype or symbol, typography and colour define corporate visual identity, according to Melewar and Saunders (1999). As the two parties equally own the strategic alliance (www.renault.com), both Renault and Nissan kept their names in order to reduce any perception of loss or too much sacrifice on one side; this is considered a key determinant of the success of post-merger integration. Furthermore, this approach can help avoiding any possible weakened corporate image.

Renault-Nissan must keep the different brand identities separate from the corporate identity so that the final customer identifies with the individual brand and other audiences with the corporation. This 'branded' corporate image is shown in Figure 10.5.

Architecture and location

At consumer level (that is, dealerships) there should be no changes due to the branded corporate image. However, at levels dealing with other audiences (for example, headquarters, research and development centres and production sites), it is assumed that the Renault-Nissan logo should be used (as with DaimlerChrysler).

Corporate communications

It is vital in a merger to communicate intentions and important messages to all key stakeholders, including customers, investors, suppliers, employees, the media, the local community and the government, in order to gain their continued support. Corporate communication has been termed 'an instrument of management by means of which all consciously used forms of internal and external communication are harmonized as effectively and efficiently as possible, so as to create a

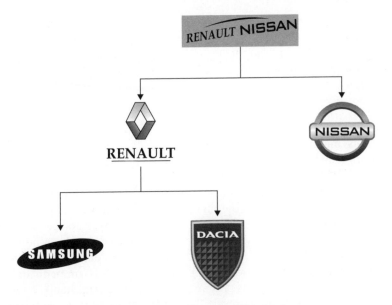

Figure 10.5 Renault-Nissan corporate visual identity structure

favourable basis for relationships upon which the company is dependent' (van Riel, 1995). The strategic alliance has laid these communication foundations. The Renault-Nissan strategic alliance, having focused upon these issues in the past, means that the eventual merger would greatly benefit from the corporate communication channels already in place.

Customers. As the structure at dealership level would not change, customers of the Renault-Nissan group should not be overly affected by the changes, providing strong branding is maintained. There would be no visible merger at dealership level; therefore, customer service should not be affected by the transformations ongoing at corporate level, which may help to maintain the strength of the brands.

Employees. This is an area where the prior strategic alliance could be beneficial to the merger. Employees need to have a strong sense of direction and an understanding of the corporate identity of the merged company; the strong leadership shown by Ghosn should enable this (and, therefore, help to safeguard key talent). Having already worked alongside each other during the alliance through cross-company teams, it is expected that the employees would have a better understanding of each other's cultures and would react well to any changes. Both companies have carried out redundancies before and during the alliance; therefore, few would be needed post-merger, ensuring good morale levels. The effect of Ghosn should not be under-estimated as he has already managed any political maneouvring during the alliance and has set the foundations for a smooth merger.

Investors. Both companies' investors (composed predominantly of private investors) seem focused on share-price performance and good improvements in shareholder returns, particularly now that the French government no longer has a controlling stake in Renault – formerly their share was 53.0 per cent but is now 25.9 per cent (*Investor Day*, 2002). This means that both sets of investors can be satisfied by the same corporate strategies, and the aim of the merged company must be to meet the shareholders' performance expectations and produce clear objectives (as they have produced for the strategic alliance). Having already witnessed the success of the alliance, investors can be confident of similar achievements with the merger. The influence of the French government could cause problems owing to its presumed wish for long-term stability and, therefore, employment; however, there have been no disagreements over the alliance, which should bode well for a potential merger.

Government, media and local communities. Corporate communication to these key stakeholders is vital in order to maintain good corporate and brand images. Renault-Nissan is a marriage of equals and the fact the two main brands are still maintained creates little negativity. The redundancies and plant closures normally associated with a merger have already occurred during the restructuring of the two companies before and during their strategic alliance and, therefore, few such negative aspects will reoccur after the merger, which is a considerable advantage. This should satisfy both the French and the Japanese governments.

Suppliers. Renault-Nissan's clear strategic direction is in the direction of joint procurement. By 2003, Renault-Nissan Purchasing Organization already made 70 per cent of the group's purchasing requirements (Renault, 2003a) and the use of joint platforms and parts for similar models show that substantial benefits can be (and have been) achieved in this domain. The prior strategic alliance will clearly aid the merged company in this respect.

Renault and Nissan's prior strategic alliance should benefit the corporate communication of the merged group in relation to all stakeholders. Primarily this is because many difficult issues that can adversely affect corporate communication have already been dealt with (for example, redundancies) and key stakeholders have a complete understanding of the strategic direction of the firm due to the coherent communication during the alliance phase.

Firm, product and services

Brand strategies and performance

Strong branding, separating both the two main brands from each other and from the corporate image or brand, is crucial (as mentioned in the Communication and Visual Identity section), to the success and strength of the merged company. Good corporate communication and development of a focused corporate identity by Renault-Nissan (aided greatly by the prior strategic alliance) may motivate and safeguard key talent who can install each individual brand ethos in the car models and marketing, thereby maintaining the strong brands. As stated in a Renault-Nissan press release (Renault, 2003a), 'the consequences of an unfocused corporate identity, resulting in the loss of key talent. . . [could affect the merged firm's] . . . ability to maintain these brand values'.

Conclusion

The application of Melewar and Jenkins's (2000) framework in analysing the theoretical corporate identity of a post-merger Renault-Nissan has suggested that a future full merger between the two companies should be successful on corporate-identity grounds. That is to say, that the firms are a good fit in the majority of model areas with very few areas of significant contrast. Under the strong leadership of Carlos Ghosn, this should lead to the development of a sound corporate identity helping to avoid many of problems associated with the 'soft issues' of integration that often thwart merger and acquisition attempts. The exact roles of the two players within the merged company will have to be more accurately defined, but it must be noted that the Renault-Nissan alliance is exceptionally strong and close, which implies that a future merger is highly likely to be successful.

The model has highlighted the numerous advantageous effects of a prior strategic alliance in the formation of a post-merger corporate identity. Aspects of the model particularly benefiting from the alliance include corporate communication (to all key stakeholders), organizational culture and behaviour. The previous corporate relationship between the firms has meant that key stakeholders (particularly employees) have a clear sense of the direction of the group and, having worked alongside each other during the alliance period, they have an understanding of their partner's differing cultures. The closeness of the relationship before entering into the full merger means that many of the difficult soft issues of integration have already been dealt with (for example, redundancies), which clearly puts the firms in a better position than those with no previous levels of cooperation.

One obvious limitation of this study is that it is carried out on a strategic alliance that, as yet, has not fully merged, making some aspects of the argument more theoretical than they would otherwise be if a full merger had occurred. Many strategic alliances are predicted to become full mergers in the future; however, as they are relatively new, few have done so as yet. This means that there a very few examples to support the ideas forwarded in this paper.

It would clearly be interesting to carry out a similar study when Renault and Nissan have actually merged in order to identify which areas in the formation of a new identity were actually aided by the prior strategic alliance. In a more general sense, a study into the success rate of mergers that have developed directly from prior alliances would be informative, particularly in comparing whether post-merger soft integration benefited from the prior corporate relationship.

Appendix 10.1: The Strathclyde Statement

Every organisation has an identity. It articulates the corporate ethos, aims and values and presents a sense of individuality that can help to differentiate the organisation within its competitive environment.

When well managed, corporate identity can be a powerful means of integrating the many disciplines and activities essential to an organisation's success. It can also provide the visual cohesion necessary to ensure that all corporate communications are coherent with each other and result in an image consistent with the organisation's ethos and character.

By effectively managing its corporate identity an organisation can build understanding and commitment among its diverse stakeholders. This can be manifested in an ability to attract and retain customers and employees, achieve strategic alliances, gain the support of financial markets and generate a sense of direction and purpose. Corporate identity is a strategic issue.

Corporate identity differs from traditional brand marketing since it is concerned with all of an organisation's stakeholders and the multifaceted way in which an organisation communicates.

Source: Balmer, 2001, pp. 248–91.

References

Balmer, J. M. T. (2001) 'Corporate Identity, Corporate Branding and Corporate Marketing: Seeing Through the Fog', *European Journal of Marketing*, 35 (3/4), pp. 248–91.

Booz-Allen & Hamilton Inc. (2001) 'Merger Integration: Delivering on the Promise', *Investor Day*, 24 July.

Economist, The (1999a) 'Renissant?', 18 March.

Economist, The (1999b) 'Merger à la Française', 16 September.

Economist, The (2000a), 'Marriage à la Mode' 29 April.

Economist, The (2000b), 'On the Rocky Road to Marriage', 18 May.

Economist Global Executive, The (2002) 'With Allies Like These', 22 April.

Harbison, J. R., A. Viscio, P. Pekar and D. Moloney (2000) 'The Allianced Enterprise: Breakout Strategy for the New Millennium', *Viewpoint*, Booz-Allen & Hamilton Inc.

Investor Day (2002) 24 September.

Kelly, J., C. Cook and D. Spitzer (1999) 'Unlocking Shareholder Value: The Keys to Success', KPMG Global Research Report, at www.kpmg.com, last visited 11/10/06.

Melewar, T. C. and J. Harrold (2000) 'The Role of Corporate Identity in Merger and Acquisition Activity', *Journal of General Management*, 26 (2), pp. 17–32.

Melewar, T. C. and E. Jenkins (2000) 'Defining Corporate Identity: The Search for a Holistic Model', *Advanced Issues in Marketing* (Warwick Business School) pp. 1–25.

Melewar, T. C. and J. Saunders (1999) 'International Corporate Visual Identity: Standardisation or Localisation?', *Journal of International Business Studies*, 30 (3) pp. 583–98.

Nissan (2003) Press Release, 27 February, www.nissan-global.com, last visited 11/10/2006.

Olins, W. (1995) *Corporate Identity: Making Business Strategy Visible Through Design* (London: Thames and Hudson).

Renault (1999) *Annual Report 1999*, www.renault.com, last visited 11/10/2006.

Renault (2000) *Annual Report 2000*, www.renault.com, last visited 11/10/2006.

Renault (2003a) 'Renault-Nissan Purchasing Organization va Réaliser 70 per cent des Achats de l'Alliance', Press Release, Renault-Nissan Group, 1 October, www.renault.com/presse, last visited 11/10/2006.

Renault (2003b) *Atlas 2003*, www.renault.com, last visited 11/10/2006.

Renault (2004a) *Atlas 2004*, www.renault.com, last visited 11/10/2006.

Renault (2004b) *Atlas September 2004*, www.renault.com, last visited 11/10/2006

Renault-Nissan Alliance (2004) *Report 2004*, www.renault.com, last visited 11/10/2006.

van Riel, C. (1995) *Principles of Corporate Communication* (New York: Prentice Hall).

van Riel, C. and J. M. T. Balmer (1997) 'Corporate Identity: The Concept, Its Measurement and Management', *European Journal of Marketing*, 31 (5/6), pp. 340–53.

11

Corporations as Storytellers – Stakeholders as Image Builders: Towards Impressive Corporate Communication

Roy Langer and Richard J. Varey

Abstract

Studies of national images and identities suggest a careful consideration of historical and contextual aspects when planning, mastering and
evaluating corporate images and identities – including a classification
of image types. We argue for a reconsideration of these contributions
if corporate communication is to be other than auto-communication,
fixes or acronyms. Our discussion draws on company examples such as
Hamburg-Mannheimer, Rambøll, Shell, Burger King and Scandinavian
Airlines.

Communication theory and reception analysis suggest an understanding of corporate communication more as a common domain than as
a specific management device or scientific management technique. By
understanding communication as dialogue, corporate communication
should be understood from the impression side and corporate images
should be considered from a stakeholder perspective. Corporate images
are bound to the corporation's discursive history and the social memory of the respective public. They cannot be changed like products or
product images, because they have to be based on coherence and consistency between a corporation's business foundation, its culture and its
identity. To communicate this unique and distinct relationship should
be the future focus of corporate communication.

Introduction

Image is reality
(Bernstein, 1984, p. 1)
Control is an illusion, and messages belong to those who listen
(Knuf, 1999, p. 28)

We examine the basis for managing identities, images, and communication through a review of corporate discourse from the perspective of media studies and research on national images.

We start with a short case. The German insurance corporation Hamburg-Mannheimer entered the Danish insurance market in 1997. Hitherto, this market had been nationally monopolized, shared among major Danish insurance corporations. But in 1998 this German corporation captured almost 70 per cent of all newly signed Danish life-insurance contracts. With this explosive growth and instant market presence Hamburg-Mannheimer became one of the big players in the Danish insurance market within a year.

Just a few months after the move, the situation again changed profoundly. The German corporation was very busy in launching a major image campaign, with corporate advertisements in all major Danish media. In its campaign, the corporation was trying to convince stakeholders and stockholders about the seriousness and honesty of their sales employees and about the competitive advantages and quality of their products. Despite these attempts, the corporation's image seemed to be heavily damaged and future prospects withered compared to just four months earlier. What happened?

In December 1998, the Danish magazine *Money and Private Economy* published an article about the entry of Hamburg-Mannheimer into the Danish market for life assurance. Under the title 'A Bad Offer from Germany', the corporation's sales strategy and sales methods, and the product itself, were the subject of major criticism.

On 17 and 18 January 1999, Danish public service *TV-channel DR 1* covered the topic in its major evening news programme. Hamburg-Mannheimer was accused of 'pyramid selling' practices and using misleading information about its non-competitive products. Furthermore, its salespersons were accused of lacking education and knowledge about the product and the market. Thus the initial dramatic success of Hamburg-Mannheimer could – according to the journalists – mainly be explained by irresponsible business methods and bad ethics in promising potential customers the moon and the stars. To document these accusations, the TV journalists had recorded salesmen in action, using hidden cameras and other undercover methods. A week later, the corporation reacted and initiated crisis management by producing one-page image advertisements in all the major daily Danish newspapers, answering directly all the accusations one by one by presenting its own perspective on the issues raised. According to the corporation, just the fact of being Germany's second-largest life insurance corporation, with six million satisfied customers, could guarantee quality and seriousness. 'We are totally sure' is the headline.

But just a few weeks later, on 1 March, another 45-minute programme on the same TV channel once again documented the earlier accusations. This time, journalists even smuggled an 'undercover agent' with a hidden camera into the organization. Here he attended a course in sales techniques, where the trainer instructed the sales persons as follows: 'Sales technique is actually manipulation, if one takes it totally down to bottom. If you use sales technique consistently, it is manipulation, and if you are really good at it, you can get people to buy almost everything.' (Denmarks Radio, 1999b)

A psychologist (presented as a communication expert) called these instructions 'mental rape' and 'psychopathic behaviour'. The makers of the programme used the same perspective, labelling the video clips from the hidden camera with expressions such as 'sales weapons' and 'tricks used on innocent victims'. Likewise, the salesmen of the corporation were presented as 'damned effective' and 'unscrupulous brain-washing' agents. After the programme, leading spokesmen of the Association of Insurance and Pension (Corporations) – *Hamburg-Mannheimer* is by law a member of this association – declared that they wished to exclude the corporation.

There are no official statistics available to tell us about the economic costs of the crisis for Hamburg-Mannheimer. Up to a point, the company later gained rehabilitation by the fact that the makers of the programme were charged by the Danish police for manipulating documents and translations from German to Danish in the programme. Also, the journalists responsible received serious criticism from other media professionals and professional organisations for their investigative methods. But apart from this, there can be no doubt that the public media debate had a major negative effect on the reputation and – in the end – on the sales figures of the company.

We need not here detail our interpretation of the journalist's reports or the corporation's responses to them. Neither do we evaluate the quality of the corporation in question or the quality of its products.

Instead, we focus attention on some interesting general aspects in this case:

- Firstly, the public scandal about Hamburg-Mannheimer tells the observer something about the relationship between the media and business life. In getting and presenting a story, journalists are increasingly using an agenda defined beforehand (including the conclusion of the whole story). Furthermore (and related to this), an increasing use of unconventional methods, such as undercover research including hidden cameras, can be observed.
- Secondly, the case illustrates the cultural dependency of a corporation's image. The sales strategy of Hamburg-Mannheimer, primarily based on direct customer contact in his/her private surroundings (door-to-door sales), is, if not popular, at least acceptable in the former West Germany. It is vulnerable to criticism, however, in Denmark, where this strategy is unusual. But this sales strategy is one of the basics of the corporation's existence, of its identity, culture and business foundation. Thus, this case illustrates a discrepancy between a company's foundation and its culture-bound image.
- Thirdly, this case illustrates national images. Research by one author (Langer) on images of Germany and Germans during recent years shows clearly that being a German corporation penetrating the Danish market makes things more difficult for the corporation, because of existing negative images in the general Danish public. As Bernstein (1984, pp. 122–4) suggested, a corporation's image can be affected by the country of origin or the industry of which the corporation is part.

There is an increasing number of similar examples showing corporations fighting for their image, working on damage control, and conducting crisis management (for example, Shell, Texaco or McDonald's). The crisis threshold for negative media exposure has fallen due to sociocultural changes (political consumerism) and due to changes in the agenda of journalism (changing news values). But, in addition, the increasing strategic use of the public media by corporations in order to gain competitive advantage through image-building (of one's own corporation) and image-eroding (of competitors) processes is contributing to this development. Thus media awareness seems to be a two-edged sword, both enforcing and spreading a corporation's positive image and endangering it. Most examples of crisis management and damage control illustrate vividly how difficult (or maybe even impossible) it seems to be to manage corporate images and corporate communication, thus questioning the widespread faith in the ability (of anyone) to control communication and its effects.

We suggest that certain historical-identity aspects of some corporations (including their national origin) might expose these corporations more than others to be in the firing line of critical media awareness. Moreover, and as one of the consequences of these aspects, we suggest a clear distinction between different types of images, based on an analysis of a corporation's historically grown identity. Our scepticism towards the ability to control communication is founded in our respective research backgrounds which motivated us to collaborate when entering the field of corporate communication and corporate-reputation management. Whereas one author has worked on issues in marketing, critical communication theory and sustainable development in both the UK and New Zealand, the other author has a professional background from media, communication and cultural studies in Germany and Denmark. These backgrounds motivate our scepticism towards large parts of the managerial literature on corporate images and corporate communication, as we reflect upon how corporate discourse about images can be informed by insights into the nature of images and their construction in and by communication from other research traditions. Hence, this chapter examines how insights from cultural studies on national images and identity and from media studies could enrich the discourse about corporate culture, by asking four questions:

- How can the relationship between identity, images, culture and communication be described and explained conceptually?
- Are all images the same in terms of stability and mode of construction?
- Which basic understanding of, and perspective on, communication should be the foundation for the discourse about corporate communication?
- Which objectives can be raised for further practice and research on corporate communication?

Images – empirical and conceptual findings from cultural studies

The Hamburg-Mannheimer example illustrates the confluence of national and corporate images. National images used in marketing communication can have a spill-over effect on product or corporate images (such as when positive values or national symbols are transferred to the product or its producer). Apart from this, the long tradition of cultural studies on national images and identities seems also to offer other relevant insights for the discourse about corporate images and identities and vice versa, as branding techniques from corporate life become increasingly important in building up and maintaining certain national images. In line with this, London-based PR expert Wally Olins argued in his book *Trading Identities. Why Countries and Companies are Taking Each Others' Roles* (Olins, 1999) that learning from each other's experiences makes sense, because nations increasingly adopt corporate techniques, whereas companies increasingly take over responsibilities (such as social and environmental care) formerly exclusively seen as duties of the state.

The importance of images as the communication of identities is increasingly recognized. Media researcher Neil Postman (1986), for example, described the shift from a word-centred culture to an image-centred culture, where verbal communication is replaced by (mainly visual) images as points of orientation in social-life domains. (Visual) images transcend linguistic barriers and will most likely be the medium of the future. Christensen (1994, p. 163) characterizes this process as follows:

> We are living in a time where communication and identity are two sides to the same story, where each form of existence seems to be dependent on what can be expressed about its existence, and where professional communication therefore becomes a decisive dimension in the individual's organising principles (translation by Langer).

From 1995 to 1999, one author empirically studied Danish constructions of 'Germany' and 'Germans' in Danish media discourses (Langer, 2000). This research was based on an empirical data corpus of around 4000 texts gathered from all major Danish newspapers and TV channels. These media texts were subjected to a quantitative analysis aimed at identifying topical and narrative macro-structures of image constructions. Certain discursive strands were chosen for qualitative in-depth textual analysis. The topical selection of these strands was based on which themes had been identified by previous research as crucial in Danish images of Germans and Germany. To ensure a historical dimension in the analysis of the pre-understanding and context of these images, further texts constituting the history of these discourse strands were included in the analysis.

The starting point for the study was an expectation that changing sociocultural surroundings – in this case the end of the post-war period — would enforce new constructions of national images and identities in Europe. Actually, the empirical findings could not confirm this expectation, at least not in terms of a rather fast and fundamental change of historically grown images. Only minor changes could be observed, and both images and identities appeared to be rather stable and resistant to sociocultural change. Danish constructions of Germans and Germany mainly continued historically grown and negative stereotypes and images. On the other hand, the positive image of German industrial products did not change either – despite Germany's economic crisis since the early 1990s.

Thus, the study confirmed several conceptualisations of national cultures, identities and images in the literature on cultural studies of nationalism and ethnicity. As in other research communities, scholars working on national identities and images have had a long, and still ongoing, discussion about whether or not (national) culture is something innate, something people have, or something people construct, i.e., whether there exist national characters or national habits, or whether national identity is just something people choose.

Most of the scholars (for example, Anderson, 1991; Billig, 1995; Eriksen, 1993; Langer, 2000) in this research community agree that national cultures, identities and images are social products of continuous reconstruction processes. But these are neither arbitrary nor random constructions. Rather, they should be seen as constructions that are dependent on a number of sociocultural and historical aspects. Thus, culture can be seen as a complex programme for the interpretation of social surroundings, depending on the actual context; pre-understandings (social memory knowledge) and ongoing constructions.

Culture consists of control mechanisms, rules and conventions for the plurality of choices from which individuals can select when trying to establish and interpret concrete interrelationships through actions. It is materialized in socially relevant applications when it reaches the public sphere, and these media play a decisive role in the construction processes of cultural identities (Schmidt, 1996, pp. 9–10). These constructions are shaped by historical discursive sediments creating a pre-understanding of the topic, by the concrete setting of the communicative or discursive event (situational context), and by the broader sociocultural context in which these reconstruction processes take place.

Hence, the construction of images and identities does not start from scratch and is part of the cultural programme. In the study of Danish media images of Germany, one author could observe discursive sediments of historical experiences determining the current construction of identities and images. Here, references pointing back to historical events occurring 50 years or even 125 years ago play an important role in the current reproduction of identities and images. Most European constructions of national identities and images are basically a result of specific sociocultural changes during the 19th century. Starting among intellectuals at the end of the 18th century, nationalism became the religion of modernity during the last century. Ernest Gellner (1998, p. 94) described it as 'a phenomenon of *Gesellschaft* using the idiom of *Gemeinschaft*: a mobile anonymous society simulating a closed cosy community'. The construction of national identities is based on the construction of a national history, traditions, rituals and myths, and a definition of common values and rules that are designed to connect everyday life with a national destiny.

In the case of Danish national identity this construction process was mainly based on constructing and pinpointing the differences with Germans and Germany. Simultaneously, certain images of Germany and certain Danish self-images were constructed. These images were to become revitalized at the dawn of the third millennium, when national identities are under pressure because of sociocultural change (increasing mobility, globalization). Instead of new image constructions, the empirical findings indicated an increasing use of references to the grounding myths of Danish national identity and Danish social memory.

Dröge (1967, pp. 151-3) offers a distinction between different types of images that might be helpful in interpreting their reproduction, as he distinguishes between persistent images, culture-epochal images, and images that are determined and can be changed by current developments. In this typology, national images can be defined as culture-epochal images as they go hand-in-hand with the construction of the nation state. They are not persistent images, as modern nation states have only existed for 200 to 300 years. Neither are national images flimsy and weak constructions underlying fundamental changes caused by current events. Culture-epochal images are an integrated part of a culture. They can only change in part, but never fundamentally – unless the very foundations of the culture are changing. In this context, it seems worthwhile to note that the majority of researchers are rather sceptical when evaluating the ability to manage images in terms of national 'public-relations' initiatives (cf. Langer, 2002). Cultures and identities can be changed by those who construct them, but images belong to the public(s) or stakeholders and not to those who are connoted by them (except auto-images).

Summing up then, we find that cultural studies on national images portrayed in the media can inform our understanding of corporate culture, identity and images. This research shows them as being shaped by historical discursive sediments creating pre-understandings, the concrete setting of the communicative or discursive event (situational context), and the broader sociocultural context in which these reconstruction processes take place. Hence, there is a complex interrelationship between culture, identity and image, in which both real history and the discourse history of these images are important additives in their ongoing reproduction by stakeholders. Although we recognize the complex interrelationship between culture, identity and image, we will in what follows focus on attempts to apply corporate communication in corporate image work (note specifically Cornelissen, 2002a and 2002b, and Gioia, Schultz and Corley, 2002a and 2002b, for recent debates about the concept of organizational identity).

The concept of image in corporate literature

According to a Danish communication expert Christensen (2002, p. 29), strategic development of corporate communication starts with an analysis of the corporate image pyramid (Figure 11.1).

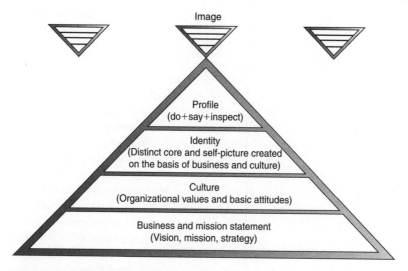

Figure 11.1   Christensen's image pyramid
Source: Christensen, 2002.

On the most basic level in the existence of each corporation, we find its ideational business foundation – selling life insurance door-to-door, for example. This foundation gives birth to a particular corporate structure and culture, based on assumptions and values, and expressed in norms and traditions directing the patterns of interactions. For example, the members of the sales staff of an insurance corporation are called 'partners'; these partners do not get any regular fixed salary but only commission from their sales. A corporation's identity can be seen as its conscious self-image, and the profile is those parts of the identity that the corporation emphasizes in its external communication in attempting to gain a certain image among consumers and the corporation's shareholders and other stakeholders. Finally, image is defined as 'a mental template that reflects the company as if it was a person with a foundation (source), culture (behaviour), distinct core (why it is here) and profile. One's own picture is always influenced by the view of the others (the public reputation of the company)' (Christensen, 2002, p. 29).

This image pyramid is seen as the basic condition of communication management aiming to convince shareholders, employees and other stakeholders of a corporation's image. However, in much corporate literature, corporate communication is seen just as a management and marketing instrument in order 'to find an identity', as a senior representative from the German Drägerwerk AG declared (Böttcher, 1991, pp. 5–6) or, as German researcher Baumann (1991, p. 7) states, in order 'to support an increase in the efficiency of labour among the employees'.

The sender perspective

Most researchers and executives seem to share what is known in communication and media studies as the 'sender perspective', declaring corporate communication as a managerial tool constructed by their own chosen actions and with planned, deliberate, intended effects. External communication is seen as a matter of techniques and, in its most radical form, this extreme self-confidence as a sender is expressed in handbook titles such as *How to Handle the Media* (Macnamara, 1996). This is also true for most parts of the corporate storytelling literature, which is often based on a structuralist approach to storytelling and branding developed in the 1950s and 1960s (Heugens, 2002; Langer and Thorup, 2006). Subsequent developments in narrativity and communication research arguing in favour of models that are less controlled by the sender and less schematic (for example, Varey, 2002a, 2000b, 2003), have had little influence on research-based corporate storytelling discourse that often expresses managements' version of corporate stories (Denning, 2000,

2004, 2005; Jensen, 1999; Kunde, 2001). Organisations are viewed from the management perspective as bodies: the management is the head, deciding how the other body parts should behave, and by monitoring and standardizing internal and external communication 'the values discipline the corporate body by collective seduction' (Christensen and Morsing, 2005, p. 102).

As a result, very often there is a discrepancy between the proudly presented 'us-feeling' as documented in high-gloss corporation brochures and corporate stories on the one hand, and employee identification and integration mainly based on voluntary submission to formal pressures and adaptation on the other (Rieger, 1991). Being aware of these differences also involves awareness of the concept of power in regard to the launching, implementation and apprehension of corporate policies.

For example, in 1995 the Danish corporation Rambøll, a firm of contractors and consulting engineers with about 2000 employees, announced its new holistic management philosophy. This value-based philosophy was based on opinion formation in the corporation and focused on the corporation's image and employees' and customers' satisfaction as potentials for future success. Starting as an idea labelled 'systematic common sense' by the managing director, the new philosophy was the prerogative of the top management during the first couple of years. Later the holistic philosophy was communicated throughout the organization, in top-down processes. But a recent investigation among the employees showed that holistic and value-based management has not changed much at the bottom of the organization. 'Holism is something for the corporation,' said a blue-collar interviewee commenting on the recent development, meaning, when referring to 'the corporation', the management group. Another interviewee added that in her opinion, employees had been listened to more before the era of 'holistic management' (Denmarks Radio, 1999a).

This sender perspective, the foundation for the change to holistic management at Rambøll, can also be found in most of the literature on corporate communication and identity (Varey, 2000a). Thus corporate communication is in danger of becoming nothing more than one-way communication (which in fact is not communication but information distribution) or, as Christensen (1994) described it, even self-referential auto-communication, where the corporation is both the sender and receiver in corporate communication processes. In both cases, corporate communication is not real communication in the sense of dialogic exchange (Ballantyne and Varey, 2006). As a result, it becomes difficult to distinguish corporate communication from traditional public relations, as has been discussed for some years now (Lewis, 1998; Thomson, 1997; Grunig, 1993a), instead of viewing corporate communication as communication in the tradition of Kennedy (1977). The sender perspective's intention to control and predict communication has been criticized in the wider management literature (Cornelissen, 1999; Grunig, 1999; Knuf, 1999; Varey, 2000a), but it remains strong. Communication is widely taken to mean the transmission of information and the reproduction of intended meanings. This view is premised on ancient classical assumptions of causality and linearity – of absolute and classifying categories – instead of relative and relational categories. Such a basis introduces intentions and causality into our understanding of communication. This reductionist thinking is seen vividly in stimulus-response models of human influence that do not adequately explain human interaction.

The interaction perspective

Social-constructionist thinking (see Gergen, 1999; Langer, 1999; Varey, 2000a, 2000b, 2006, for example) sees the world as a complex set of interrelated social phenomena constructed by people in interaction, that is, in joint social action. A wealth of constructive thinking can be discovered in Nordic, Germanic and eastern sociologies and social philosophies (see Langer, 1999, for a Nordic and Germanic perspective). This is an alternative to the western psychological perspective in management thinking that is both dominant and misleading (Varey, 2000a). Circular (interactional) rather than linear (transmissive) models are more helpful in understanding human communication and what is required for responsive and responsible management of communication for productive business enterprise. Causal assumptions can be discarded in taking a view of communication in and of corporations (that is, 'corporative communication') as both stimulator and stabilizer. However, social, political and cultural phenomena can be more richly understood if their linguistic and discursive (interactive) nature is addressed with a constructionist perspective on social reality. Communication cannot be understood without reference to knowledge, understanding, information, meaning and sense. A social constructionist theory of communication is a broadened framework for the analysis of communication in a complex and holistic fashion.

Images revisited

Christensen (1994) explains that images are weak, floating, relational, flexible and flimsy constructions without any direct relation to reality, and that images have to be renewed constantly through communication. Thus he is repeating one of the key themes in postmodernist thinking. And indeed, social and personal identities seem weaker and less lasting than ever before. Still, maybe this impression does not come from a lack of inner consistency or stability – perhaps people are just increasingly changing between different identities.

But corporate images are not at all weak and flimsy. At least, they do not have to be and they should not be, if they aim to be other than self-referential auto-communication. As Bernstein (1984) suggests, images have to be consistent and have to be related to a corporation's identity and culture. And they are bound to the public and not bound to what the corporation believes:

> Strictly speaking a corporation cannot create an image. Only a public can 'create' an image in that it consciously or unconsciously selects the thoughts and impressions on which that image is based ... The corporation cannot create the image. It can create the elements of the identity for the corporation (and all the identity for the brand) (Bernstein, 1984, p. 56).

More recently, Cornelissen (1999) and Grunig (1993b) described images in a similar way as perceptions and interpretations on the receiver's side. The common use of the term 'perception' to mean understanding is dealt with by Vickers (1984), for example, who talks of *appreciation* to extend our explanation of the cognitive process beyond data capture to include interpretation and judgment or evaluation that leads to choice in courses of action. Knuf (1999) frames this agenda by saying that it is time to consider corporate communication from an *impression* paradigm, one that favours recipiency, interpretation and relational continua. In such an agenda, storylines, discursive sediments, myths and the processes of semiosis among stakeholders are key issues for communicative practice and analysis.

Taylor's (1993) socio-semiotic approach tries to reconcile the opposing functionalist and interpretive movements by concentrating on the organising properties of communication (see also Cooren, Taylor and van Every, 2006). Corporations can then be seen as symbolic processes and social facts, as co-operative systems in pursuit of common interests and goals, and as an array of fractionalized groups with diverse purposes and goals.

Bernstein's distinction between the construction of brand images and the construction of corporate images has to be underlined. Perhaps the very core of corporate images (that is, their basis in organizational foundations and organizational culture) is forgotten when talking about the constant adjustment of corporate image to changing conditions of existence. Neglect of history and the very business foundation as the determining aspects of corporate image makes it impossible for corporations to make the whole discourse about corporate communication fruitful. Maybe this discussion is similar to the debate maintained between public relations and integrated marketing communication, and maybe we should look back again at ideas that were considered novel in the early 1980s but that did not enjoy the sustained research that could have supported them as viable constructs (cf. Grunig, 1999). In this pursuit, we can refer back to Bernstein's classic book *Image and Reality: A Critique of Corporate Communication* (1984), in which the author drew on interpersonal face-to-face communication (instead of mass communication) to model corporate communication (Rosengren, 2000 suggests the application of a definition of human communication in this direction, also).

Changes in form are not sufficient if the content and purpose are wrong. Moreover, respect for the historical and cultural dimension makes sense, both in regard to the case of the sales strategy of the German insurance corporation in Denmark or – to take the best known example for discussing image crisis and damage control – the case of Shell. As media research has pointed out, there can be no doubt that certain features in a corporation's history may increase its susceptibility to scandal (see, for example, Lull and Hinerman, 1997, p. 11). In the case of Shell, the continuing resonance with the public of the corporation's activities in southern Africa during the apartheid era in the 1980s contributed to the successful strategy by grassroots environmental organisations to paint Shell in a bad light during the 1990s. Thus, Shell's own history and actions make the corporation more vulnerable to scandal than many others, and only a real break in the policies of the corporation (and not only the image policies and activities which took place during the 1990s) will avoid the necessity of new crisis-management activities in future. Or, as Sutton (1998, p. 13) puts it:

> Market conditions will change, strategies will need to be constantly evolved. But there are certain fundamentals of corporate communications which must stay constant over time if we want our businesses to be truly understood by audiences. And the biggest fundamental of all is a senior management which is seen to know where it's going and communicates a consistent vision and mission to prove it.

Communication, BNFL Corporate Communication Unit, The Management School, University of Salford, UK

Hatch, M. J. and M. Schultz (2003) 'Bringing the Corporation Back into Corporate Branding', *European Journal of Marketing*, 37 (7/8), pp. 1041–64.

Heugens, P. (2002) 'Managing Public Affairs through Storytelling', *Journal of Public Affairs*, 2 (2), pp. 57–70.

Jensen, R. (1999) *The Dream Society: How the Coming Shift from Information to Imagination will Transform Your Business* (New York: McGraw-Hill).

Kennedy, S. H. (1977) 'Nurturing Corporate Images: Total Communication or Ego Trip?', *European Journal of Marketing*, 31 (5/6), pp. 396–409.

Knox, S. and D. Bickerton (2003) 'The Six Conventions of Corporate Branding', *European Journal of Marketing*, 37 (7/8), pp. 998–1016.

Knuf, J. (1999) 'Re-thinking Corporate Communication', in R. J. Varey (ed.) *Excellence in Communication Management*, Proceedings of the 4th International Conference in Corporate and Marketing Communication, BNFL Corporate Communication Unit, The Management School, University of Salford, UK.

Kunde, J. (2000) *Corporate Religion – Building A Strong Company through Personality and Corporate Soul* (Tokyo: Financial Times Prentice Hall).

Langer, R. (1999) 'Towards a Constructivist Communication Theory? Report from Germany', *Nordicom Information*, 1–2, pp. 75–86.

Langer, R. (2000) *Die Darstellung Deutschlands in dänischen Medien* (Wiesbaden: Deutscher Universitätsverlag).

Langer, R. (2002) 'Place Images and Place Marketing', in J. Helder and S. U. Kragh (eds) *Senders and Receivers. New Perspectives on Market Communication* (Copenhagen: Samfundslitteratur) pp. 25–58.

Langer, R. and S. Thorup (2006) 'Building Trust in Times of Crisis. Storytelling and Change Communication in an Airline Company', *Corporate Communications – An International Journal*, 11 (4), pp. 371–90.

Larsen, M. H. and M. Schulz (1998) *Den Udtryksfulde Virksomhed* (København: Bergsøe 4).

Lewis, S. (1997) 'Strategic Overview: Where We Are Ahead', in T. R. V. Foster and A. Jolly (eds) *Corporate Communications Handbook* (London: Kogan Page), pp. 3–6.

Lippman, W. (1929/1961) *Public Opinion* (New York: Macmillan Corporation).

Lull, J. and S. Hinerman (1997) 'The Search for Scandal', in J. Lull and S. Hinerman (eds) *Media Scandals: Morality and Desire in the Popular Culture Marketplace* (Cambridge: Polity Press), pp. 1–33.

Macnamara, J. (1996) *How to Handle the Media* (London: Prentice-Hall).

Olins, W. (1999) *Trading Identities: Why Countries and Companies are Taking Each Others' Roles* (London: The Foreign Policy Center).

Postman, N. (1986) *Amusing Ourselves to Death* (London: Heinneman).

Rieger, B. (1991) 'Janus-faced Corporate Identity', in T. Bungarten (ed.) *Concepts of Business Communication, Corporate Culture & Corporate Identity* (Tostedt: Attikon Verlag), pp. 140–68.

Rolke, L. (1999) 'Die Gesellschaftliche Kernfunktion von Public Relations – ein Beitrag zur Kommunikationswissenschaftlichen Theoriediskussion', *Publizistik*, 44. Jahrgang (Dezember), pp. 431–44.

Rosengren, K. E. (2000) *Communication: An Introduction* (London: Sage).

Schmidt, S. J. (1996) *Konstruktivismus als Medientheorie* (Siegen: Lumis).

Stuart, H. and L. Muzellec (2004) 'Corporate Makeovers: Can a Hyena be Rebranded?', *Journal of Brand Management*, 11 (6), pp. 472–82.

Sutton, T. (1997) 'Management of Reputation', in T. R. V. Foster and A. Jolly (eds) *Corporate Communications Handbook* (London: Kogan Page), pp. 13–16.

Taylor, J. R. (1993) *Rethinking the Theory of Organizational Communication: How to Read an Organization* (Norwood: Ablex Publishing Corporation).

Thompson, J. B. (1997) 'Scandal and Social Theory', in J. Lull and S. Hinerman (eds) *Media Scandals: Morality and Desire in the Popular Culture Marketplace* (Cambridge: Polity Press), pp. 34–64.

Thomson, K. (1997) 'Meeting Today's Audience Expectations', in T. R. V. Foster and A. Jolly (eds) *Corporate Communications Handbook* (London: Kogan Page), pp. 7–11.

Tomlinson, J. (1997) '"And besides, the Wench is Dead": Media Scandals and the Globalization of Communication', in J. Lull and S. Hinerman (eds) *Media Scandals: Morality and Desire in the Popular Culture Marketplace* (Cambridge: Polity Press), pp. 65–85.

Ulrich, P. (1995) 'Business in the Nineties: Facing Public Interest', in P. Ulrich and C. Sarasin, *Facing Public Interest* (Dordrecht: Kluwer Academic Publishers), pp. 1–8.

Van Riel, C. B. M. (1995) *Principles of Corporate Communication* (London: Prentice-Hall).

Varey, R. J. (2000a) 'A Critical Review of Conceptions of Communication Evident in Contemporary Business and Management Literature', *Journal of Communication Management*, 4 (4), pp. 328–40.

Varey, R. J. (2000b) *Marketing Communication: Principles and Practice* (London: Routledge).

Varey, R. J. (2003) 'A Dialogical Foundation for Marketing', *The Marketing Review*, 3 (3), pp. 273–88.

Varey, R. J. (2006) 'Accounts in Interactions: Implications of Accounting Practices for Managing', in F. Cooren, J. R. Taylor and E. J. van Every (eds) *Communication as Organizing: Empirical and Theoretical Explorations in the Dynamic of Text and Conversation* (Mahwah: Lawrence Erlbaum Associates), Chapter 10, pp. 181–96.

Vickers, G. (1984) *Human Systems Are Different* (London: Harper & Row).

Index